THE PATH WITHIN

RITUAL MAGICK AND THE GATEWAY TO SELF-MASTERY

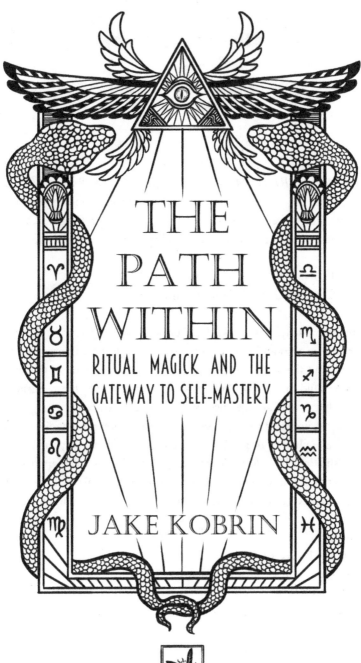

THE PATH WITHIN

RITUAL MAGICK AND THE GATEWAY TO SELF-MASTERY

JAKE KOBRIN

Chicago, IL

The Path Within: Ritual Magick and the Gateway to Self-Mastery © 2025 by Jake Kobrin. All rights reserved. No part of this book may be reproduced in any manner whatsoever without written permission from Crossed Crow Books, except in the case of brief quotations embodied in critical articles and reviews.

Paperback ISBN: 978-1-964537-16-0
Library of Congress Control Number on file.

Disclaimer: Crossed Crow Books, LLC does not participate in, endorse, or have any authority or responsibility concerning private business transactions between our authors and the public. Any internet references contained in this work were found to be valid during the time of publication, however, the publisher cannot guarantee that a specific reference will continue to be maintained. This book's material is not intended to diagnose, treat, cure, or prevent any disease, disorder, ailment, or any physical or psychological condition. The author, publisher, and its associates shall not be held liable for the reader's choices when approaching this book's material. The views and opinions expressed within this book are those of the author alone and do not necessarily reflect the views and opinions of the publisher.

Published by:
Crossed Crow Books, LLC
6934 N Glenwood Ave, Suite C
Chicago, IL 60626
www.crossedcrowbooks.com

Printed in the United States of America.
IBI

ACKNOWLEDGMENTS

This book owes its existence to the influence and contributions of many remarkable individuals. At the forefront, I owe immense gratitude to my parents, Marsha Thomas and Dr. Neil Kobrin, for their steadfast support and encouragement. Artistic inspirations like Android Jones, as well as Alex and Allyson Grey, have been instrumental in shaping my life's path, particularly in terms of psychedelic experiences, mysticism, and consciousness.

In the field of magick and esoteric studies, teachers like Damien Echols and Dr. David Shoemaker have been invaluable. Dr. Shoemaker's guidance was particularly crucial in initiating this project. I also thank Frater D. A. and others who have mentored and guided me and enriched my path.

The creation of the Magick 101 course brought forth contributions from friends, students, and teachers. While not all are mentioned in this book, I am grateful to Luna Veronica Mystic, Micki Pellerano, Gabriela Herstik, and Daniel Shankin for their insights, with hopes to include more in future works. Guest teachers Mitch Horowitz, Carl Abrahamsson, Sean Fargo, Dr. David Shoemaker, and Mark Stavish have been pivotal to this book's essence.

I must also acknowledge the impact of Duncan Trussell's podcast, *The Duncan Trussell Family Hour,* among other podcasts, on my magickal practice. My heartfelt thanks go to the friends and lovers who supported me throughout this extensive project. Your love and encouragement have been a bedrock of inspiration. Finally, to all TOTEM alumni,[1] I share a bond of solidarity in our sacred fellowship of life, art, and magick.

---

1   The Temple of the Eternal Muse

DEDICATION

This book is dedicated to my teenage self, and to all those persons who naturally stand outside of heterodoxy and who are suffering needlessly from pain, despair, and depression. There is an alternative to this, and it is my hope that this book will help you find it. If you are yearning for freedom, autonomy, self-empowerment, more options and opportunities, greater creativity, meaning, and deep significance, this book has been written for you. You have now become part of a movement to bring enchantment back into the world. Welcome!

ABOUT THE AUTHOR

Jake Kobrin is a multifaceted artist renowned for his psychedelic and esoteric artwork, which is distinguished by its intricate, meticulous details. His creations delve into the nuanced play of shadows and light, not only in the finesse of form but also in the essence of the subjects he captures. His art is a testament to embracing the full spectrum of emotions, ranging from moments of revelation and serenity to those of fear and dissonance.

A devoted practitioner of magick, Jake's artistic journey is deeply influenced by an eclectic mix of Western Esotericism, including occult and mystery school traditions, and Eastern spiritual paths like Buddhism, Hinduism, Animism, and Tantra. This rich synthesis of influences infuses his work with a unique depth and perspective.

Jake stands out in the psychedelic art community with a solid foundation in classical art, honed at the Angel Academy of Art in Florence, Italy, where he studied classical realist drawing and painting. This formal education enriches his work with a blend of contemporary vision and traditional technique.

Beyond the canvas, Jake wears many creative hats. He is a teacher, podcaster, writer, tattoo artist, musician, DJ, and designer. His diverse talents reflect a deep commitment to exploring and expressing the many facets of art and spirituality. Residing in Ubud, Bali, Jake draws inspiration from his surroundings and his roots in the Redwood Forests of Marin County near San Francisco, California, weaving these influences into his vibrant and transformative artistic narrative.

In 2022, he founded the art collective and occult order The Temple of the Eternal Muse, abbreviated TOTEM.

ABOUT THE GUEST TEACHERS

Carl Abrahamsson is a Swedish writer, publisher, filmmaker, lecturer, photographer, and musician. He has written extensively about occulture and how occultism and hidden ideas interact with our general culture through art and media. Carl Abrahamsson also writes fiction and journalism. He hosts 23rd Mind TV and works on a variety of multimedia projects with his wife, Vanessa Sinclair. He is the editor and publisher of the annual magickal-anthropological journal, *The Fenris Wolf.* He is the founder and owner and operator of the publishing company Trapartisan Books. He is also one of the founders of Thee Temple ov Psychick Youth, abbreviated TOPY. TOPY was formed as an organization of individuals dedicated to updating and demystifying religious thought and also dedicated to creating a world where individuals can be free to express themselves by whatever means they wish to.

www.carlabrahamsson.com

www.patreon.com/vanessa23carl

Mitch Horowitz is a historian of alternate spirituality and one of today's most literate voices on esoterica and mysticism. He illuminates outsider history, explaining its relevance to contemporary life and revealing the longstanding quest to bring empowerment and agency to the human condition. Mitch is a writer and resident at the New York Public Library, a lecturer and resident at the Philosophical Research Society in Los Angeles, and the Penn Award-winning author of many books, including *One Simple Idea: How Positive Thinking Reshaped Modern Life* and *The Miracle Club.*

Sean Fargo is a former Buddhist monk of two years, an executive consultant, the director of Mindfulness Program Development for Wellbrain, and a certified integral coach. He works with professionals to help increase clarity, energy, and resilience with evidence-based mindfulness practices. He has worked for and with multiple world-class companies, such as Google, Facebook, Tesla, Reddit, DocuSign, and Kaiser Permanente. He is also the founder of mindfulnessexercises.com, a free online resource of more than 750 mindfulness exercises. Sean is passionate about bringing the practices and benefits of mindfulness and meditation into daily life.

Dr. David Shoemaker is a clinical psychologist in private practice, specializing in Jungian and cognitive-behavioral psychotherapy. David is the Chancellor and Prolocutor of the Temple of the Silver Star (totss.org), a Thelemic initiatory and educational organization. He is a long-standing member of O.T.O. and A.'.A.'. (www.onestarinsight.org) and has many years of experience training initiates in these traditions. David's popular *Living Thelema* podcasts (livingthelema.com) have appeared regularly since 2010, and his widely praised *Living Thelema* book was published in late 2013. His 2016 publication, *The Winds of Wisdom,* contains a full record of his scrying of the Thirty Enochian Aethyrs, and his latest work, co-edited with Lon Milo DuQuette, is *Llewellyn's Complete Book of Ceremonial Magick.* David has co-edited many volumes of the writings of Thelemic luminaries such as Phyllis Seckler, Karl Germer, and Jane Wolfe.

In addition to his work in magick and psychology, David is a composer and musician.

Mark Stavish is a respected authority on Western spiritual traditions. The author of 26 books published in seven languages, including *The Path of Alchemy* and *Kabbalah for Health and Wellness,* he is the founder and director of the Institute for Hermetic Studies and the Louis Claude de St. Martin Fund. He has appeared on radio shows, television, and in major print media, including Coast to Coast AM, the History Channel, BBC, and the New York Times. The author of the blog *VOXHERMES,* he lives in Wyoming, Pennsylvania.

TABLE OF CONTENTS

FOREWORD XV

INTRODUCTION 19

A BRIEF NOTE ABOUT THIS BOOK 25

CHAPTER ONE: UNDERSTANDING MAGICK 33

CHAPTER TWO: ETHICAL APPROACHES TO MAGICKAL PRACTICE 67

CHAPTER THREE: YOUR MAGICKAL TOOLKIT 89

CHAPTER FOUR: HARNESSING THE POWER OF THOUGHT 105

CHAPTER FIVE: MAGICKAL MEDITATION 137

CHAPTER SIX: FUNDAMENTAL CONCEPTS 169

CHAPTER SEVEN: ESSENTIAL RITUALS 199

CHAPTER EIGHT: MAGICKAL ARTS 239

CHAPTER NINE: DIVINATION 265

CHAPTER TEN: UNLOCKING THE POWER OF DREAMS 297

CHAPTER ELEVEN: INVOKING THE DIVINE 335

CHAPTER TWELVE: CREATING PERSONAL RITUALS 357

CONCLUSION 377

BIBLIOGRAPHY 383

FOREWORD

There are far more things in Heaven and Earth, friend, than are dreamt of in the modern dogmatic materialist world.

Magick has been persecuted, ridiculed, and scorned for thousands of years in the West by the people in charge of conventional religions, because they know that the practice of magick puts people in direct contact with their immortal divine Self, which makes them unafraid of death, and thus renders them impossible to control and exploit.

Magick has been mocked not because it doesn't work, but because it works so well to empower people like you and me that it drives authoritarian control freaks crazy.

I'm so happy to present this book to you because the author, Jake Kobrin, has courageously carved a path into the dark forest for you to tread so you can find the staggering wonders of your own soul, your own Self, by the light of your own inner power.

One summer night, after a month of daily ritual magick practice involving the Lesser Banishing Ritual of the Pentagram and the Middle Pillar (two standard classics both taught in this wonderful book that you hold in your hands now), I opened my eyes to see a man ten feet tall, with the face of a blue hawk, standing at the foot of my bed.

There he was, a hawk-faced man, a rather regal and handsome creature, with a broad, muscled chest covered in teeny tiny blue feathers that fluttered in the breeze from my whirring, dusty old bedside fan. He wore a hammered-gold breastplate that gleamed with beveled jewels, a matching skirt, and a grand *nemyss* headdress in the ancient Egyptian style.

I felt a wave of deep peace and awe come over me as I looked at him.

The big blue hawk-faced Egyptian man made the "sign of silence" gesture (holding his fingers to his lips) as he looked into my eyes. He held my gaze and I suddenly understood something endlessly funny, sweet, and

Jake Kobrin

sublime about the dance of time, destiny, free will, and the beautiful simultaneity of all things—an understanding that I still struggle to explain.

It wasn't until the next day that I fully grokked whom I had encountered. I gradually realized the gentleman at the foot of my bed matched the description of Ra-Hoor-Khuit, the hawk-headed Lord of the Aeon made famous by the renowned magician Aleister Crowley in *The Book of the Law*.

That day, I realized something that changed my life forever: magick works—and not just "manifestation" magick for cash and parking spots and new lovers, but deep magick, strange magick, magick to conjure the gods, and magick to learn incommunicable secrets!

Don't take my word for it, of course. Do the magick taught in this book and find out for yourself.

One of the marvelous things about magick is it requires little faith; it simply requires regular and enthusiastic practice. It works of its own accord.

"The soul is a dark forest," quipped D. H. Lawrence.[2]

Kobrin lives his life immersed in art and ritual. He lives as someone who, like me, knows the most fabulous secret, one that we work as hard as we can to shout from the rooftops: magick works, it's for real, and with serious dedication, it can change your whole life and identity for the better in a short time.

Kobrin has managed to deftly pull off a daunting feat: he explains the ins and outs of a notoriously arcane and dense subject patiently and clearly, so *The Path Within* rewards both beginners who have just set out to learn magick and serious practitioners who desire a refresher.

In other words, in the book you hold in your hands, you've found a direct, wise, and loving guide to the world of ritual magick—also known as "high magick" or theurgy.

Theurgy literally means "god-working," and theurgical magick seeks to align our consciousness with the realm of the gods, gods who happen to be emissaries (you could also call them angels or *angelos*—Greek for

---

2   D.H. Lawrence, *Studies in Classic American Literature* (Thomas Seltzer, 1923)

"messenger") of our own larger trans-dimensional, trans-temporal divine Self. Theurgical practices in the Western Esoteric Tradition that Kobrin teaches, like the Lesser Banishing Ritual of the Pentagram and the Middle Pillar, serve as acts of devotion. Yet, unlike "prayer" as most of us know from Judeo-Christian religions, theurgy doesn't tell us to get down and grovel to a distant, silent Sky Daddy for help. Rather, theurgy entails ritually identifying as the divine Source of All Creation, and thereby becoming God.

The Lesser Banishing Ritual of the Pentagram and the Middle Pillar fulfill the famous injunction of the Corpus Hermeticum:

If then you do not make yourself equal to God, you cannot apprehend God; for like is known by like.

Leap clear of all that is corporeal, and make yourself grown to a like expanse with that greatness which is beyond all measure; rise above all time and become eternal; then you will apprehend God.

Think that for you too nothing is impossible; deem that you too are immortal, and that you are able to grasp all things in your thought, to know every craft and science; find your home in the haunts of every living creature; make yourself higher than all heights and lower than all depths; bring together in yourself all opposites of quality, heat and cold, dryness and fluidity; think that you are everywhere at once, on land, at sea, in heaven; think that you are not begotten, that you are in the womb, that you are young, that you are old, that you have died, that you are in the world beyond the grave; grasp in your thought all of this at once, all times and places, all substances and qualities and magnitudes together; then you can apprehend God.

But if you shut up your soul in your body, and abase yourself and say "I know nothing, I can do nothing; I am afraid of earth and sea, I cannot mount to heaven; I know not what I was, nor what I shall be, then what have you to do with God?"[3]

Dr. Carolyn Lovewell
June 2024, Pittsburgh, Pennsylvania

---

3   Hermes Trismegistus, *Hermetica: The Greek Corpus Hermeticum and the Latin Asclepius*.

INTRODUCTION

Magick is real, but it is likely not what you have thought it is. Magick is a form of reality hacking, a way of altering consciousness to produce changes that you desire in your life more effectively. This is distinct from *magic* without a k, which refers to stage magic, a form of illusionistic entertainment. Throughout this book, I will spell magick with an additional "k," employing the specific spelling that Aleister Crowley established to differentiate *magick*, the art and science of change in accordance with Will, from the magic performed by stage magicians and illusionists. Aleister Crowley was a British occultist, writer, and ceremonial magician who founded the religious movement Thelema.[1] His work, especially in terms of magick and the occult, has had a lasting influence, serving as a foundational text for many modern esoteric traditions. Many of the ideas and movements presented in this book originate from his large body of work.

---

1 Crowley, Aleister, *Magick in Theory and Practice* (Dover Publications, 1976). Crowley elaborates on this in *The Book of Thoth* (Weiser, 1969) 40: "Magick is the science and art of causing change to occur in conformity with the Will. In other words, it is Science, Pure and Applied. This thesis has been worked out at great length by Dr. Sir J. G. Frazer."

Jake Kobrin

If you are holding this book in your hands, you already possess a very rare and open mind. It takes courage to read a book like this, to contact ideas that run counter to most of the world's dominant belief systems and paradigms. Even more so, it takes courage and immense curiosity to practice the information and techniques presented within it, given the fact that many people, if made aware of the fact that you are choosing to read such a book and be open to these ideas, would belittle you or at the very least cringe at you for doing so.

I don't know what experiences in life led you to find this book, but it is certainly no chance encounter. You are reading this book because you are ready. This book came to you for a reason. You may be suffering in various ways in your life, whether acute or mild, a sharp pain or a vague numb aching, and are ready to transform your orientation to life into something more playful, flexible, meaningful, and creative. This is what magick and its techniques can provide for you. Magick will challenge and change your assumptions about reality, the world, your place in it, and who you are, and your habituated means of perception for how and why situations occur, why we can inhabit certain forms of experiences, and why others escape our grasp.

I'm writing this book to empower you to understand your magickal potential. I don't believe that magick is something only for the rare and special minorities, for only the fringe or the elite few. It does require study, effort, and practice, but I believe that magick is our birthright. We all have things we'd like to have in our lives, to be, to experience, and to achieve, yet many of us are stuck feeling frustrated and powerless to attain these things. Maybe you've tried some real strategies to get these things, and maybe you've put some real work into it. Maybe you feel like you've tried everything and nothing has worked. The aim of this book is to help you become more of yourself so that your life and reality fit who you truly are and can be in this world.

The ancient Hermetic axiom "as above, so below; as below, so above" serves as a foundational concept in esoteric traditions, encapsulating the idea that the laws and phenomena of different planes of Being and Life are intrinsically connected.[2] This principle provides a framework for under-

---

2   Three Initiates, *The Kybalion* (The Yogi Publication Society, 1908)

The Path Within

standing the interconnectedness of the cosmos, suggesting that what occurs on one level of reality also happens on another. Magick functions from congruence between what is within and what is without. We all have both an internal and an external component to our worlds, what could be termed *exoteric* and *esoteric*. Exoteric is relating to the world of matter and external form. This is the general apprehension and knowledge of the common person. The esoteric refers to the obscure and is only understood or intended to be understood by a small number of people with special (and perhaps secret) knowledge. Most people live only in the exoteric world most of the time. The problem is that people use strategies that focus solely on the exoteric components of reality and neglect or are not even aware of the esoteric.

Magick is the art of mastering and directing the internal, unseen, esoteric world so that changes in our outer realities conform to the inner world. Our thoughts, feelings, impulses, intuitions, perceptions of the world, and external realities dance and entwine with what unfolds in our outer worlds in intricate and mysterious ways. An inner shift, which is what the tools of magick are aimed toward, must precede any significant change in the outer world.

I see commonalities in people, and I think for the most part we all struggle with the same types of stories and afflictions. We all have tendencies and patterns that can be difficult to overcome. Sometimes we feel frustrated, like nothing is working and we are banging our heads against the same issues time and time again. This is not something to shrug away, as it can be extraordinarily painful. Magick and its adjacent practices are a useful, effective, and potentially revolutionary toolkit for our modern world. This book is a compendium of the practices that have helped change my life.

We exist in a time of great crisis and uncertainty. Our generation faces challenges that are immense and dire. In such difficult times, our ancestors often turned to magicians, sorcerers, mystics, and shamans, their tribe or culture's wise people (the word *wizard* comes from something like "wise one" or "wise-ered" in late Middle English) who possessed specialized knowledge that could help them navigate their life's struggles and uncertainties. Magick has taken many different forms and has been called many different names. Its ideas have been integrated into many other modalities, including mental causation, neuro-linguistic programming, semiotics, auto-suggestion, self-hypnosis, the power of positive thinking, ceremonial magick, and chaos magick. These are some of the tools and techniques geared toward understanding and utilizing the powers of your psyche to radically impact and create the circumstances you desire in your life.

Simply and very broadly, magick is the interaction of our consciousness and reality to cause a change in accordance with our will. It's a collection of methods and techniques, both a science and an art form, to create circumstances, states, and experiences that you desire willfully. This can be something material, like a certain amount of money or to get a certain job, or something more spiritual or less tangible, like enlightenment or the quest for higher awareness. It can also be something very novel, occult, and rarified, like the experience of traveling to other so-called astral dimensions, the experience of spirit contact, or channeling a particular entity or deity.

My definition of magick is to impress changes willfully into your consciousness through symbolic actions (such as magickal rituals) that result in changes in your external world. It's important to emphasize that I also don't deny science's validity, but in my world—much like the magicians of old in Queen Elizabeth I's time, where the court magician John Dee played the role of both proto-scientist and one of ceremonial magick's pioneers—magick and science co-exist and are symbiotic.[3]

We all have dreams, things we want to accomplish, and sometimes the odds of accomplishing these things can make these dreams and visions feel almost impossible. You already have everything you need to be able to accomplish these tasks and live the life of your dreams, and it all exists within your psyche. Magick is a study of the methods to directly impact our psyches so that the experiences we attract and are magnetized toward align with our true desires.

---

3   John Dee was a sixteenth-century English mathematician, astrologer, and occultist best known for his efforts in attempting to communicate with angelic beings through his associate Edward Kelley. In the context of magick and occultism, Dee's Enochian system has had a lasting impact, offering a complex and elaborate set of magical practices that many modern esoteric traditions draw upon.

The Path Within

Although it might be associated with things like Harry Potter and fantasy stories, the hundreds-of-years-old philosophy and practice of magick asserts that there are subtle, hidden forces that govern our world, and that, if you understand how to tap into and align with these forces and direct them, you can use these subtle occult forces to achieve anything you desire.

My practice and study of magick have completely changed my life by allowing me to have greater power and agency to envision and create the life I truly want for myself. I believe that it can positively change your life as well.

If you're reading this, I believe in you. I believe in your magick. Magick is real, it can touch your life if you are willing to open your mind to the possibility of things being different. That possibility is a doorway that you can walk through and through which you can experience radical change. Everything you've ever wanted is on the other side, but the first step is opening your mind to the possibility.

In this infinite universe where our very lives and existence are a mystery and a miracle, I believe that anything we could ever want is possible. Allow that door to open, permit yourself to temporarily put aside your disbelief, and let hope and curiosity saturate your mind. Allow yourself, like a scientist in a laboratory, to experiment with this book's contents and exercises. I believe in you.

If you are reading this, you are already blessed to have been shown that there is another option. You don't need to accept any circumstance in your life, and you have the power and agency to change it. Magick is one of the ways, if not the most effective way, to do this.

Thank you for reading this book; I'm glad it found you. I'm excited that you will join me on this journey. It's a privilege and an honor to be presenting this information to you.

Jake Kobrin
Ubud, Bali, Indonesia
October 2023

A BRIEF NOTE ABOUT THIS BOOK

This book is intended to be a beginner's accessible introduction to magick, which is a field that can often seem impenetrable and difficult to understand. In this way, I see myself in the role of a translator of sorts. If this is the first book you've ever read about magick and want a good understanding of the fundamentals, you have come to the right place, but if you have read many books on magick and have experience as a practitioner of magick already, I hope that you will also deepen your understanding and be inspired by this book.

It's also important to emphasize that nothing stated in this book is a fact, per se, and none of it is dogma. Magick has many different traditions, and many different practitioners have many different perspectives on how and why it works. While I'd advise you to maintain any of the practices presented in this book for at least one to two months consistently to be able to say you gave them a serious try and made an effort to work with them, if you do not see immediate and tangible results after this period and you do not enjoy doing the practices, I would suggest letting go of them. I notice immediate and tangible effects from the practices within the same day (or hour) of doing them in contrast to the days in which I don't. This is why I uphold the practices as a routine and discipline every single day.

And finally, here is a disclaimer before I continue: there are exceptions and alternative perspectives to every statement in this book. There is nothing in this book that I claim in any way to be absolute truth, and I will probably look back on it years from now and be astounded at how much my ideas and perspectives have changed.

Be warned that if you do the exercises in this book with enthusiasm, it may change your life permanently and the effects may be irreversible. Continue at your own risk.

TRANSFORMING MY BODY WITH MAGICK: MY STORY OF LOSING 100 POUNDS

It was a sweltering summer when I was fourteen years old, and I was in misery and despair. Weighed down by my large body of over 250 pounds, I was plagued by chronic back pain and suffered from depression, agoraphobia, and insomnia. My anxiety was so strong that it felt as if I had opened a portal to some other demonic realm, and my room seemed to be infested with flies. I was alone and isolated, too shy to reach out to people and ashamed to look them in the eyes. I was convinced that nobody was interested in showing me love or compassion, and I felt trapped, unable to see any way out. It is difficult for me to remember these experiences without shuddering.

Little did I know that the biggest transformation in my life was on the horizon. Over the next ten years, I explored different healing modalities and spiritual paths, including ayahuasca ceremonies and holotropic breathwork. I slowly began to understand the power of magick and the importance of the inner world. Now, I can look back on my struggles with a newfound understanding, and I am grateful for the transformation that has taken place.

The Path Within

When I was a teenager, I was deeply ashamed of my weight, and I felt extremely uncomfortable in my body. At the time, it seemed that loneliness and isolation were the only things that shone for me, and I struggled with a deep sense of hopelessness and despair. I had no friends, and I had shut out my family. I felt completely alone.

I didn't know then that there were other ways out of my situation, that magick and spiritual paths existed and could be explored, or that the inner world was of such importance. I felt so trapped and helpless that I resorted to diets and health specialists, trainers, and exercise regimens, but none of it worked. It was only when I was able to start making changes within my heart, mind, and psyche that I was able to start seeing external changes.

Between the ages of sixteen and nineteen, I transformed much like a caterpillar entering the chrysalis and dissolving into a network of imaginal cells before emerging as a butterfly. I lost more than a hundred pounds and changed many aspects of my life, psyche, and personality. The practice of magick was instrumental in this transformation, and I have become a fundamentally different person from who I was then.

I want to empower you to know that, regardless of who you are or your struggles, you can also transform your life for the better. As I look back on this period, I know that I have a long way to go to reach my full potential, but I am confident that I will continue to grow and evolve.

At the age of sixteen, I, at the time a self-proclaimed Satanist obsessed with the Norwegian black metal culture of the early 90s, found myself in an unfamiliar place. My father, a Ph.D. psychologist, had brought me to the Spirit Rock Meditation Center in Woodacre, California, founded by the renowned spiritual teacher Jack Kornfield.[4] Though I had up to this point held a fixation on extreme metal bands, which allowed me to discover Aleister Crowley and begin my infatuation with occultism, I was ready to experience something different. I had already begun meditating with the

---

4   Jack Kornfield is a prominent American author and teacher in the Vipassana movement of Theravada Buddhism. While not directly aligned with magick or occultism, his teachings on mindfulness and spirituality offer valuable perspectives on inner transformation, which can complement and deepen esoteric practices.

instructions from Aleister Crowley's *Book Four* and I thought that joining my father would give me an opportunity to deepen my practice.[5]

Following Jack's instructions, I meditated among the upper-middle-class Marin County adults. Though I was wearing a black leather jacket with patches of bands whose band members had burned down churches and murdered their bandmates, as I sat next to lawyers, therapists, tech executives, and CEOs, I felt a sense of peace and a quality of ease and rest. Although my mind initially struggled, like trying to teach a puppy to sit, I soon found myself able to reach altered states of consciousness of deep relaxation and clarity with the Buddhist meditation techniques that felt a bit like taking Valium.

This was life changing. I felt full of pain and anguish, but during meditation, I experienced a sense of peace for the first time. My curiosity about magick had been sparked by Crowley's *Book Four,* and a tangential interest in lucid dreaming led to powerful experiences of non-ordinary states of consciousness and transpersonal and archetypal domains. I was deeply impacted by these experiences, and it has shaped the course of my life ever since.

The Dharma was the remedy I had been searching for, and meditation was the instrument I needed to make dramatic alterations in my life. What followed was remarkable. I started meditating, not because I wanted to be a good meditator or Buddhist, or achieve enlightenment, but because it made me feel content. It gave me solace. In that stage of my life, meditation, magick, and lucid dreaming were the only things that did that besides art and music. As I began to meditate regularly, initially once a day (then twice a day) for twenty minutes, then thirty minutes, then one hour, and after that, for more than one hour every day, I started to recognize a shift in my consciousness that eventually caused a remarkable transformation in my body.

Meditation is a vital part of the practice of magick and is the cornerstone of the process of Dissolving and Reconstituting, as prescribed by the Solve et Coagula formula. The Solve et Coagula formula is an alchemical concept that means "dissolve and coagulate," signifying the process of

---

5   Crowley, Aleister, *Magick in Theory and Practice* (Dover Publications, 1976)

The Path Within

breaking down components and then bringing them back together in a new, purified form.[6] In the context of magick and occultism, it symbolizes the cycle of death and rebirth, as well as the transformative power of spiritual enlightenment. Meditation constitutes the *Solve* or "dissolving" part of that equation. When I focused my mind in a deep and still place, it quieted and dissolved the endless narrative in my head that perpetuated the self-concept of being fat, depressed, and so on. This gave me a chance to consciously create a new version of myself.

We all have a self-concept that drives us and determines the decisions we make—this is generally referred to as the *ego*.[7] The ego is the pilot of our lives, and it will defend itself fiercely. Even the slightest sign of something that does not match the self-concept is incredibly threatening to the ego. This is why it is so difficult to change our lives—we are so used to reinforcing our self-concepts with our thoughts, actions, and beliefs that it can be hard to break away from them.

The practice of magick is about taking our consciousness to a level above that of the self-concept. It is through meditating and seeing the ego's insubstantiality that I lost one hundred pounds when nothing else worked. I stopped seeing myself as a fat and depressed person and instead shifted my focus to experiencing life as pure awareness—observing my thoughts and feelings without attachment or self-definition. This process of discarding a self-concept that was not in line with my desired outcome was essential in achieving my goal and is a key component of any self-transformation or healing path. One of the most widely read books on this subject is the book *Psycho-Cybernetics* by Maxwell Maltz, who was not an esoteric person but rather a plastic surgeon and found that external shifts in a person's body and appearance did not always bring about internal changes to self-esteem and self-concept unless effort was made to change this through various techniques of visualization and meditation.[8]

---

6   Jung, Carl, *Mysterium Coniunctionis, Collected Works of C. G. Jung, Vol. 14* (Princeton University Press, 1977)

7   Jung, Carl, *Aion: Researches into the Phenomenology of the Self, Collected Works of C. G. Jung, Vol. 9, Part 2* (Princeton University Press, 1959)

8   Maltz, Maxwell, *Psycho-Cybernetics* (Prentice-Hall, 1960)

Jake Kobrin

I used meditation to help me form new habits and behaviors that helped me lose weight and become healthier and happier. I still put in the effort to maintain and improve my health, but I was not even able to begin the process until I started engaging in meditation and magick. I had tried diets and exercise before, but nothing worked. Once I started to meditate, however, I was able to loosen the grip of my identity and my ego and reach a zero-point consciousness that was beyond the constructs of identity. This allowed me to shift my identity and perceptions of myself and live my life differently.

From my experience, I have come to understand that our minds and states of consciousness have the power to bring about change in our lives, even in our health. I have also seen how magick can shift our consciousness, identity, and ego, allowing us to access the deeply embedded and subconscious beliefs that define our reality.

The power of magick is mysterious and perhaps unknowable, yet it undeniably has an effect on the causal plane—the root of all that manifests in the physical world. Through my own experience, I have seen that if you want to create change in your life and in the world, you must first affect it at the root level. Austin Osman Spare was a British artist and occultist who developed a system known as "sigil magick," which combines artistic expression with occult practices for manifesting will. In the domains of magick, occultism, meditation, and spirituality, his words still ring true today: "Unless desire is subconscious, it is not fulfilled, no, not in this life."[9]

The truth of this statement was made clear to me when I lost more than a hundred pounds with little effort. I had programmed my subconscious to believe I was already thin and healthy, and my body responded accordingly. Magick does not have to be complex; a small shift in consciousness can have a profound effect on reality. Rituals, spells, and other occult practices can be powerful and enjoyable, but they are not always necessary for magick to work. I created this change in my body and my life through a shift in my consciousness. Magick rituals, spells, and workings can be powerful tools, but they are merely an embellishment to the fundamental truth that belief

---

9   Spare, Austin Osman, *The Book of Pleasure (Self-Love): The Psychology of Ecstasy* (IHO Books, 2001)

The Path Within

is the key to creating a new reality.[10] This heretical statement is neither definitive nor meant to demonstrate disrespect for the profound and beautiful symbols and rituals of high magick, which I have deeply studied and by which my life has been powerfully transformed and enriched. I mean to say that although these symbol systems are powerful, magick can still be done effectively without them, as Austin Osman Spare and the chaos magicians discovered and propounded.

I have used the same principles to affect many areas of my life; I believe that whatever we desire to experience or achieve is possible at a cost and through the right channels. Step through that door, set aside your doubts, and let hope fill your heart. This life is but a dream, and this book was written to help you become a lucid dreamer. A lucid dreamer is someone who is aware that they are dreaming while the dream is still occurring, often gaining the ability to control elements of the dream itself. This form of dreaming allows for conscious interaction with the dream environment, providing opportunities for exploration, self-discovery, and even problem-solving. We will explore techniques and exercises to achieve this later in the book.

---

10   Radin, Dean, *Real Magic: Ancient Wisdom, Modern Science, and a Guide to the Secret Power of the Universe* (Harmony, 2018)

CHAPTER ONE

UNDERSTANDING MAGICK

Magick has been defined in different ways by different cultures around the world throughout time. A fundamental principle in magick, encompassing its various forms and traditions, is the necessity of transcending societal conditioning to either reclaim or become keenly aware of our influence over our environment. It's a process of acknowledging that we are active participants in shaping our reality, in tandem with our surroundings and the people around us. This power of creation is inherent to each individual and cannot be outsourced or relinquished to others. Embracing and asserting this personal power is a transformative step that marks the transition into being a true practitioner of magick, thus becoming a magician. Magick is also the practice of using symbols to alter states of consciousness in oneself or other people.[11]

---

11 Moore, Alan, Interview by Rowan Hooper. *"Haunted Resonance: An Interview with Alan Moore"* (The Quietus, 2018)

Jake Kobrin

This is in no way a new practice. Magick has likely been around since the beginnings of human civilization.[12] In our ancestry, it was a way of survival that was passed down from generation to generation.[13] Magick is used to communicate with the unseen, which includes communicating with spirits and otherworldly beings. Magick was first used by shamans who would go into trances to communicate with the spirits. This then evolved into priests and other religious leaders who became the main source of magick and its practices. Today, magick is practiced by many people all over the world. It is seen as a way to connect with the divine and to create positive change in the world.

As time went on, magick became more and more hidden from society. It was mainly practiced in secret by those who were interested in its ways. This was because it was often seen as heretical or as a threat to the dominant power structures of the time. In the Renaissance, magick made a comeback as people became more interested in its ways and practices. However, it was again forced underground during the seventeenth century.

One of the most fundamental ideas of magick is that everything a person does affects them on more levels than the most apparent or visceral. Whenever you create change, it affects not only the obvious or physical aspects, but also deeper, unseen levels of your being. Magick also traditionally has a lot to do with connecting your nature to the greater forces of nature. By doing this, you realize that there is no difference between them. Traditionally, a shaman is someone who was in tune with these forces and acts as a guide to others who want to learn about them.

To me, magick is about finding your path and being true to yourself. You can use different techniques from various traditions to do this. It's helpful to study different magickal systems and find one that you resonate with, but ultimately the magick lies within you. There are many different ways to practice magick, and each person needs to find the path that works

---

12   Eliade, Mircea, *Shamanism: Archaic Techniques of Ecstasy* (Princeton University Press, 2004)

13   Abrahamsson, Carl, *Source Magic: The Origin of Art, Science, and Culture* (Park Street Press, 2023)

best for them. Part of the intention of this book is to provide a wide array of perspectives and practices that you can experiment with and then discern what is most aligned with your disposition and path in life.

WHAT IS MAGICK?

Delving into magick is to embark on a rich and multifaceted adventure, one that encompasses a myriad of interpretations, practices, and age-old traditions. At its core, magick is about consciously shaping and molding our reality through our thoughts, expressions, and actions. While this process may occur subconsciously for many, those who practice magick do so with deliberate intent and heightened awareness. Engaging in magick unlocks dormant capabilities within us, enhancing our lives in ways that are often unexplored but hold immense potential.

Magick operates through mechanisms that remain largely enigmatic to modern Western science, yet it effectively brings about change in congruence with one's will. It is not a supernatural occurrence, but rather a natural one within the reach of anyone prepared to commit their intention and energy. Magick merges the mystical with the empirical, acting as a conduit between the spiritual realm and the domains of scientific exploration. It is the art of channeling energy in order to effect transformation within ourselves or the world around us. The ethical dimension of magick is shaped by the intentions of its practitioner, rendering it a morally neutral force.

Broadly speaking, magick is the study and application of cosmic principles in everyday life, setting it apart from the scientific pursuit, which tends to focus on the physical and material world. Magick posits that science, while invaluable, captures only a fraction of the vast cosmos, leaving the intangible aspects largely unexplored. It is both an intellectual exploration of the universe and a hands-on approach to implementing this knowledge in pragmatic scenarios.

Numerous mystics and philosophers from diverse cultures and epochs have proposed that consciousness, rather than physical matter, is the foundational fabric of the universe. This perspective views the brain as a receptor of consciousness—similar to how a radio antenna picks up various frequencies—rather than the sole originator of awareness. Embracing this viewpoint invites us to transcend material-centric approaches to healing and well-being. By honoring both the physical and metaphysical aspects of existence, we pay homage to the role of consciousness and the invisible dimensions that weave through our universe.

WE ARE ALL DOING MAGICK ALL THE TIME

I have come to the conclusion that there is no real difference between magick and any other intentional or willful action. Every result, no matter how small or mundane, is a result of a combination of both internal and external factors, such as our thoughts, emotions, and desires, and physical actions like driving to a café or exchanging money for goods. This means that by making decisions and locking into a certain direction in life, we are actually doing magick or using our will to achieve a desired result.

Aleister Crowley's book *Magick in Theory and Practice* provides a good example of this concept: for instance, if someone wants to write a book and share it with the world, they must will it to be so by using both esoteric and exoteric means, such as writing a manuscript in a language that will be understood and then calling on spirits such as printers and publishers to help spread the message.[14] Magick can be any action (not only those of ritual or esoterica) that bring about the desired result in the life of the person taking the action.

The practice of magick is really about understanding the conditions that must be in place in order for a desired outcome to manifest and then

---

14   Crowley, Aleister, *Magick in Theory and Practice* (Dover Publications, 1976)

taking action to align the patterns of our minds and habits of life so these conditions may arise. Rituals can be helpful in some cases, providing momentum for the desired outcome, but are not a prerequisite for magick. Therefore, any intentional action or act of will is an act of magick.

We are constantly influencing the creation of our lives and experiences through our thoughts, beliefs, decisions, and perceptions, so it is beneficial to be aware of this process and use it consciously. Magick is something we all do, whether we are conscious of it or not, and the more we practice it, the more effective we can be.

HOW DOES MAGICK WORK?

There is no unifying official theory of how magick works. However, these are some useful models:

The first model is the *animistic model*. This is what they practice and believe where I live in Bali, for example. Everything, whether it is your motorcycle, a tree, or a stone, is spirited, meaning that there is a spirit or a perspective within everything—a sort of living quality to everything in the universe—and the universe itself is conscious. When you do magick, you are interfacing with the universal consciousness or the consciousness of the things, the spirit-embodied things that surround you.

The next model is the *psychological model*. The psychological model came into favor in the twentieth century, and it's still a perspective that many magicians hold. Crowley, for example, oscillated between a psychological model of magick and a spirit-based model of magick throughout his entire career, causing internal conflict for him.

The psychological model states that our subconscious drives dictate the manifestation and unfolding of our lives. Practicing magick creates shifts in your consciousness, imprinting ideas into your subconscious that manifest in your life through your decisions, beliefs, and perceptions of reality. In

Jake Kobrin

short, changing your operating beliefs and the kind of mental software that you are operating on will result in changes in your life and reality.

The next model is the *spirit-based model of magick*. The spirit-based model of magick was the primary perspective on magick up until the twentieth century. It is still a model of magick and spirituality perpetuated by many modern magicians in many cultures throughout the world. It wasn't traditionally believed that the magician had any special magickal powers themselves. Instead, they were able to commune with, command, and have control over a variety of hosts of supernatural agents, including spirits, ancestors, demons, angels, Archangels, gods, goddesses, and so on. It wasn't that the magician was able to use their magickal powers to influence the world, but rather that they would have the skills and abilities, as well as the passwords and rituals, to command, bind, and collaborate with the spirits that govern our world and the realms outside of our ordinary perception. This is still a very popular model of how magick works, and it's essentially the oldest and most universal model.

Another way of explaining magick is what I'd call the *divine consciousness model of magick*. This was exemplified through the systems of initiation as presented by the Hermetic Order of the Golden Dawn. The Hermetic Order of the Golden Dawn, commonly referred to as the Golden Dawn, was a secret society devoted to the study and practice of occult Hermeticism and metaphysics during the late nineteenth and early twentieth centuries. This magickal order was based in Great Britain and focused its practices on theurgy and spiritual development. As a result of its influence, many of the rituals and theories that we explore today have their origins in the Golden Dawn. In particular, its teachings have been an important source of inspiration for contemporary traditions such as Wicca and Thelema, and it has become one of the largest single influences on twentieth-century Western occultism. Even now, there are still active Golden Dawn lodges in existence.

The idea of this model is that when you are able to raise your consciousness to the level of that of a God, you realize that the most fundamental aspect of our consciousness is synonymous with the consciousness of the great creator. We are God, and the realization that we are God then gives us creative power and agency over our Universe, like waking up inside a lucid dream and then gaining control over the dream space.

The next model suggests that we basically give ourselves permission slips, or there are tricks of the mind involved in doing ritual, implying that magick is similar to the placebo effect. This is similar to the psychological model, where we trick ourselves into having a greater level of confidence or ability to do things that we want.

Quantum physics has also influenced modern-day magicians and their perspectives on how magick works, especially within the tradition of chaos magick. The idea of quantum entanglement or sympathetic resonance is that everything is connected and any two things, though they might seem separate, are inherently linked. When you do something to affect change to a symbolic representation of something, like a voodoo doll, you're affecting change for that which is indirectly connected to it—such as the person the voodoo doll is representing.

Another model made popular through New Thought is the idea that thoughts themselves are causative, our thoughts are themselves powerful, and we can think things into being. The book *Think and Grow Rich* is a popular example of this.

The two most popular models for explaining magick are the spirit-based model, which is more of a classical approach, and the psychological model, which is a more modern-day approach. Most magicians lean towards one perspective or the other. However, as you can see, it is quite mysterious how magick works and why, so you can experiment with and explore all of the different models and perspectives to see which one suits your understanding. Very likely, your understanding will change over time as you continue your practice.

Peter J. Carroll, a chaos magician, famously wrote that "magick works in practice and not in theory."[15] This statement serves as an important reminder that to be a successful practicing magician, one must be able to accept irrational paradoxes and transcend the rigid beliefs and systems of knowledge that tend to dominate modern thought. In other words, a

---

15 Carroll, Peter J., *Liber Null & Psychonaut* (Weiser Books, 1987)

successful magician must be open to the idea that, in order to practice magick, one must be willing to accept and use knowledge and methods that may not fit into accepted scientific or philosophical models. Magick is an experiential form of knowledge rather than something that can be understood through the traditional theoretical frameworks.

WHAT MAKES MAGICK WORK...OR NOT

This is not an explanation of how magick works, but rather we will look at some of the necessary conditions for any desired result to come into manifestation. Every desired change has its own unique and specific conditions. If you desire physical health and fitness, you must first have an able body. You cannot run if you do not have legs or if you are dead. Secondly, you must undertake a regimen of exercise in the proper amount, the proper regularity, and the correct way. Other factors, such as sleep and diet, must also be curtailed to operate efficiently within the context of the goal that you have in mind. And finally, an adequate amount of time, with consistent practice and exercise, must be undertaken for your specific fitness goal to be realized. If you are not reaching your goal, you can therefore assume that the problem might be the natural condition of your body, the type of exercise you are participating in, the amount of exercise, your diet, your sleeping habits, and the amount of time you have undertaken these patterns with consistency.

Every desired outcome has a specific set of circumstances defined by natural laws for it to be realized. To do magick, one must understand these conditions and conform one's life to be in accordance with those conditions through action. Otherwise, it is impossible for the desired outcome to occur.

Successful magick occurs when the right conditions are met for your desired outcome. A failed act simply means the necessary conditions and actions were not in place. To give another mundane example, if you desire wealth but are spending more money than you are earning and not saving,

The Path Within

accumulating, or investing your savings, then one or more of the requirements to fulfill your desire for wealth is not being observed.

Complete awareness of these conditions, both qualitatively and quantitatively, is the first and primary requirement for bringing about any change. The next requirement is the ability to take the right actions to engage the required forces. Not only do you need to understand the causes and conditions of any desired outcome, but you must also possess the means to take those actions. For example, I may intellectually understand everything that is necessary to fly a rocket ship to the moon, but if I do not possess a rocket, the wealth or means necessary to acquire one, or any practical, tangible experience of being an astronaut, I cannot fulfill my desired outcome.

MAGICK WORKS THROUGH NATURAL MEANS

As I said before, magick can help increase the occurrence of improbable events, but it cannot induce impossible ones. Like most things in nature, magick takes the path of least resistance. It is possible, under the right conditions, to create spells or rituals to bring yourself money, love, wisdom, contentment, or anything else you would like. However, it does not arrive instantaneously.

Magick often follows the path of least resistance, manifesting its outcomes through natural and sometimes unexpected means. Consider a scenario where you perform a magick ritual to find a new job opportunity. A few days later, while attending a casual social gathering, you strike up a conversation with someone who, unbeknownst to you, is looking for an employee with your exact skill set. They invite you to apply, leading to a successful job offer. This is a prime example of how your ritual paved the way for a serendipitous meeting. In practicing magick, it's crucial to be open about the channels through which your goals may materialize while being clear and precise about what those goals are.

I do not believe it is possible to use magick to manifest or change absolutely anything under any conditions. However, in the right circumstances, you can utilize magick to produce a phenomenon that is indistinguishable from your perspective of manifesting something. In other words, although a properly done ritual will inevitably deliver an approximation of your desired outcome, it is not always possible to manifest everything through the use of magick. I can't do a ritual and be able to levitate out of my chair right now. But if I did a ritual to fly, I might find myself on an airplane or something like that. Sometimes rituals can manifest in almost funny or ironic ways.

In addition to performing your rituals, I would recommend that you exhaust all mundane means of achieving your desired goals before, and certainly in addition to, using ritual magick. All decisions and actions that are taken to carry out one's will are acts of magick, regardless of whether they involve rituals or not.

THE TRUE WILL

One reason why an act of magick may not be working is that it is not in alignment with the True Will. The True Will is a concept that is central to the type of magick that was taught by Aleister Crowley and in fact, is the meaning of the word *Thelema*, the name of his magickal tradition. The Law of Thelema, a Greek word for "Will," was delivered to Aleister Crowley in a channeled text called *Liber Al Vel Legis* or *The Book of the Law* and is the foundation of a technical system of magick, philosophy, and religion that Aleister Crowley helped perpetuate in his lifetime and is still practiced by thousands of people today.[16] The True Will is a deep concept, and is, in essence, The Will of the Higher Self. The Higher Self is, of course, the totality of existence, and is also synonymous with what magicians often call the Holy Guardian Angel (HGA), another complex subject. The True

---

16   Crowley, Aleister, *The Book of the Law* (Dover Publications, 1976)

The Path Within

Will is, therefore, what springs forth naturally through you when you are in alignment and harmony with your HGA or Higher Self and, given that the Higher Self is also coequal and coterminous with the entirety of existence or God, the True Will is also the Will of the Universe itself. This is a fancy way of saying that sometimes our desires are frustrated because the desires of our limited, egoic, and small sense of self are opposed to the Will of the Divine and what it intends to manifest through our existence. Crowley famously said "[a] Man who is doing his True Will has the inertia of the Universe to assist him" because one who is doing their True Will is enacting the Will of the Universe itself.[17]

The True Will is something similar to the Stoic idea of *Eudaemonia*. Eudaemonia (also spelled *eudaimonia*) in Greek philosophy and Aristotelian ethics is the condition of human flourishing or of living well. Crowley, and many quite ancient sources of Western wisdom, uphold the idea that we have a kind of essence pattern that we naturally gravitate towards. In other words, there are behaviors and inclinations that are naturally a part of our essence and temperament, and others that are not.

In Crowley's *Magick in Theory and Practice*, he describes somebody who is attempting to realize the desired outcome of being a painter, when the True Will of that being is not in accordance with that desire. Therefore, the desire will ultimately fail, or at least will be met with great obstacles and complications. On a more practical level, he suggests that perhaps this person *is* a painter, but they do not adequately and thoroughly understand the causes and conditions of success that are necessary to manifest the desired outcome of having a career as a painter.[18]

Every person is different and unique. Every human being is intrinsically independent with their own character and motion. Understanding your individual makeup and temperament is very important to understanding which actions are worth undertaking and which are not. Some desires are better to let go of because they are not in alignment with your True Will. It is a long process of deep acquaintance with yourself to thoroughly understand and live in accordance with your True Will. The practices and rituals

---

17 Crowley, Aleister, *Magick in Theory and Practice* (Dover Publications, 1976)
18 *Ibid.*

Jake Kobrin

of ceremonial magick are one way to deepen that understanding, but there are many ways to learn and understand this, including the wise use of psychedelics and plant medicines, meditation, psychotherapy, and rigorous self-examination—especially through journaling. Ultimately, one must test their own ideas of what their True Will is throughout their life and pay attention to what feels right and natural within their intuitive heart, and what does not.

A person is wasting their energy if their conscious will conflicts with the True Will. If they do so, they have no chance of effectively influencing their surroundings. It is very important that we live in accordance with our own nature and explore and discover what that nature is, rather than be swayed by external forces such as socialization, family, cultural roles, and responsibilities. Generally speaking, the dictates of the ego lead one astride from the True Will. It requires a practice of reorienting one's consciousness away from their mental fabrications and ego assumptions to a deep state of surrender and listening to the small voice of guidance within that may lead them towards the fulfillment of their True Will. In a way, the Universe, God, or whatever name you wish to give to Higher Intelligence has an invested interest in you fulfilling and living in alignment with your True Will. The Hindu epic *The Bhagavad Gita* demonstrates this by Krishna, the manifestation of God, urging Arjuna to fulfill his True Will of acting in the role of a soldier, despite the fact that Arjuna's ego mind opposes this role at first. Many people would dispute that this story is an example of Dharma rather than True Will due to the fact that the two concepts have distinct origins, Dharma being Buddhist and True Will being Thelemic. In a Buddhist, Vedic, or Hindu context, Dharma usually represents a spiritual duty that one has to perform in life and the path to liberation.

The Path Within

DIFFERENT TYPES OF MAGICK

There are many different types and traditions of magick, including Western ceremonial magick, witchcraft, chaos magick, Thelema, Wicca, Druidic magick, Norse magick, Eastern folk magick, indigenous shamanism and sorcery, ancient Greek magick, New Thought, and many other varieties. There is evidence to suggest that nearly every culture that has ever existed in human history has practiced different forms of magick that are unique to that culture. You learn magick through doing magick and being attentive to the results and consequences of your practices. It is less important that the way you are practicing is technically and traditionally 100% correct. What is important are the results that you get from your personal practice. If you're doing a ritual and it's slightly different than what you read in a book from the late 1800s, but you're getting good results from doing it that way, keep doing it by all means.

You can also engineer your own rituals. Magick is a bit like cooking. You first learn by following recipes and, through this, you learn how basic ingredients fit well together. But at a certain point, you need to become a chef. You need to be the one to spearhead your own ritual practice and design your own rituals. What I hope to do in this book is to present some traditional rituals, but also give you an idea and an understanding of why those rituals work so that you can begin to construct your own practice and rituals. Later, we will explore the basic structure of ritual form, which is essentially universal in the tradition of magick as it is practiced across all world cultures. A great historian of magick, Dr. Steven Skinner, compares magick to the smelting of iron: the process is essentially the same whether you do it in Japan, India, or Germany. There might be slight differences in the traditions, but the formula and how it works is essentially the same.[19] So, if you actually look into the way magick is being and has been practiced all over the world, you will find the same essential components, even though they might vary culturally and their symbols might vary dramatically.

DIFFERENCES BETWEEN HIGH MAGICK AND LOW MAGICK

The concept of the ego, or what we might call our "lower self," is just a fragment of our true, expansive nature. We often identify with our physical characteristics, mental capabilities, and the environment around us, but our essence extends far beyond these confined elements. There's no real separation between our everyday self and our higher self, often equated with divinity. We are intrinsically connected to the cosmos, and we have the potential to align with our higher selves, achieving a state commonly known as *enlightenment*.

The practice of high magick, or theurgy, provides a route to this profound recognition of our inherent divinity. This form of magick engages directly with divine entities or energies, facilitating personal insights into the divine that go beyond just benevolence and inspiration. In high magick, the integration of contrasting elements—such as light and dark, the tree of life and the tree of death, and the natural ebb and flow of breath—is essential in understanding divinity. Importantly, high magick emphasizes the need to embrace our shadow aspects. Recognizing and integrating our duality is key; neglecting our shadow side can lead to an unbalanced spiritual practice. High magick involves facing these darker aspects through structured and intentional practices, which may include interactions with demonic entities in a controlled environment.

In magick, it's crucial to distinguish between the highly improbable and the outright impossible. While magick does not make the impossible

---

19   Skinner, Stephen, *Techniques of Graeco-Egyptian Magic* (Golden Hoard Press, 2014)

achievable, low magick can influence events that appear highly unlikely. This might manifest as chance meetings or fortuitous events. Low magick leverages a profound understanding of the universe, beyond the physical, to influence such outcomes. However, it's important to understand that low magick is not about performing stage illusions or tricks that claim to enable physical impossibilities like levitation or telekinesis. Those expecting such feats from this book may be left wanting.

In magickal practice, the lower self is as important as the higher self. Balancing and nurturing both aspects is crucial for a practitioner to create positive change in the world. Magicians employ various methods to achieve this balance, from exploring altered states of consciousness to attempting to manifest non-physical entities, both benign and malevolent. They may also engage with these entities to accomplish specific tasks, offering gratitude through various means such as specific scents, symbolic offerings, or expressions of intense emotion.

BLACK MAGICK VS WHITE MAGICK

In addition to the distinctions between low magick and high magick, it may be useful to define black magick versus white magick. A lot of people have different interpretations of what these things mean. What I am describing is my own personal definition and perspective.

White magick is similar in its goals to Eastern yoga, and it's practically synonymous with mysticism. It is aimed at union with the higher self or God and other self-realization ambitions within the Western Esoteric Tradition. White magick is generally aimed at the purpose of achieving "knowledge and conversation with the Holy Guardian Angel," which, for the sake of convenience, I will say is similar to achieving gnosis, enlightenment, or Godhead. It could also be called *apotheosis*, the exaltation of the aspirant.

Jake Kobrin

Aleister Crowley has penned the useful quote: "There is a single main definition of the object of all magick ritual. It is the uniting of the microcosm with the macrocosm."[20] The microcosm is the individual. The macrocosm is God, the divine, the universe, the totality of existence, et cetera.

Black magick, on the other hand, is done with the express purpose of causing either physical or non-physical harm to yourself or another person. The law of karma applies just as much to magick as to life in general, in that, if you cause harm to another person through the use of magick, this usually results in some harm being done to yourself. On a deeper spiritual level, when you seek to harm another person, you are separating them from yourself and perpetuating an experience and perspective of alienation and separateness. People who have practiced black magick often say that they know when their spell or their ritual has worked because something bad happened to them.

Black magick, or malefic or baneful magick, is generally not necessary. I would recommend that you enchant for forgiveness or for compassion, for example, before enchanting to do harm to another person. Enchantment is casting a spell or enacting a ritual in order to create a desired change. In essence, it is a way of manipulating the forces of the universe to bring about a desired change. Although I will not use language such as "spell" or "spell casting" very often in this book, I will occasionally make reference to the practice of magick as "enchantment" or "to enchant." In certain very rare situations, like if somebody is a totalitarian dictator that is creating harm for millions and millions of people, it might be for the benefit of others to do harm to another person. But this is a very complicated subject that I don't feel I have the moral or ethical authority to gauge.

Crowley argued that all magick that is not directly aiding you in achieving knowledge and conversation of the Holy Guardian Angel ("K&C with the HGA" in short) —in other words, black magick is only for the gratification of your senses or for your ego.[21]

Grey magick is practical magick done to further your lot in life or to advance yourself in this world. It's okay to do grey magick for yourself or for others. We all have desires in life and it's okay to go after them. But it's

---

20   Crowley, Aleister, *Magick in Theory and Practice* (Dover Publications, 1976)
21   *Ibid.*

The Path Within

recommended that you do divination beforehand to check on the potential consequences of your grey magick. For this, you can use Tarot cards, I Ching, Norse runes, and lots of other forms. We will explore divination more deeply later in the book. Sometimes when you intend to perform grey magick, you may do black magick, causing harm to other people by accident. The way to avoid this is through a careful divination process beforehand.

However, if we're to accept the existence of a higher self or Holy Guardian Angel—an entity, energy, or consciousness that transcends our everyday understanding and may know the future or what's best for us— it might seem like our personal choices or efforts (such as divination) don't have much significance. After all, if our higher self knows the best path and can influence events, then why bother with our own conscious decisions or attempts to foresee the future?

It's important to recognize the value of both elements in our journey of self-growth and exploration. Here's a way to reconcile the two: consider the possibility that our divination process and our higher self's guidance aren't necessarily contradictory, but rather two elements of a single complex system. Our divination process could be a tool or a mechanism to tune into our higher self's wisdom and intuition, to understand its suggestions or nudges.

Through such practices, we're not trying to counteract the wisdom of our higher self or change a predestined outcome but align more closely with it. It's about finding harmony with that higher wisdom, learning to listen to it, interpret it, and integrate it into our daily lives.

So, from this perspective, both the divination process and the guidance of our higher self are integral parts of our spiritual and personal growth. They represent the intersection of our conscious intentions with the higher wisdom that guides us. Maybe it's even the hand of our higher self that guides our divination tools and reveals to us its knowledge. In any case, I find it useful to perform divination beforehand and have held back from performing magick at times based on the results of divination regarding potential rituals.

An example from Donald Michael Kraig's *Modern Magick* is as follows: you do a ritual without divination to receive a thousand dollars. Your uncle dies in a car crash, leaving you with the amount you enchanted for. In this case, you actually did black magick because you caused harm to another person without meaning to. Divination beforehand could have given you the perspective necessary to change your approach.[22]

Any magick that works for you and feels right and good to you is good magick. This may seem contradictory with our discussions on white, black, or grey magick. Instead, they offer two complementary ways to approach magic: one emphasizes ethical considerations and societal norms (white, black, and gray magick), and the other promotes personal resonance and individual growth (magick that feels right and good to you). Both approaches can coexist in a balanced magickal practice, providing valuable insights and checks for the practitioner. It's up to you to explore and find the right balance between tradition and intuition arrived at through experience.

THE CLASSICAL MAGICKAL ACTS

There are five classic acts in magick: evocation, divination, enchantment, invocation, and illumination.[23]

- **Enchantment:** This involves spell casting or manifesting desires into reality through the use of ritual.
- **Divination:** This practice aims to enhance your ability to receive information, often through symbolic sources like Tarot cards.
- **Invocation:** Here, you seek to attune and merge your consciousness with an archetypical or significant nexus of thought, such as the mind of a deity or an Archangel.
- **Evocation:** This entails the intentional conservation of spirits or entities and using them to carry out your will.

---

22 Kraig, Donald Michael, *Modern Magick: Eleven Lessons in the High Magickal Arts* (Llewellyn Worldwide, 2001)
23 Greer, John Michael, *The New Encyclopedia of the Occult* (Llewellyn Worldwide, 2003)

The Path Within

- **Illumination:** This involves meditative practices and Yoga, also known as white magic, focused on self-improvement and expanding perception and consciousness for inspiration and direction, ultimately aiming for the exaltation of the individual spirit.

ADDITIONAL MAGICKAL PRACTICES

Alongside the classical acts, other significant practices contribute to the richness of magick.

- **Banishing:** This is the magickal cleansing of space and the creation and maintenance of magickal boundaries.
- **Creation of Talismans and Amulets:** These are objects imbued with magickal power, attracting (talisman) or repelling (amulet) specific magickal qualities for various purposes.
- **Astral Projection:** This practice uses visualization and altered states of consciousness to visit or scry other realms or dimensions, usually to gain information and communicate with entities that reside there.

Magick is an endlessly fascinating subject; it's a rabbit hole you can dive into, continuously discovering new insights and techniques. While it's important to absorb theoretical knowledge, remember that magick is a practical field. Avoid being an "armchair magician" —someone who only reads about magick without putting it into practice. Engage in rigorous, thorough recording of your results and learn from your experiences. In this way, you understand not just how magick works generally, but specifically how it works for you.

Magick's effectiveness extends beyond technical knowledge or skill. The key to success is the intensity of energy you put into your practices. This truth applies not just to magick but to all endeavors. To truly imbue an object, project, or book with magic, you must bring your full authenticity to it and pour your heart into it. A crude ritual performed with fervor and passion will always surpass a perfect ritual performed without any feeling or energy.

THE EVOLUTION OF MAGICK BY GUEST TEACHER CARL ABRAHAMSSON

Magick, or the so-called Occult, is part of the human psyche, soul, life, and culture: always has been, and always will be. So, what you will experience here is hopefully not a "crash course" that leaves you exhausted, but rather a trip into a multicolored and multifaceted gemstone that will whet your appetite and curiosity even more.

I will take you on a history trip, a technology trip, and a suggested development trip. They will all merge, and I can only encourage you to continue studying both theory and practice when it comes to all of these things: magickal or philosophical history, which includes technological aspects as well as your never-ending personal journey of development and empowerment.

This history of magick is impossible to separate from general human culture, period. If we track what we know of biological evolution and integrated cultural expressions, it has always been a question of survival. We may not feel that this is the case today, but it might be more poignant than ever before in history. That is exactly why magick and the Occult have become visible and present to the great extent that they have. Magick is an integrated part of our survival mechanism.

When our forefathers and foremothers tried to figure out how to survive, communal efforts were necessary, and that required not only

The Path Within

fighting, hunting, and staying alert but also huddling together, surviving nights and winters, procreating, and realizing the concept of continuity and cyclical processes. In huddling or staying safe, we see the cathartic function of expressed art: of storytelling, of emerging ritual and art, and in communication with the unseen. As we all know, when it's dark in nature, it's really dark—and threatening. The conceptualization of gods and spirits was a human attempt to communicate with the unseen in order to be protected, gain control, and survive. It was there right from the beginning.

We know that cave paintings were very likely magickal in essence; they were created to bring good luck in hunting and protection. The creative externalization of the will to live is one early definition of magick that we should always hang on to. Because, as we will see, not much has really changed. The same goes for other externalizations: singing, dancing, and making jewelry and other ornaments which are not necessary for function, but elevate the mind or spirit of both the individual and tribe and, in many ways, promote strength.

As societies became more complex, with tribes interacting peacefully rather than violently, we see the emergence of a specialized role: the Shaman. The Shaman was a specialist in communicating with the realms that the other members were now too busy to explore themselves, except for special occasions and initiations.

The Shaman went into a trance by different methods, usually by manipulating rhythm and frequencies that allowed for a displacement of the so-called normal way of thinking and acting. Their function became one of an outsider, almost a jester, but also one revered and respected because the Shaman also brought back information that was necessary. Whatever gods or spirits there were, the Shaman was the one who could communicate with them. This also included medical knowledge, knowledge of the cycles, and the use of an intuitive orientation to explore more.

The integration of psychedelic mushrooms and other agents in the development of the human brain and consciousness has been debated, but science in general now seems to think that there is a direct correlation between

Jake Kobrin

psychedelics and human development. The tribe's Shaman was the original psychonaut: one who traveled inside and came back with information and mythic fodder necessary as existential glue in a life of extreme hardships.

With migration followed dissemination of culture and habits, sometimes clashing, sometimes merging. But as the overall structures became more complex, the Shamanic function or role remained. Jumping forward thousands of years, we can see the emergence of the institution of integrated priesthood and also that of Shaman-as-magician—the one working outside the system. An important foundation of societies is the specialization of individuals. Farmers farmed and passed on that knowledge, hunters hunted, metal workers passed on their unique knowledge, and priests, midwives, and healers did also. In a world where we could huddle with our little families and still be safe, the distinct Shamanic role became a little bit more opaque. The storyteller, artist, and healer of emotional ailments all became auxiliary functions emanating from the same core, and many of the parts grew into their own full functions.

The humans as societal beings developed or realized a new concept: the culture and mind-frame of power. In order to survive within the tribe (now that external threats were more or less under control, but of course not eradicated), you had to have power. Rulers took power. Violence and brute force became the new game. It was no longer a question of fighting for procreation. Material objects, clothes, weapons, lodgings, and behavior all became stratifying power signifiers. The previously Shamanic function became relegated to an almost jester-ly function, while the priesthood that was concerned with the same questions and behaviors became a power in itself, immersed in a dynamic that we can still see in our own cultures today.

The outsider-ship of the Shaman, which also included wise women (very often connected with midwifery) became both a blessing and a curse. People in general revered the esoteric knowledge while those threatened by it—hegemonic power structures in the same business—tried to ostracize it even more.

Cultures were different in their development and assessment of new findings. We can see parallel strains of exploration concerning both the

The Path Within

inner and the outer. Finding patterns, joining the cosmic dots, mapping the existential cycles, and elaborating the findings in art for instruction and posterity have all been there, albeit in slightly different forms and expressions. Astronomical analysis was imbued with meaning and religion within astrology, manipulations of the Elements, and various experiments with produce, fruits, herbs, plants, soil, and seeds developed both farming and medical advances. Most of this development wasn't shamanic in itself— if you disregard it amplifying a healthy, holistic outlook—but rather an example of a kind of proto-science in which communal efforts played a big part. The Shaman always lurked in the shadows, though, increasingly ostracized, except for in cultures that weren't part of general routes of trade and knowledge, and hence were "spared" what we today would call "modern progress."

Some five thousand years ago, Mesopotamia was the hotbed of civilization, including the development of cities and cuneiform writing, which also included historical writing. The land was not only fertile and a center of trade, but it also attracted cultures from the East and West. The main cultures were Persian, Babylonian, and Assyrian, all flexing their muscles, waxing and waning. Sumerian and other polytheisms of the region were related to the ones of the Egyptian, later Greek and Roman, empires, and Hinduism: systems in which the different forces of greater nature take on individual god forms very much resembling humans with distinctly human traits, strengths, and weaknesses.

Some 2,500 years ago, a big shift in consciousness occurred, and it seems to have taken place globally. Of course, not at the same exact point in time, but it is kind of remarkable that we have key influencers like the Buddha, Lao-Tse, Pythagoras, Plato, emerging Jewish mysticism, plus the still vital Egyptian culture and the emergence of the Roman Empire, all roughly at once. It's as if many foundations were laid out concerning human empowerment and potential parallel to the emergence of massive new cultural structures. Whether to balance out or to inspire, we will never know, but it all certainly had to do with the development of writing and the use of paper: historical writing and the expanded preservation

Jake Kobrin

of ideas, philosophy, and science. (And, of course, fiction and poetry.) Perhaps there had been similar quantum leaps before and in other parts of the world, but we have no real historical records of it.

The centuries before and after the birth of Christ were very conducive to cultural exchange largely thanks to increased trade and the Roman Empire. The Mediterranean region was a veritable hotbed of cultural exchange, and that also included ideas that could be called *hermetic*—meaning esoteric explanations and speculations about how the macrocosmic experience is connected to the microcosmic experience. In the wake of Egyptian culture, the mythic figure of Hermes Trismegistus ("thrice greatest Hermes") emerged as an archetype of sorts for what we know as a "magician." The ideas of a cosmic Oneness seeped into Gnosticism and Greek philosophy. The Jewish cultures began interpreting their language and writing as keys to connect to the divine through what became known as Kabbalah. In all of this there was exchange and curiosity, a branching out as well as in.

After a few centuries of budding Christianity, the Roman Empire was no more, and the new religion began its purge of other cultures and other religious behaviors. Monotheism grabbed hold of the cultural spheres, amplified from the seventh century and onward as Islam emerged. The big religions fought each other and all the pagans they could find, and in a way, it's still going on, much to the detriment of humanity and overall health.

Any occurrences of magick and occultism, proto-science, philosophical speculations, and so on were more or less banned and squashed. Of course, there were times when a more liberal attitude reigned, and it always brought a renewed interest in the old, perhaps even timeless, wisdom from the Mediterranean region and, of course, from beyond.

The Renaissance, circa 1300–1500, was especially interesting from our magickal perspective. The Italian city-states defied the rigid grips of the Vatican and allowed for art and philosophy to bloom. Integrated in this became what is known as Neo-Platonism—a reconnection to Greek philosophy and also the philosophy that the Golden Age Greeks had admired, such as the Hermeticism stemming from Egypt. The validation and use of inner visions and meditations became *en vogue* again, with it, heretical

The Path Within

ideas of personal freedom, individuation, and unhampered artistic and scientific expression.

That this was eventually clamped down on was inevitable. Here we find the beginning of occultism as we know of it today. Proto-Magicians, artists, and scientists had to rewrite their narrative and go underground by establishing a system of symbols and code, as well as a behavior cloaked in secrecy. Again, the transcendental behavior became connected to a survival instinct: not only survival for those involved but also the perennial wisdom from the East, West, and beyond that now had to be protected.

Slightly before the Renaissance, we had the Knights Templar protecting Christian pilgrims on their way to Jerusalem. During hundreds of years, between the twelfth and fourteenth centuries, they became a wealthy organization that through its mere wealth and power challenged the Vatican's hegemonic rule. Not only did they invent an efficient form of banking, where people could carry a letter of deposit or credit instead of money and cash that in Jerusalem, for instance. They also "trafficked" or interacted with Muslims in ways that weren't condoned or sanctioned. They were soon rumored to be receiving esoteric teachings from this different culture, and perhaps also in exchange for their own esotericism and secrets. This was enough to initiate their downfall. The Catholic Church clamped down and killed the main Templar leaders. In the mythic recounting of this strange tale, the remaining surviving leaders went underground and created a strict secrecy, only to emerge many hundreds of years later as the first Freemasons, celebrating their Templar past in their teachings and initiation rituals.

In the seventeenth century, the Rosicrucians appeared, promoting the teachings of the enigmatic Christian Rosencreutz. Likewise, the Bavarian Illuminati popped up and left a mark that is still felt today in an assortment of conspiracy theories. Both these movements honored the Hermetic past, but also mixed in ideas of social reform and a more or less secretive Christian mysticism—depending on how rigid the Christian tyranny was at that time and space.

We also need to remember the pioneering scientists who developed chemistry through alchemy, astronomy through astrology, botanical knowl-

Jake Kobrin

edge from age-old herbalism, and so on. What they had to deal with in the dark, so to speak, because of oppression and power struggles brought many of the incredible scientific advances we can enjoy today.

The very same became true of the Freemasons, especially during the eighteenth century. They had grown out of a mythic esoteric past, through communal glue in various medieval trade and artisan guilds, and onto the political scene by the very leverage of societal power. Although not in any way overground, they did manage to influence policies in Europe and what was to become the US. Many of the founding fathers were Freemasons and integrated their ideas into new constitutions and attitudes. Both the American and French revolutions carried strong Masonic ideals.

The rational enthusiasm of the Enlightenment brought with it an empirical mindframe and a materialism that in many ways pushed esoteric speculations to the side, or perhaps even underground again. This time it wasn't so much the tyranny of a violent inquisition but rather the ridicule of an industrialized era that regarded monetary wealth as an expression of progress. This backlashed within culture through German romantics, Gothic horror, pre-Raphaelites, and eventually the big boom of magick towards the end of the nineteenth century. With hotspots in Paris and London, the Rosicrucian salons, spiritualism, seances, occult orders, the emergence of romantic Satanism, and, of course, the Theosophists and the Golden Dawn, the market was suddenly flooded with the Occult in both old and new shapes and sizes.

As a parallel strain of psychology in general (and psychoanalysis in particular) grew, the desire to look deeper within also manifested through Buddhism and other Asian movements that now became visible in Europe. This longing to know more about oneself both on personal and cosmic planes had been a perennial presence within Occultism and philosophy. Now they could be out in the open to a much higher degree, and this led to even more radical findings.

During the twentieth century, we could see a dissolution of many of the old sets of rules. Nietzsche had hammered in the re-evaluation of all values, beyond good and evil. The chaos that ensued in the First and Second World Wars created a topsy turvy apprehension of what it really means to be human, and many people looked for solutions in unconven-

The Path Within

tional ways: the Lebensreform movement of Germany, the beatniks of the 1950s, and the hippies of the 1960s, peace movements, civil rights, and social reform movements, and so on. These were all imbued with either religious or decidedly occult input, from Eastern religions and philosophies to concrete ritual magick and experiences with altered states of consciousness. The Shamanic sensibility was thrown headfirst back into the mix—perhaps as a safeguard after the atomic bombs had shown what human beings could do if left unchecked.

During this century, we had the Golden Dawn, Crowley and his AA group, the Ordo Templi Orients (OTO), Gurdjieff, Theosophy, Anthroposophy, and other groups. Solitary magicians like British artist Austin Osman Spare were key bridge figures between old and new, and between arcane systems and artistic expression. Spare became a main source of inspiration for the British new wave of the 1980s, with Thee Temple Ov Psychick Youth (TOPY) and the chaos magicians of the Illuminates of Thanateros (IOT).

In the US, Anton LaVey's formulation of Satanism in his Church of Satan brought an unadulterated love of the dark mysteries to center stage, as he emphasized his philosophy of individual liberty via public rituals and sexual provocations. Whatever the draconian forces had tried to suppress over the centuries now suddenly all came back to bite them in their moralistic behind.

Today we are living in a technological culture that was largely developed via the inspiration of psychedelic drugs. The enhanced connectivity potential of psychedelics brings us back full circle to the Shamanic perspective. Things happen for a reason, and today we are faced with environmental problems that seem very hard to deal with—perhaps they are even insurmountable. The connections to nature itself need to be re-enlightened, and the internet is one way of facilitating the exchange of ideas and information that is necessary to make any shifts happen.

The big boom of the psychedelic 60s was equally one of acceptance of Eastern philosophies, and in this, we could see integration from other parts of the world as well, like in the case of Central American sorcery via the writings of Carlos Castaneda. And today we are immersed in the magics of the African diaspora systems, stemming from Africa but trav-

Jake Kobrin

eling via the Caribbean and South America and on to the West's young adepts who are all looking for solutions to the same perennial problems or challenges as ever before: individuation and survival.

That this has been a superficial and partial Western-focused overview is obvious. But it tracks a spirit or value that still remains. The Shamanic approach is the quintessential key to this spirit. Any and all systems in any and all times in any and all cultures are but derivatives of the proto-Shamanic approach. We are inherently connected to a greater whole, and by understanding this, we can shape our lives to achieve meaning and fulfillment. However, it's essential to recognize that this is an exchange, not a one-sided transaction.

Let's move into what I call the technological side of things. Each culture has its own technology. It could be an outer one, as in tools, and it could be an inner one, as in approaches. The same is valid for the magickal spheres and cultures. There are techniques that integrate the use of certain tools, and whether they are symbolic or "real" can be argued back and forth forever. Suffice it to say that traditionally in the West, we have Elemental representations in the forms of magickal "weapons." This can be a bit of a misnomer, as the word "weapon" has quite a few meanings we don't necessarily appreciate. Perhaps this is a remnant of a paranoid past when the ritual tools in question could actually be used as weapons of defense too.

The wand represents Fire, the will. The cup, Water, the emotions. The disk, Earth, materiality. The dagger, Air, the intellect. On each altar, there should be actual fire too, as a symbol of the fire of survival that has kept us protected through thousands of years. In a way, this could be seen as representing the immortal Spirit of nature, the light that we need to see in darkness.

When you begin, begin simple. The tools of your magickal trade will evolve over time. You will find finer things and objects that are more attractive to use. Just remember that they are tools to be used, not merely decorations that look cool in your magickal corner.

Concerning the space: not everyone has a designated temple space that is overflowing with energy and beauty even when you're not there. That is completely beside the point. Even if you bring your tools out now

The Path Within

and then because you don't have the space to keep them out permanently, what really matters is your investment in working with them. You can't really buy a prefab kit or ready-made magickal success. You have to create it yourself by trial and error. If we keep up the economic analogies, you have to invest in your own work.

Any tool you have is an extension of yourself and your will. That's why it's good to look at your altar as yourself. Is it aesthetically pleasing? Is it balanced? Are you happy with it? One of the cornerstones of the hermetic philosophy that still emanates from Thrice-Greatest Hermes is "as above, so below." That basically means that as we're all in the same cosmic boat; whatever you do at the helm will be felt in the stern. Your actions not only have implications but also applications. So, if you improve your altar as a representation of yourself and your potential, that will affect you in similar ways.

An initial analogy will be to your own body, and vice versa. You are your own best tool, for all kinds of magic. This is true for your body as well as for your mind. The Elemental matrix is valid for all kinds of analysis it seems. Symbolically, you clear the air and focus with your ceremonial dagger, and you stand firm on your disk for your working agency. The flame illuminates your vision, while the cup and dagger represent the dynamic forces of libido—the very life drive that goes well beyond strictly sexual connotations but can certainly include them, as well as the generative organs.

From a mind-based perspective, again the dagger is focus, and the disk a down-to-earth approach of not flying unreasonably high in the ritual. The flame is the original spark of life, the proto-will that guides your own will. Your own will is the wand, so treat it kindly and with respect. The cup is your emotions and fantasies, your desires and hopes, no less worthy of kindness and respect.

Again, we could find many different analogies in the process of interpretation, but the main lesson is that it is all you. Always all you. Whatever you change, you change on more levels than the most apparent or visceral. That said, your body and mind are tools themselves. They should be kept in pristine health and strength so that they function as well as possible.

Your individuation is also an important tool. That is, how you act vis-à-vis yourself in the journey of finding out more about yourself. And there is

Jake Kobrin

always more to find out. We don't stop one day and realize we're perfect. If someone claims that, just keep walking. We constantly evolve and are affected by outer as well as inner circumstances, by health, illness, other people, life choices, chaos and disorder, and so on. Your awareness of this kind of meta-perspective as a useful tool is invaluable. Look at yourself while you move onwards, and keep questioning what you do, so you don't do it for other reasons than those you've formulated to and for yourself in temple space and temple time.

Also, don't separate too much from what the tools of your trade are. If you are in a meaningful place in life, you already have tools of study, work, or both. Very few people are full-time magicians who occupy themselves with the technology and philosophy of magick 24/7. An ideal is to be in the magick 24/7—but that is an entirely different thing.

Are you a nurse? A teacher? A plumber? An academic? Then the tools of your trade, whichever they are, are also tools of your magick because you are always the vehicle of your own will—or should be.

You've probably heard the old cliché that "it's all in the mind." This means, in my opinion, that magick is how and what we perceive about the outer world, which is interpreted and sent back in a kind of cyclic cosmic regurgitation. Using mind-altering drugs can illustrate that. It feels magickal and certainly out of the dreary rational sphere, but is it beneficial to your actual will? If so, then fine. But if not, it's not really magick, but rather some form of colorful escapism.

That said, the mind is an integral, integrated tool. We can expand it, contract it, it's a central of sorts for receiving and interpreting data. I don't mean this specifically about the brain or in the neurological sense, although we could absolutely argue that the real tool in all of this is actually the brain itself. But if we stick to the mind, and perhaps also accept that it's all in there, then that provides us with plenty of food for thought, and action as well.

A key to knowing the mind is transcending it. You probably know "transcendental meditation," at least as a phenomenon. As with all medi-tation, it's meant to temporarily stop the chaotic disorder of a free-flowing, associating mind for reasons of stillness, health, and a deeper insight. So far, so good. But that leads to a mystical state of mind, not a necessarily

The Path Within

magickal one. We want to change things, be active, learn, indulge, and go places, not stop the vehicle proper.

Luckily, there are other ways of transcending the mind that are more in line with magickal approaches, the main one being ecstasy. No, I'm not talking about the drug but about the strong, shocking, and immediate euphoric elevation of the mind via outer manipulation. One such manipulation is sex, for instance. In ecstatic mind-frames, we are temporarily open to a meta-programming of ourselves. The body allows for a transcendence that our will makes use of via the mind in its neutral gear, so to speak. I won't go into detail here about what to do once this is achieved, but I want to emphasize that the mind and body are absolutely on par as tools, and when combined, they are an actual force that the symbolic Elemental weapons merely represent in their totality.

Many magicians like to work with what I call an "associative feedback" system. This is a set of symbols or artistic representations that are filled with meaning for the magician. It could be a Tarot deck, the I Ching, or runes, for example. Working with them in traditional or innovative ways can create extensions and associations in your own work of interpretation that at times can be very revealing indeed. No secrets here: just experiment and see what comes up.

Now, over to what I called the development trip. As you are all on different levels of entry—some may be adept and experienced, some may be complete novices—I'm going to generalize quite a bit here. However, good advice is good advice, wherever and whoever you are. You are about to embark on a journey that will definitely change your life. Though I certainly don't mean that in any ostracizing, stigmatizing way, or any moralistic way in which you are threatened with the demons of hell or the wrath of your mother if you don't stick to the curriculum.

I would advise you to always remain true to yourself. If you feel attracted or compelled to seek out a group that promises teachings and you feel trust for it, by all means go ahead and explore. In the initial phases, that can be great, like going to elementary school, high school, and maybe even college. Always remember that structures serve their own purposes and exist independently of your personal path. What should matter is that

Jake Kobrin

you always be true to yourself. You carry your magic, they don't. They may help you develop in a system that you feel comfortable in but if that in any way decreases or deviates, you should probably check and re-check your own position.

Many of the established systems of teaching also exist in book form, so that theoretically, you could begin on your own. It is a commonly held belief that the master appears when the student is ready. This I cannot guarantee, and I don't think you should hope for it either. Seeking out human relations within specific esoteric environments can be fun and rewarding for all involved, but you should ask yourself: "is this person a good representative of this system and what it claims to provide? Is it working out for them?"

Some basic recommendations: Yoga, meditation, and physical exercise (but not too much or aggressive). Never strain yourself. Joyfully move on, happy to explore. People who claim "no pain, no gain" are merely masochists, not prophets of health or wisdom. This is equally valid in the gym as in the magickal temple.

Connect to your dream life. Record your dreams. Don't interpret them for the sake of it; just acknowledge that they exist in your mind, too, and yet they have a different narrative. What can you learn from them? Sometimes it can be constructive to twist the perspectives a bit: what if you look at your waking two-thirds as merely a necessary exhaustion so you can be healthily asleep and dream as much as possible? That the dream world is the "real" one and the waking one merely a tiresome illusion and physical strife?

As an extension of both meditation and dream work, try to learn to see things with your inner vision. This is also why meditation practices are helpful. If you can somewhat still your mind, you can be more adept in visualizing a scene or scenario that you want to happen. Remember Hermes? "As above, so below." That also means "so within, so without." If you're skilled enough via practice, you should be able to visualize things even in ecstatic mind-frames. Then the doors not only of perception, but also of conception, will be wide open for you.

Get a diary. Write in your diary. Read your diary. This should have been mentioned among the tools, because it may be more valuable than

The Path Within

any wands, daggers, cups, or disks. You do not have to be methodical about it. Just write. Please disregard whatever Crowley wrote about "the method of science, the aim of religion." That may have been his trip, but that doesn't mean it's yours. Keeping a diary is an extension of communication with yourself that with time will be very cherished. Laugh at your mistakes! Marvel at your achievements! Join the emotional dots! Remember all the things you've forgotten! I started writing my diary in 1987 and have been doing it since then. I'm glad I have, because how else could I have remembered all the weird things I've done?

You've probably heard a lot about banishing, invocation, and evocation—terms from magickal history that seem to be important. They are, but only specifically within the system in question. Each system has its own routines. A ceremonial magician in the Western Tradition banishes the temple before invocation or evocations begin, and then banish again afterward. A Voodoo practitioner may be greeting the ancestors (physical as well as adopted) before anything else happens. And there may be a blood sacrifice, whereas that would be looked upon with dread among the vegan witches, whose sexual revelries might terrify the bookish ceremonial magician. No system is worth more than the other. We do what we do because we feel a resonance and affinity with the specific system in question. The magick lies in our own "vibing" to the frequency that the egregore or center of that system emits. When we tune in, we can communicate. To tune in, there are simply different ways in different egregores.

Also, just for the sake of it, please do connect somehow to Shamanism as such, read about it, try it, attend classes and courses, learn the traveling techniques and get out into nature. Even if that does not end up being your preferred magickal toolbox and environment, it is something from which everything else stems: the roots of the tree, if you will, in which you straddle a particular branch of your liking.

What is magick all about, then? It's basically about the connection between your nature and greater nature, and the ensuing realization that there is essentially no difference between them. Welcome to the eternal gang of transcendental renegades! The Shaman exists inside you. Always has, always will.

CHAPTER TWO

ETHICAL APPROACHES TO MAGICKAL PRACTICE

Before getting into the meat of the book, in which we will explore some of the most powerful and fundamental theories, concepts, and practices of magick, I wanted to first talk about ethics. Magick can be extraordinarily powerful, and just as there are characters in stories that use magick for good, and others for evil, it can be a tool of either healing or destruction that can either benefit the practitioner and others or hurt both. While most of the people reading this book will not want to use magick to create pain for others or in an exploitive way, we all have the capacity to use magick in a way that will affect the lives of others. I have found most books about magick to be lacking in any meaningful discussion of ethics, and so I wanted to include this chapter as a foundational and essential subject to explore before we really begin.

ETHICS AND MAGICK

Although some traditions of magick do have ethical implications, such as the Wiccan Rede "An' it Harm None, Do What Ye Will,"[24] the form of magick that I am presenting here is generally neutral, more of a toolkit than any kind of hard-ironed spiritual path or tradition. Therefore, having a personally rooted sense of ethics and values is the most important first step on the path. Without an ethical code, the dangers of magick are significantly greater and magick can potentiate harm for yourself and for others and can turn wayward practitioners into selfish, cruel, self-righteous, bigoted, and unhappy people. There are already enough miserable people in occult communities, and that is not what I am trying to promote here. My primary goal is not to turn you into a magician, but to help you become a happier and more empowered person. Developing your own personal code of ethics is essential—not just for practicing magick, but for your overall well-being and happiness. Your heart and soul are at stake. Beware, for there be dragons.

There is no one universal ethical right or wrong. There are many different codes of ethics that are culturally specific. For example, some people believe that sex before marriage is ethically wrong. I do not agree. In his book *Ethics for the New Millennium*, the Dalai Lama writes:

> *Let me say that no one should suppose it could ever be possible to devise a set of rules or laws to provide us with the answer to every ethical dilemma, even if we were to accept religion as the basis of morality. Such a formulaic approach could never hope to capture the richness and diversity of human experience.*[25]

---

24   Cunningham, Scott, *Wicca: A Guide for the Solitary Practitioner* (Llewellyn Publications, 1988)

25   Dalai Lama XIV, *Ethics for the New Millennium* (Riverhead Books, 1999)

The Path Within

The Law of Thelema states, "do what thou wilt shall be the whole of the Law,"[26] meaning that adherents of Thelema should seek out and follow their own personal true path and find and determine their True Will. Unfortunately, many people have taken this phrase out of context to mean "you can do whatever you want." You can, in fact, do whatever you want, but there are consequences to all of your decisions, and you have to live with them. Some of these consequences are very undesirable. In the true sense, this is not what "do what thou wilt shall be the whole of the Law" means at all, but rather that we must discover our unique soul's path and stick to it with unwavering and devout discipline in order to live out our true purpose in this life. Just as the Law of Thelema suggests that there are many paths and it is up to each and every one of us to discover what way of life is right for ourselves. It is, therefore, necessary for each of us to discover and decode our own values and systems of ethics.

The starting point of ethics is to understand that you want to be happy and free from suffering. You ultimately want things to go well in your life and to avoid misfortune and situations that would cause you pain. Likewise, then, you can see that all human beings, and possibly all sentient beings, want this same thing. To understand and practice ethical behavior, we have to be able to empathize and consider other people's feelings, desires, and suffering. We must operate from this perspective of *sameness,* not from a place of self and other. We have no way of discerning what is right or wrong if we cannot take into account the feelings of others. The Dalai Lama stated simply that "what determines whether an act is ethical or not is its effect on others' experience or expectation of happiness. An act which harms or does violence to this is potentially an unethical act."[27]

I am deeply inspired by Buddhism and often refer to my practice as "chaos dharma" —an eclectic blend of elements from a wide range of cultures and traditions, some of which I've invented along the way. I have spent time reading and reflecting on ethical teachings from the East and the West, and I can safely say that none of my efforts have been wasted. My ethical outlook has been shaped by my upbringing, stories, and myths—

---

26   Crowley, Aleister, *The Book of the Law* (Dover Publications, 1976)
27   Dalai Lama XIV, *Ethics for the New Millennium* (Riverhead Books, 1999)

including J. R. R. Tolkien's Lord of the Rings, which conveys Christian values such as humility, virtue, courage, self-sacrifice, fellowship, and community. I have explored ethical philosophies from a variety of sources, including secular, Buddhist, Jewish, Christian, and Stoic perspectives.

You'd be surprised how much ethical concerns take part in your magickal practice. When we are affecting change in the universe, we are affecting the entire universe and therefore must be cautious and considerate of the ramifications of those actions. This is especially true when you are doing magick that affects another person specifically, such as a love charm or a malefic curse. In my mind, neither love magick (to make a specific person fall in love with you, usually against their will) nor malefic or baneful magick (magick that seeks to punish or harm other people) is a good idea. Yes, I have done magick to acquire the attraction of specific love interests. Yes, it works. But it is usually a really bad idea. You might end up perpetuating suffering for yourself and the other person by creating an entanglement that goes against the nature of both people, or you might acquire that person's affection to find yourself very incompatible with them. An alternative for this would be to enchant for love, partnership, or connection in an open and non-specific way, without dragging the object of your infatuation unwillingly into it. In the case of malefic magick, just don't do it. Not only is it morally and ethically unsound, but by the magickal principle of "whatever you do to others comes back to you tenfold" you are just cursing yourself. Enchant instead for justice, reconciliation, or forgiveness.

ETHICAL FRAMEWORKS ACROSS TRADITIONS

Various traditions offer systems for ethical living, such as the Yamas and Niyamas from the Eight Limbs of Yoga or the Judaic Ten Commandments. The Golden Rule— "do unto others as you would have them do unto you" —can serve as a practical guide for ethical conduct. Alternatively, its

The Path Within

negative formulation— "do not do unto others what you would not have them do unto you" —can also be a useful compass for the right action. These ethical principles can be helpful to contemplate, inspiring you as you develop your personal system of ethics.

I encourage you to explore ethical teachings from different wisdom traditions for a more comprehensive and robust perspective. For the purpose of this discussion, we will focus on Buddhist ethics, specifically the Five Precepts.

BASIC BUDDHIST ETHICS

"The non-doing of any evil, the performance of what's skillful, the cleansing of one's own mind: this is the teaching of the Awakened."
—The Dhammapada, translated by Thanissaro Bhikkhu

In this section, we delve into the fundamental ethical principles of Buddhism, known as the Five Precepts. While it is not my intention to present one ethical system as superior to others, exploring these Buddhist principles can offer valuable insights.

The Five Precepts of Buddhism

The Five Precepts form the foundation of ethical conduct in Buddhist life, especially for those who have taken monastic vows.[28] They are:

1. **Refrain from taking life:** This precept advises against killing any living being. It is the reason why many Buddhists choose vegetarianism.
2. **Refrain from taking what is not given:** This precept discourages stealing.
3. **Refrain from the misuse of sexuality:** This precept advises against engaging in lustful behavior or committing adultery.

---

28   Harvey, Peter. *An Introduction to Buddhist Ethics.* (Cambridge University Press, 2000)

Jake Kobrin

4. **Refrain from wrong speech:** This precept discourages lying or gossiping about others.
5. **Refrain from intoxicants that cloud the mind:** While some Buddhists completely abstain from intoxicants, generally this precept advises against alcohol and other substances that encourage harmful behavior.

These precepts are subject to various interpretations and are not meant to be adhered to rigidly. They are intended to inspire you to understand and define your own ethical code, governing your life and magickal practice.

While I don't strictly adhere to these precepts all the time, they influence and inspire my ethical perspectives. I don't identify as a Buddhist in the strict sense, but I find immense value in the ideas, philosophies, and practices of Buddhism.

The universality of Buddhist practices, such as the Five Precepts, offers a rich foundation of ethical guidelines that resonate with individuals from diverse backgrounds. In adopting elements of Buddhism into personal belief systems, it's essential to approach with respect and sensitivity, acknowledging its origins and cultural significance. While integrating these practices into one's life, especially in a context like magick and esotericism, it's important to avoid cultural appropriation by not misrepresenting or trivializing these beliefs. Instead, one should aim to honor the depth and integrity of these teachings. By doing so, we can enrich our spirituality and ethics, drawing on Buddhist wisdom while maintaining a respectful and authentic connection to its roots.

The Path Within

THE FOUR CARDINAL VIRTUES

People often talk about the cardinal directions, the Four Elements, and many other associated correspondences. Magick in general has a lot to do with resonances and correspondences, which is a concept that we will speak more about later on and throughout this book. Related to ethics and the pursuit of happiness is the Stoic concept of the Four Cardinal Virtues.[29] These cardinal virtues are Wisdom, Justice, Courage, and Temperance. I think you could make the case that these could be vaguely mapped out to the Four Elements, an essential magickal concept that we talk about later on. Prudence aligns the most with the Element of Earth, Justice to Air, Courage to Fire, and Temperance to Water.

- Courage means bravery, fortitude, honor, and sacrifice.
- Temperance suggests self-control, moderation, composure, and balance.
- Justice relates to fairness, service, fellowship, goodness, and kindness.
- Wisdom encourages knowledge, education, truth, self-reflection, and peace.

These virtues can be invoked through magickal processes, by calling in their corresponding Elements in the practices that we will explore throughout this book. These are virtues to aim our lives towards, like a compass that can guide us in navigating our sometimes confusing and complicated lives.

In Western magick, another famous concept is the idea of the Four Powers of the Sphinx. These four powers are To Will, To Dare, To Know,

---

29 Holiday, Ryan, *The Obstacle Is the Way: The Timeless Art of Turning Trials into Triumph* (Portfolio/Penguin, 2014)

Jake Kobrin

and To Keep Silent. Aleister Crowley, who is perhaps not always the most ethical person who was, wrote in his *Book of Thoth*:

> *The great secret of magick, the unique and incommunicable Arcana, has for its purpose the placing of supernatural power at the service of the human will in some way. To attain such an achievement, it is necessary to KNOW what has to be done, to WILL what is required, to DARE what must be attempted, and to KEEP SILENT with discernment.*[30]

Likewise, I think that these Four Powers could be mapped out to the Four Elements, the Four Directions, and the Four Cardinal Virtues in the following way:

Element	Direction	Power	Cardinal Virtue
Air	East	To Know	Justice
Fire	South	To Will	Courage
Water	West	To Dare	Temperance
Earth	North	To Keep Silence	Prudence

Throughout your magick, and in your life in general, these Four Cardinal Virtues are useful shorthand for the types of behaviors and attitudes most beneficial to strive towards, cultivate, and emphasize. The Stoic philosophers believed that these four virtues are the foundation of a good and happy life.

---

30   Crowley, Aleister, *The Book of Thoth: A Short Essay on the Tarot of the Egyptians* (Samuel Weiser, 1974)

HAPPINESS AND WELLNESS

I will talk about something that I rarely hear addressed within occult or magickal literature: happiness and wellness. Why are you interested in learning magick? Most likely you want to learn magick because you believe it will make you happy, on some level. You may want to feel a greater sense of agency and control in your life or discover a sense of personal power. Maybe you have goals you want to lend extra power towards achieving or material aims you want to realize. Maybe you want to feel a deeper connection to your spiritual nature. In any case, chances are you want any of these things because you believe they will make you happy.

In his best-selling book *The Art of Happiness,* the Tibetan Buddhist leader His Holiness the Dalai Lama XIV said: "Whether we live a day or a century, a central question always remains: What is the purpose of our life? What makes our lives meaningful? The purpose of our existence is to seek happiness."[31] He proposes that no matter who you are, of what caste or country, religion or race, age or gender, what unites our human community is a fundamental drive and desire towards our own and shared happiness.

So how does this relate to our magickal practice? Magick can help cultivate greater happiness, wellness, and harmony in your life, but it also can detract you from it and potentially cause greater suffering. Any spiritual practice, including magick and its adjacent disciplines of witchcraft, Qabalah, theurgy, tantra, and all kinds of spell casting and ritual practices, that do not ultimately lead to greater fulfillment and happiness, and personal and collective wellness and harmony, should be discarded. That is why I am emphasizing this at the very beginning of your exploration

---

31 Dalai Lama XIV and Howard C. Cutler, *The Art of Happiness: A Handbook for Living* (Riverhead Books, 1998)

with magick. Magick is a tool. It is, in my opinion, morally and ethically neutral. It is not good or bad in and of itself. The results of your magick, and how your magick will affect you and your life, will depend on your intentions, your values, your motivations, and your decisions. Ultimately you are the one with the responsibility to whether or not your magick will lead to a happier version of yourself or a more miserable one.

To again quote the Dalai Lama: "Only the development of compassion and understanding for others can bring us the tranquility and happiness we all seek."[32] This means that self-serving actions, especially those that exploit or harm others, inevitably create suffering for ourselves and others. Conversely, actions motivated by altruism or self-sacrifice for the good of others and the community lead to genuine happiness. This idea is at the core of many of the world's spiritual, religious, and ethical traditions. In your magickal practice, rituals driven solely by personal gain, without considering their impact on others—especially those intended to harm—sow seeds of suffering. However, magickal endeavors aimed at helping others will contribute to both your happiness and the well-being of the world.

This does not mean that you should never do any magick for yourself, because you as much as anyone deserve happiness and all of the good things that the opportunities of life afford you. But it is important to observe, scrutinize, and calibrate what actions and motivations actually bring you happiness and what do not. You may be tempted to enchant for things you don't really need, which you may have strong desires for but will not ultimately bring you happiness or fulfillment. For example, many of the things that people are programmed by society and culture to believe will make them happy don't, and when you realize this, you can ask yourself, "does this align with my purpose to be happy and contribute to the happiness of others?" If not, let it go. I have met many miserable millionaires. I have met miserable billionaires. The story that our culture sells us—that material wealth accumulation and social status will make us happy—negates the inner dimension of our lives and is a complete falsehood. You don't need to be a social scientist to discover that this hypothesis is inaccurate, just get around a bunch of rich people and see

---

32 Dalai Lama XIV, *Ethics for the New Millennium* (Riverhead Books, 1999)

how they're doing. That's not to say that wealth is not a worthy and noble pursuit, or that it cannot contribute to happiness, but it is only one of the many pieces that come into play for happiness to occur.

A way to overcome the selfishness of any desire you may wish to perform magick for is to understand that we all want essentially the same things. Every human being wishes to be happy, safe, healthy, and prosperous, and to feel connected through love and community. So, for example, if you are about to travel and wish to perform a ritual for your travels to go smoothly without obstacles or complications, you might realize that many other travelers are traveling that day and that they all also wish to reach their destination without obstacle or difficulty. So, you may change the intention of your enchantment to accommodate these people as well. Instead of enchanting only for your own benefit, for your own travels to go smoothly and easily, you may want to enchant on behalf of all travelers: to perform a ritual so that all who are traveling that day do so with ease and grace and arrive at their destinations safely and without complications. Based on the idea that selfish motivations create suffering while altruistic motivations contribute to happiness, enchanting and performing a magickal ritual in this way on behalf of the well-being of others is likely to make you feel better and contribute overall to a happier heart and mind, and you do not lose anything because the enchantment still benefits you as well.

A perspective that many Eastern and Western thinkers have in common which brings happiness is that there is greater importance in cultivating wholesome inner states of mind and cultivating virtue, compared to the relative insignificance of changing external conditions. The Stoic philosopher Seneca in *On the Happy Life,* which was written in 58 AD, makes the analogy that inner virtue and a strong, ethical moral character, are like the light of the sun, while external circumstances provide pleasure only in a small way like a tiny fire. He says: "What absurdity lies in not being content with the daylight unless it is increased by a tiny fire. What importance can a spark have in the midst of this clear sunlight?"[33] There are heroic examples, both historically and in our modern era, of people who were able to

---

33   Seneca, *On the Happy Life* (Original work published 58 AD). Translated version referenced.

Jake Kobrin

cultivate happiness in even the most dire external circumstances given the strength of their inner character, such as the still actively teaching Tibetan Lama Garchen Rinpoche, who was able to maintain perfect happiness while being tortured in a Chinese communist prison for twenty years.[34] He would famously reject any deals the Chinese government would offer him, such as disclosing the location of his fellow monks and lamas in exchange for his freedom, saying, "why would I want to leave when it is so nice here?" despite the fact he was regularly tortured and brutalized by the Chinese and constantly watched his friends be subjected to the same hardship. The deeply moving *Man's Search For Meaning*, written by Austrian psychiatrist Viktor Frankl, describes how his ability to remain altruistic and motivated to be of service to his fellow prisoners allowed him to survive the deepest suffering imaginable during his internment in the Nazi concentration camp Auschwitz.[35] Keeping this in mind, it may be of greater value to do magick for the cultivation of inner qualities, such as virtuous character traits and the strength of heart and mind, rather than for comparatively trifling external acquisitions.

Pondering happiness and wellness is a worthwhile endeavor: let us explore and nurture them both within ourselves and those around us. According to research and my own observations, many components go into creating it: kindness, self-esteem, trust, affection, benevolence, selflessness, a purpose that benefits others, sympathy, not obsessing over control, not taking things to heart, preserving our energy, being optimistic, living in the moment, maintaining healthy boundaries, fostering healthy interactions and habits, diet, an inviting and wholesome environment, activities appropriate for our individual temperaments, and economic stability. All these can help us to construct a lifestyle that brings more joy and wellness for ourselves and those we care about.

It is up to each and every one of us to explore and discover that which makes us truly happy. Grief, sorrow, and misfortune are inevitable aspects of life that practicing magick cannot protect you from, and our

---

34 Garchen Rinpoche, *A Spacious Path to Freedom: Practical Instructions on the Union of Mahamudra and Atiyoga* (Snow Lion Publications, 1998)

35 Frankl, Viktor, *Man's Search for Meaning* (Beacon Press, 1959)

human predicament and the collective story are wrought with tragedy and loss. But this grief does not have to harden us or prevent us from living life in an openhearted way which can allow us to be open and vulnerable, to be touched by life. Living from an open heart, in which we are rooted deeply enough in the transcendent and larger aspects of our True Self so that we can be truly touched by life in all of the myriad forms that it presents itself, is how we can begin to live life in a way that is happier, more compassionate, and more connected with each other and with the whole web of existence.

To me, a big part of happiness is feeling myself to be worthy of it, and a big part of that is knowing in my heart that I am a good person who does good to others and the world and that I, therefore, deserve good things in return. To have high self-regard and self-esteem. To feel good about myself. Having the discipline and resolve to observe behaviors that I deem to be morally and ethically correct through a balanced mind and altruistic actions is one of the things which helps me feel deserving of and willing to feel happiness. For this, it is necessary to formulate and live by a code of ethics.

PUTTING ETHICS INTO PRACTICE

What are your values? What are your codes of ethical behavior? What must you aim towards? What high ideals do you strive to enact? What behaviors are not in alignment with your personal ethics? Write all of these down. Begin to journal about and reflect on this.

I have a practice where in the morning, I read out loud to myself a list of about twenty minutes worth of ethical precepts, affirmations, prayers, and intentions that define my own personal code of conduct. There are passages from Zen Buddhist Ghatas, a prayer from the Christian Saint Francis, as well as passages from the Golden Dawn—some of which I composed myself for my own usage. I will not present this to you because

Jake Kobrin

it's too personal, but it has short "I vow to..." lines such as: "Today I will be self-reflective, honest, and scrutinize myself to eliminate ways, patterns, and behaviors which are harmful," "Today I will take no actions towards another person that is not how I would want to be treated," and "Today I will not take anything personally, and understand that the actions of others are beyond me and not about me." There are 125 lines like this (perhaps more or less at the time you will read this, as I am always revising the list) in addition to five paragraphs that were added from other writings that inspired me that I did not compose, taken from the sources I mentioned before, and I read it before the altar (metaphorically speaking) at the very beginning of each day at the conclusion of my meditation and ritual practice.

This type of practice, although I am not following any specific tradition, reflects many of the world's spiritual and religious traditions. In Thelema, it is common for magicians to recite passages from the *Book of the Law* (Liber AL) or other texts such as *Liber Cordis Cincti Serpente* (Liber LXV) either during morning practice, or four times daily at the conclusion of the Liber Resh Ritual—the adorations of the four phases of the Sun. The Liber Resh ritual is a way of celebrating and uniting ourselves with the sun's fourfold cycle across the day.[36] While we will not be going into further detail here, you can find plenty of information on this ritual elsewhere, be it in books or on the internet. In Buddhism, Christianity, and other religious traditions, it is likewise common to have a series of prayers, psalms, or stanzas that the practitioner would repeat out loud to themselves each day and likely have memorized (though doing so is not necessary).

Doing something like this is incredibly beneficial and, in the sense of magick being the art of affecting change in accordance with your Will, is an incredible magickal act. In this sense, the change you are enacting with your Will is towards yourself—your own character.

---

36   Duquette, Lon Milo, *The Magick of Aleister Crowley: A Handbook of the Rituals of Thelema* (Weiser Books, 2003)

The Path Within

Here's an assignment for you. I would like for you to reflect upon, analyze, and write out what your ethical principles are. Write whatever you can think of. Just get it out of your head and onto the page. After you have your first draft written down, you can come back to this document again and read it to yourself each morning. As you read it each morning, don't hesitate to change it, add to it, or remove certain things from it.

Next, formulate and compose a more formalized "ethical script" for yourself. My "script" begins with "Dear God, lord of the Universe, I swear a solemn and sincere vow and the oath that today…" followed by the 125 vows that I personally composed, though they are inspired by Buddhist ethics and other teachings, such as: "Today I will cultivate virtue through moral, ethical, and altruistic behaviors." You can compose your ethical script in a similar format. Also, if there are any passages, blessings, affirmations, or prayers from any holy books (I consider *Lord of the Rings* to be a holy book—so your holy book doesn't necessarily have to be a religious scripture), you can include these as well and choose to recite them each day. The idea is for you to be reminded of your core principles, of what is the most important for yourself for each day in your life, not only for your magickal practice, but certainly including it.

This is your new code of conduct that you will bind yourself to. You will not be bound to any God or deity or even a priest, but you will be bound to your own word and the vows you make to yourself each and every day. Each new day and every night, you will be released from your oath unless you decide to make it again the next day. I find this practice keeps me firmly oriented toward ethical behavior that increases my happiness and well-being and disciplines me away from behaviors that would do harm to myself or others. I look forward to reading my vows each morning, even though I am under no obligation to do so. I don't always conform each day to the vows completely, but I forgive myself for any mistakes or failings and try again each day. Reading them is easy, but sometimes the test of putting the vows into practice in life can be much more difficult. Have patience and be kind to yourself.

EXERCISE: CRAFTING YOUR PERSONAL ETHICAL CODE

This exercise focuses on identifying and articulating your personal ethical principles. The purpose is to create a daily practice that aligns your actions with your values, helping you live more intentionally and in harmony with your beliefs. By defining your ethical codes and integrating them into a regular practice, you cultivate a deeper understanding of your principles and strengthen your commitment to them.

Needs:
- Writing materials (journal, pen, or digital device)
- Quiet space for reflection
- Optional: Inspirational texts or quotes

Setup:
- Find a comfortable and quiet space where you can reflect and write without interruptions.
- Have your writing materials ready.

Instructions:
- Begin by contemplating your core values and ethical principles. Consider questions like: What do I stand for? What behaviors align with my personal ethics?
- Write down your thoughts freely, capturing all ideas that come to mind about your values and ethical codes.

The Path Within

- After your initial reflection, revisit your notes and start formulating a more structured "ethical script." This script should include affirmations or vows that resonate with your beliefs, such as: "Today I will act with kindness and integrity."
- If desired, incorporate passages, blessings, or affirmations from various sources that inspire you. These could include religious texts, philosophical works, or any material that holds personal significance.
- Once your script is complete, make a commitment to read it aloud to yourself each morning. This practice serves as a daily reminder of your ethical commitments.
- Feel free to revise your script as you evolve. Add, remove, or modify parts of it to keep it aligned with your current state of being.

Follow Through:
- Store your script in a place where you can easily access it each morning.
- Remember, this is a personal and evolving document. Allow it to change as you grow and learn.

Optional:
- If you're comfortable, consider sharing your script with a trusted friend or mentor for feedback.
- You might also want to create a digital version of your script for easy access, especially when traveling.
- For those interested in integrating this practice into a broader spiritual or magickal routine, consider reading your script as part of your morning meditation or ritual practice.

THE RIGHT USE OF MAGICKAL FORCE

Many people embark on learning magick in order to fulfill their desires. But if we look deeper, we can understand that desire—fulfillment is merely a tool that helps us come closer to our Sacred Self.

At the core of magick is our True Will, our highest purpose and true nature. Nobody can tell another person what their True Will is, as it is something we must discover and articulate for ourselves. What is important to remember, however, is that magick is a path toward realizing our True Nature and, with it, discovering our true purpose in the grand scheme of the Universe.

Any activity that aids you in gaining self-knowledge can be seen as a magickal tool. Keeping a daily journal, analyzing your dreams, and seeking guidance from therapy or coaching are all invaluable tools in the practice of magick. I think this quote from the twentieth-century American mystic Neville Goddard sums up what I am trying to say very well:

> *What would be good for you? Tell me. Because in the end, every conflict will resolve itself as the World is simply mirroring the Being that you are assuming that you Are. One day you will be so saturated with wealth, so saturated with power in the World of Caesar, you will turn your back on it all and go in search for the Word of God.*[37]

Neville Goddard suggests that, instead of seeking to gain power in the external world of material possessions and status, one should instead turn towards the divine essence within each of us and seek to develop and nurture the power of the Word of God. By learning to direct this inner power, we can intentionally create our realities and fulfill our desires without the risk of generating negative karma or bad consequences for ourselves.

---

37 Goddard, Neville, *A Lesson in Scripture* (October 23, 1967)

The Path Within

When it comes to the use of magickal force and its application to one's spiritual practice, opinions vary greatly. People inspired by Eastern traditions such as Hinduism, Yoga, Vedanta, and Buddhism might argue that, based on said traditions, craving is a leading cause of suffering. Thus, if magick is used to obtain something desired, more suffering may be created. Additionally, one might use magick to manipulate another person's will and take advantage of their free will or to manifest something that ultimately does not bring desired satisfaction, leading to suffering.

These are issues that novice magick users are likely to encounter and are why, in traditional orders, such as the Order of the Golden Dawn, students would only be taught practical magick once they had achieved the sixth degree, which could take several years to accomplish.[38] The idea is that one must first purify their consciousness and gain clarity of thought before one is prepared to use magick.

Many people come to the practice of magick to gain greater control over the material world. It can be thought of as a kind of driving school for a Ferrari, as the technology of magick can be applied to the acquisition of whatever your will is and to enact change in both internal and external ways. However, there is a Trojan horse in the practice of magick, in that through its exploration, you realize that you have the potential to cause change and that you are fundamentally and inherently creative in a powerful way. This realization can then lead to a shift in awareness and the eventual asking of the question, "who am I that I can affect and impact reality in this way?" This is ultimately the true goal of all spiritual practices, including magick, of realizing your True Self and True Nature.

As you explore the various techniques available to you and explore your divine creative essence, you will come to realize that you possess a divine spark of creativity. This spark is part of the same divine intelligence in all living things and all places. Unfortunately, it is often the case that we pursue the material world in search of something to bring us comfort, security, or pleasure without really understanding what our True Will is. The issue with this is that none of these things are solid or

---

38   Zalewski, Pat, *Golden Dawn Rituals and Commentaries* (Rosicrucian Order of the Golden Dawn, 2010)

Jake Kobrin

permanent, and although they may bring us temporary pleasure, they will eventually disappear.

This can be seen as part of the journey to discovering our True Self, for when we have used up all of our desires in the physical world, we must then turn inward and seek the divine union. We realize that only through this inner exploration can we find a permanent answer and that no matter how much we strive for external gratification, we will never be truly satisfied. It is through this understanding that we can begin to find our True Will, something that is beyond the physical world and beyond the boundaries of time.

If one engages in magick, it is important to approach it playfully, for it is an opportunity to tap into the essence of the divine and awaken to a new level of understanding. Through this practice, one will understand that life is fluid and that there is tremendous potential and power in one's creative abilities. Things are never as fixed and rigid as they appear, and this is a truth that magick can help to reveal.

When considering the phrase "do what thou wilt shall be the whole of the Law," it should not be mistaken for a license to act upon any fleeting desire, but rather as a profound call to uncover and live by your True Will. This is the higher, divine purpose that aligns you with the universe's flow. Practicing magick in this light means engaging in a journey of self-discovery, where the True Will must be illuminated and embraced. The work of the magician is to ascend in consciousness and come into greater awareness of the Higher Self, what magickal traditions refer to as the Holy Guardian Angel, akin to the Stoic concept of eudaemonia, or "right living." Before embarking on any practical magick, one must deeply reflect and ensure that all actions serve this divine purpose, never imposing on the free will of others. Magick, in this sense, is not simply a tool for personal gain, but a means of aligning with a higher, spiritual purpose.

Throughout this book, we will go in-depth on different ways to do magick and access particular states of consciousness. But for the beginning magician, the task is to discover and become aligned with their True Will and then to endeavor to reach the Knowledge and Conversation with the Holy Guardian Angel.

The Path Within

As you contemplate enacting a ritual for a desire of yours, it is important to ask yourself if any part of you conflicts with this desire. It may be necessary to go through some negotiation work to resolve this conflict. It is strongly advised that you do not proceed with any magickal force if there is any part of you that conflicts with the desire. It is important to take the time to reflect and truly think of what you want and if this desire is in alignment with your Higher Self and True Will. Having a reliable divination tool, such as Tarot cards or the I Ching, can help to provide clarity as to whether you should proceed with this ritual or not.

While I cannot stop you from doing anything you wish to do, if there is any suffering that arises from the wrong use of magickal force, then it is part of the process of discovering our True Nature and how to use magick effectively, safely, and responsibly. Exploring our desires can give us clues about who we truly are and what our real purpose is. I hope that your exploration of magick is empowering and that it helps bring you into greater alignment with your True Nature. It is also my hope that magick is enjoyable—that it is like waking up from a dream to realize your internal divine essence and creative potential. And having experienced this power, it is important to spread the light and knowledge to help empower the world and be part of the great re-enchantment project.

CHAPTER THREE

YOUR MAGICKAL TOOLKIT

This chapter is all about building your own magickal toolkit, a key part of your magickal pursuits. Know that the tools you use are more than just objects; they're a reflection of your intentions and energies. Your toolkit is where the physical meets the spiritual, aligning with your personal style and goals. Here we will put together a set of tools that not only assist in your practices but also resonate with who you are and what you aspire to achieve.

To fully benefit from this book and hone your skills as a magician, it is essential that you keep a magickal journal. This journal will serve as a written record of all your magickal work, experiments, goals, dreams, insights, and progress. It will also prove to be an invaluable tool of reflection and an important resource for future reference.

Jake Kobrin

The type of journal you use to document your magickal practice and experiences can be as simple or as elaborate as you like. Some people prefer to decorate their journals with images and symbols that have a special meaning to them, while others prefer to keep them plain and simple. Ultimately, it is a matter of personal preference.

Regardless of the type of journal you use, there are a few important things you should always include. Firstly, you should record the date of each entry. This allows you to keep track of your progress and look back on your work overtime. Secondly, you should include a brief description of the work you did, such as the ritual you performed, the spell you cast, the meditation or visualization that you did. Thirdly, you should record any insights, realizations or messages from your Higher Self that you had during your work. Fourthly, you should document any results that you achieved from your work, such as changes in your circumstances or the way you feel. Finally, you should record any goals you set for yourself, and any steps you took to achieve those goals, such as a plan of action or a list of things you need to do.

The most important thing to remember when it comes to your journal is that it is for you and you alone. It is a place to be honest with yourself, to track your progress, and to record your thoughts and feelings. It is not a place to be critical of yourself or compare yourself to others. Instead, it is a tool for personal growth and development.

When it comes to writing in your journal, you can do so in a simple lined notebook or on a digital platform such as an iPad, a Microsoft Word or Notes document, or an app. You can also record information about the phases of the moon, astrological details, the planetary day and hour, weather, your emotional state, and any rituals performed. Additionally, you can record your thoughts and feelings about the rituals and their results at a later date.

The Path Within

THE DREAM DIARY

You will need a separate dream diary to write down what you remember of your dreams every morning. It is okay if you can't remember your dreams every morning. You can use a voice memo app to help you remember your dreams, and then transcribe them into your dream journal. Recording your dreams is important because it strengthens your connection to the astral dimension, and it is a prerequisite to lucid dreaming. Your dreams can also teach you things about yourself. It is recommended that you not share your dreams with anyone, except a trained and qualified specialist or therapist, but you can if you feel like it is relevant. We'll explore this exercise more deeply in the chapter on dreamwork.

Dedicating a Space for Practice
If you're going to do some magickal work, it's best to have a specific space set up for it that you use every time. That way, it becomes an anchor that will help you get in the zone for your ritual work. Your space should have a magickal circle (which can just be a rope or rug), an altar, and a meditation cushion or chair. The altar should face East, and both the altar and the meditation cushion should fit inside the circle. You should also have a way to banish and consecrate the space, which we will explore later on in this book.

Before We Get Started
There's a wealth of resources on magick available, including books, video tutorials, and online courses. Typically, these resources will introduce you to foundational magick rituals like the Lesser Banishing Ritual of the Pentagram and suggest starting with Tarot card studies. You're also likely

Jake Kobrin

to encounter a recommended reading list based on the Golden Dawn tradition. While all these resources are valuable, they represent just a fraction of the vast world of magick.

Rather than immediately diving into existing literature and practices, I propose an alternative approach. Set aside all other resources, except for this one, after you finish this chapter. Before delving into the practices and theories outlined here, take a moment to form and experience your own thoughts about magick. To start, sit down and ponder what magick would truly look like in your life. How would you practice it? How would it alter your reality and daily living? Get a journal and pen, find some solitude, and write down these reflections, shaping your personal understanding and aspirations for magick.

For your first exercise, I encourage you to invent your own rituals. Let them be an extension of your imagination and creativity. You might find that these self-crafted rituals resonate more deeply with you than conventional methods. This approach is how I began my magickal practice: creating from within made the experience more exciting, immediate, powerful, and fulfilling.

Looking back, after learning traditional magickal techniques, I realize some of my early, spontaneous rituals were remarkably effective. Remember, even the most ancient and revered magickal systems were once someone's innovation and are not inherently superior to your own creative ideas.

When I talk about rituals, I refer to any symbolic and meaningful action aimed at inducing change in one's life. This could range from traditional religious practices, like the Jewish Tefillin prayer, to more personal acts like meditation or appealing to deities. Your ritual can draw from established traditions or be entirely novel. These rituals employ suggestion and symbolism, akin to self-hypnosis, to impact the subconscious. Physical symbols can be used to represent emotions or situations; for example, an object can be used to symbolize grief and then discarded as a way to release the associated pain. Rituals are embedded in our daily lives, from birthday wishes made while blowing out candles to athletes' pre-game rituals.

The Path Within

Now, pause your reading, and in a notebook, jot down your perceptions of magick and your motivation for practicing it. Be bold in creating a ritual and give it your all. Embrace your creativity and intuition, experimenting with what you can manifest. Remember, magick is essentially the fusion of will and imagination.

Magick, as a creative act, leads you into uncharted territories beyond prescribed instructions and paths well-trodden. It is an art form that challenges and expands your creativity. Always keep this in mind as you walk the path of a practicing magician.

EXERCISE: PRELIMINARY JOURNAL QUESTIONS AND CREATING YOUR FIRST RITUAL

This exercise is designed to deepen your connection with magick through introspection and the crafting of a personal ritual. It aims to uncover your inherent magickal abilities and explore them in a meaningful, self-directed way.

Needs:
- A comfortable pen or another preferred writing instrument
- A journal (ensure it's a physical one, as the tactile experience is vital)
- Optional items for your ritual, as per your preference (e.g., candles, incense)

Creating a Sacred Space:
- Choose a tranquil space where interruptions are unlikely.
- Ensure comfort and readiness for a reflective session. You may wish to light a candle or incense to demarcate this time as sacred.

Instructions:
- Begin by detaching yourself from this book or any other distractions.

- Sit comfortably with your journal and writing instrument at hand.
- If it enhances the experience, create a sacred atmosphere in your own way.

Journaling and Self-Reflection:
Ponder over these questions, allowing each to resonate before you jot down your responses:

- Envision magick in your life. What does it look like?
- How would you practice magick?
- In what ways could magick transform your daily existence?
- How would the reality of magick reshape your living?
- If magick were tangible and real, how would it manifest?

Process:
Take your time with each question. Allow your thoughts and feelings to flow freely as you document them in your journal. This is an exploratory process to shape your understanding and expectations of magick.

INVENTING YOUR PERSONAL RITUAL

Brainstorming:
Think about a personal need, wish, or desire. Use your journal to brainstorm a ritual that could manifest this. Your ritual can be as unconventional or traditional as you like, incorporating any symbols or objects that resonate with you. Consider time, place, and atmosphere.

- **Recording Ideas:** Document every idea, no matter how eccentric. This is a creative process—let your imagination run wild.

- **Performing the Ritual:** Conduct the ritual as envisioned. If immediate performance isn't possible, plan for a later time.
- **Reflection Post-Ritual:** Reflect on the ritual in your journal. How did it feel? Note any insights, realizations, or specific guidance that emerged during the ritual.
- **Documenting and Reflecting:** Celebrate the completion of your first ritual. Acknowledge this step in your path to becoming a full-fledged magician.
- **Future Reflections:** Leave space in your journal for future entries. In the weeks or months ahead, return to reflect on the ritual's effectiveness. If it didn't work as hoped, consider what changes you might make next time.

This exercise isn't just about performing a ritual; it's about initiating a dialogue with your inner self and the universe. It's a quest for discovery, where each step, each thought, each symbol holds significance in your magickal practice. Remember, this is your personal exploration of magick; let it be as unique as you are.

BASIC PRACTICES

Some basic practices that can help people get started with magick, which we will explore in this book, are Yoga and meditation, working with Tarot cards, understanding and being in tune with the phases of the moon, and keeping a diary. Yoga in this sense doesn't mean stretching and physical practices, which is known as Hatha Yoga, but rather refers to the broad array of esoteric practices and meditations from the East that are intended to lead the practitioner back towards union with the divine.

Many magicians like to work with an associative feedback system, which is a set of symbols or artistic representations that are filled with meaning for the magician, such as the Tarot or the Qabalah. A lot of what people do in magick is based on interpretation. Certain tools are traditionally used to represent different things, but it is up to the person using them to decide what they mean. It is all about finding what works best for you and using it to your advantage. You can use tools from your everyday life to help you with magick, as long as you are aware of how they affect you. Meditating and transcending the mind is also key to understanding magick.

Each culture has its technology, and in the West, we have Elemental representations in the form of magickal weapons. This means that each Element (Fire, Water, Earth, and Air) is represented by a different weapon (Wand, Cup, Disc, and Dagger respectively). These weapons are symbols of our Will, Emotions, Materiality, and Intellect. We use them to clear the air, focus, stand firm, and illuminate our vision. We also use them to represent aspects of ourselves in finding out more about ourselves. These tools are just representations of something bigger, and what matters is your investment in working with them. Your mind and body are also tools that should be kept in pristine health and strength. One key to knowing the mind is to transcend it, and one way of transcending the mind is through ecstasy. Ecstasy here means to transcend the experience of separateness through various methods including fasting, meditation, or ritual, and occasionally the use of mind-altering plants or chemicals. It does not refer to the drug MDMA, which is known by its street-name "ecstasy."

EXERCISE: ESSENTIAL QUESTIONS THROUGH MORNING PAGES

The Morning Pages exercise, inspired by Julia Cameron's *The Artist's Way*, is a practice of creative introspection designed to connect you with your inner self. It involves daily, free form writing to explore and express your thoughts

The Path Within

and feelings. This exercise is particularly valuable for those on a magickal path, as it aids in the discovery and connection with your True Will—the essence of your being and your role in the universe.

Needs:
- Journal or notebook
- Pen or pencil
- Quiet, comfortable space for writing

Setup:
- Choose a peaceful time in the morning before starting your day.
- Have your journal and writing instrument ready.
- Sit in a comfortable, quiet place where you can write undisturbed.

Instructions:
Start each morning by writing three pages of longhand, stream-of-consciousness writing. Don't worry about coherence or style—simply let your thoughts flow onto the page. Use the following prompts to guide your writing, but feel free to deviate as needed:

- **Understanding Your Motivations:** What draws you to magick? Formulate a clear statement of your intent and desired outcomes.
- **Discovering Patterns in Your Life:** Write a brief autobiography focusing on key events and choices. Look for recurring themes.
- **Reflecting on External Perceptions:** Consider how others see you and which observations align or conflict with your self-perception.
- **Exploring Character Assessment Systems:** If comfortable, delve into systems like astrology or personality tests for additional insights.
- **Recognizing Happiness and Unhappiness:** Reflect on past experiences that brought joy or dissatisfaction. What do these say about your values?
- **Studying Inspirational Figures:** Identify individuals who embody qualities you admire and explore what they reveal about your aspirations.

Follow Through:
Keep your Morning Pages journal in a dedicated spot for easy access each day. Remember, this is a personal and evolving practice. Adjust your approach as you discover more about yourself.

Optional:
You may want to digitize your writings for ease of review and reflection. If you find certain prompts more helpful than others, focus on those, or create your own based on your unique preferences and needs. Consider integrating this practice into a broader routine of meditation or magickal work to enhance its effectiveness.

THE DESIRES LIST

In the following activity, we will be constructing a list of our wishes for our life. This list is of great importance, as it will help us to make contact with our genuine and essential selves. We should dedicate a period of self-reflection, contemplation, and meditation while doing this, and should revise the list regularly. When we are done, we should read it out loud twice a day to aid in its manifestation. Additionally, when something from our list is achieved, we should celebrate it and give thanks. Our list should also be regularly updated, whenever we think of something new or decide that we no longer want something. Furthermore, it is important to keep our list to ourselves and not share it with anyone. Finally, when something from your list is granted, make sure to express your gratefulness.

    I would then additionally recommend elaborating this list into four separate lists. The first list should be titled *Have and Want* and should contain everything in your life that you have, enjoy, and are grateful for.

The Path Within

The second list is *Have and Don't Want* and should contain all of the things you have in your life that bring you pain, frustration, or that you otherwise don't want anymore. The third list is *Don't Have and Want* and should contain everything that you haven't yet manifested into your life but desire to own or experience. Lastly, make a list titled *Don't Have and Don't Want,* which can be anything from "being tortured in a Chinese prison" to "lung cancer." It's anything that you don't have in your life and that you don't want in your life. After you make these lists, you can compare them to each other; it is an interesting activity to see a more balanced view of your desires.

EXERCISE: CRAFTING YOUR DESIRES LIST

Creating a Desires List is a fundamental practice in magick, serving as a powerful tool for self-discovery and manifestation. This exercise involves listing your wishes and aspirations, helping you connect with your true and essential self. By identifying and regularly revisiting your desires, you align your actions with your deepest yearnings and facilitate their realization.

Needs:
- Journal or notebook
- Pen or pencil
- Quiet space for contemplation

Setup:
- Choose a peaceful environment where you can reflect without interruptions.
- Have your journal and pen ready for writing.

Jake Kobrin

Instructions:
Begin by contemplating your life's desires. Think about what you truly want, without restraint or shame. Write down everything that comes to mind, covering all aspects of your life. Organize your desires into four categories:

- **Have and Want:** Things you currently have and appreciate.
- **Have and Don't Want:** Aspects of your life that cause discomfort or dissatisfaction.
- **Don't Have and Want:** Desires and aspirations yet to be fulfilled.
- **Don't Have and Don't Want:** Things you wish to avoid or never experience.

Regularly review and update your list, adding new desires or removing ones that no longer resonate with you. Read your list aloud (only the Don't Have and Want part) to yourself once or twice daily to reinforce your intentions. Keep your list private, as this is a personal practice of self-discovery.

Follow Through:
Store your Desires List in a secure and accessible place for daily reading and regular updating. Remember, this is an evolving document that reflects your growth and changing perspectives.

Optional:
You may find it beneficial to create a digital version of your list for easy editing and reflection. Consider integrating this practice into your daily meditation or magickal rituals to enhance its effectiveness. If you find certain categories more relevant or insightful, focus more on these in your reflections and updates.

The Path Within

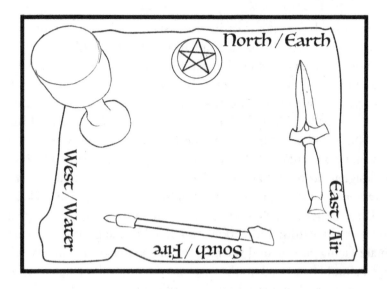

ALTAR SET UP

An altar is a special place that you can create in your home, designed to focus on your magickal goals. It can be as simple or as elaborate as you like, ranging from a corner of your room, a dedicated room, to a table or shelf. You can decorate your altar with items that are meaningful to you, such as candles, crystals, images, and symbols. You can also use your altar to store your journal, tools, and supplies. It is a place to go to meditate, to pray, to do rituals and spells, and to connect with your Higher Self. Most importantly, your altar is your own personal space and should be respected as such.

The altar that we will use is a simple one that represents the four cardinal directions and the four Elements. The altar is a symbolic representation of the entire Universe. We will use the four traditional Elemental Weapons of the Wand, the Dagger, the Cup, and the Pentacle to represent these four basic Elements. Alternatively, you can use other objects to symbolize these attributions, such as incense to represent Air, and a crystal or rock or even coins to represent the Element of Earth. Occasionally a candle is used to represent the Element of Fire. It's not important what the altar necessarily looks like, or how expensive your tools are, what is important is that these four Elements are represented.

Traditionally a black double cube altar is used. This is a big black box about 480 x 240 x 240 mm with no other details or inscriptions. You can easily make one out of plywood or buy a cupboard at a store like Ikea that you designate as your altar. In this case, it is not so important how it looks, but rather that you create the intention for this to be your magickal altar.

The Elements each correspond with one of the four directions, known as the cardinal direction. You should arrange your altar so that you are facing east behind the altar when you perform your magick. The dagger should be placed on the eastern side of the altar, representing Air. The wand should be placed on the south side of the altar, representing Fire. The chalice or cup should be placed on the western side of the altar, representing Water, and the pentacle or coin should be placed on the north side of the altar, representing Earth. You can also put a candle or two on the altar in the center. My altar is covered with a ceremonial altar cloth and has a bell upon it that I use to signal the beginning and end of my magickal work.

ROBES

Though wearing robes while performing magick is not a requirement (you can also always go "skyclad," also known as naked), it is often seen as beneficial to getting into the right mindset for rituals. It is suggested that robes should be acquired that have not ever been used for any other purpose and would be best suited to one's magickal work. A traditional ceremonial magick

The Path Within

robe, called the Tau robe, is black and resembles the Greek letter Tau with drooping sleeves and a flared bottom. Some systems have different colored robes that indicate different grades that individuals have been initiated into, or different roles they might perform in the order. In addition to the robe, a hood can be included and act as a kind of sensory deprivation device for meditation. Having a specific outfit that is only worn during magickal ritual can be a useful tool for getting into a specific frame of mind.

MOTTO

It is also beneficial to distinguish and keep separate all elements of a magickal world, such as choosing a magickal motto. This motto is often chosen to reflect an intention and can be taken during an initiation in a magickal grade order system. Although this is not required, if one feels inspired, they can choose one. Generally, the magickal name would take the prefix Frater (brother) for men and Soror (sister, or sibling) for women. However, for those who don't identify strictly with the binary genders or prefer a non-gendered term, there isn't a well-established Latin alternative. One option could be *Sodalis*, which translates to "comrade" or "colleague" in Latin, but does not have an inherent gender implication. As language and societal norms continue to evolve, it's possible new non-binary or gender-neutral terms will emerge in the future within magickal traditions.

The mottos are generally chosen to reflect an intention that you have and want to be reminded of during your magickal work. For example, Crowley had many mottos, but his most famous was *Frater Perdurabo* meaning, "I shall endure until the end."[39]

---

39 Duquette, Lon Milo, *The Magick of Aleister Crowley: A Handbook of the Rituals of Thelema* (Weiser Books, 2003)

Jake Kobrin

In this chapter, we've covered an array of subjects including starting your Dream Diary, setting up your altar, and creating a Desires List. We've looked at carving out your own practice space, digging into some thought-provoking journal questions, and designing rituals that resonate with you. Along the way, we tackled the basics of magick, the meaning behind your tools, and the importance of having a personal motto. With exercises like the Morning Pages and shaping your Desires List, the goal was to help you connect more with your magickal intentions. All these pieces fit into your Magickal Toolkit, making your magick practice more personal and powerful. Whether you're new to this or building on what you know, these tools and exercises are here to enhance and evolve your magickal practice.

CHAPTER FOUR

HARNESSING THE POWER OF THOUGHT

If you can take control of your thoughts, beliefs, and meta-programs, you can radically change your life. Entire disciplines, including neuro-linguistic programming, cognitive-behavioral therapy, and the New Thought movement, which includes the popular documentary and book *The Secret*,[40] have been created to create a methodology around this idea. In theory, the core idea is that the beliefs, attitudes, thoughts, and ideas that we hold in our minds are what create our actions and behaviors in the world, and eventually manifest in the lives we inhabit. In practice, we will explore a few different methods which include mindfulness of thoughts, visualizations, and affirmations.

---

40   Horowitz, Mitch, *Occult America: The Secret History of How Mysticism Shaped Our Nation* (Bantam Books, 2009)

Jake Kobrin

I wanted to introduce this section before introducing some of the more ritualistic and aesthetically occult practices in this book because these techniques can be done anywhere and everywhere at any time, and do not require any complex or verbose rituals to execute. All you need is to be conscious and considerate of your thoughts and beliefs at any moment and see where those thoughts lead you. Our thoughts directly impact our behaviors, and our beliefs directly impact our thoughts. In the discipline and methodology of neuro-linguistic programming (NLP), which delves into the intricate landscape of human behavior and communication, we find an array of ideas and methods that unpack the complex web of our actions and interactions, bringing together a diverse array of tools and techniques. At its core, NLP operates on a structured hierarchy of logical levels that shape and influence a person's actions, experiences, and outcomes. These logical levels are, from highest to lowest: Purpose (source), Identity (how you think of yourself), Beliefs and Values (such as your motivations, capabilities, and skills including your knowledge and competency), Behavior (which includes your actions and reactions), and the Environment (which includes external factors and restraints). All of these ingredients lead up to the specific circumstances which produce a result.[41] Much of magick is about looking at, becoming aware of, and consciously shifting the factors which are subtle and usually unexamined, understanding that these subtle factors have an impact on everything above and below it in the chain of causation. NLP has many compatible ideas and techniques to that of magick.

Allow me to present an example. Let's say that you have the desire to be in a committed and healthy relationship. There are certain specific factors that lead to this desire being realized. Some of those factors are dependent on a certain way of thinking, holding certain beliefs and ideas about yourself and the world, and having a particular level of awareness. In fact, all of the NLP ingredients that I listed earlier must be aligned in order for that result to occur. If you believe that you are undesirable,

---

[41] Farber, Philip H., *Meta-Magick: The Book of Atem: Achieving New States of Consciousness Through NLP, Neuroscience, and Ritual* (Weiser Books, 2008)

The Path Within

or that there are no good available people out there, then you are likely to confirm that through your biases. However, if you believe that you are fully capable and worthy of being loved and in a loving relationship and see the world as full of people you could potentially meet and connect with and share amazing romantic experiences with, you will likewise see this reflected in your life through your awareness and focused attention.

The saying "where focus goes, energy flows" is a cliche self-help statement, but it is very true, and it is a statement that is especially applicable when it comes to magick.[42] Magick is, in its essence, a way of shifting our attention, awareness, focus, and consciousness to shift those logical levels, so that a specific result can occur. At a simplistic level, in practice, this looks like being aware of your thoughts and making sure that your thoughts are positive, not negative, and are directed toward where you want to go.

A good analogy is riding a motorcycle. If you are driving a motorcycle, you want to make sure you are looking in the direction of where you want to be headed, or else the motorcycle will be steered where you don't want it to go. With your thoughts and attention, it is the same. This takes practice, awareness, and effort. If you hear yourself thinking "I don't want to be sick," you can pause, say in your mind "erase that thought," and then replace it with a more positive thought such as "every day I am feeling more and more healthy." When you begin to experiment with this process, you will see that we quite literally can program our experiences of our lives and realities, by shifting our thoughts. This is one of the simplest and most effective forms of magick that there is. When we introduce the practices of meditation in the later sections of this book, those practices will help to develop and increase the amount of awareness that you have over your thoughts, beliefs, and attitudes.

---

42 Robbins, Tony, *Awaken the Giant Within: How to Take Immediate Control of Your Mental, Emotional, Physical and Financial Destiny!* (Free Press, 1991)

"SOLVE": CLEARING OUR BLOCKS

The alchemical formula *Solve et Coagula* is a powerful concept that speaks to the importance of clearing our blocks. In its simplest form, *Solve* stands for breaking down and dissolving that which no longer serves us, while *Coagula* stands for building something new. This principle applies to all aspects of life, and it is especially important to our process of personal growth.

To break down our blocks, we can use a variety of methods from the traditional to the avant-garde. Traditional methods include therapy, cognitive behavioral therapy, somatic releasing, NLP, and Gestalt therapy. For those who are more open to alternative approaches, psychedelics and plant medicines in safe settings with trained guides and practitioners offer a powerful way to clear blocks.[43] Additionally, Dr. David Hawkins created a form of kinesiological testing that allows people to discover their blocks and then clear them using energy points on the body.[44]

At its core, the process of breaking down our blocks and limiting beliefs is about removing the brakes from our life's momentum. These blocks and beliefs (for example, "I'm not good enough for a relationship" or "I am unable to make enough money to follow my dreams") are the breaks that hold us back from our goals and dreams. Therefore, it is important that we continue to do the process of clearing our blocks. While it is important to actively create what we want, it is equally important to shed and banish the limiting beliefs and blocks that keep us from achieving our dreams. Clearing our blocks is like taking the brakes off a vehicle, allowing it to charge forward smoothly with momentum.

---

43   Pollan, Michael, *How to Change Your Mind: What the New Science of Psychedelics Teaches Us About Consciousness, Dying, Addiction, Depression, and Transcendence* (Penguin Press, 2018)

44   Hawkins, David R., *Power vs Force: The Hidden Determinants of Human Behavior* (Hay House, 2012)

The Path Within

It is said that the real power of a magician lies within, and the best way to access that potential is to work on oneself in addition to your work with magick. By engaging in therapy and coaching, magicians can heal deep-seated traumas, clear blocks, and release any obstacles that may be standing in their way. In doing so, they will find that their desires can be more easily achieved. Healing and therapeutic work is essential for any magician, as it will help them to unlock the true power of their magick.

AFFIRMATIONS

In magick and personal transformation, affirmations hold a curious position. They are simple, powerful statements designed to harness the power of positive thinking and intention. However, they often face skepticism for their seemingly simplistic approach to complex issues. Critics argue that repeating a phrase like "things are being made better in this moment" or, as Émile Coué, who was a pioneering French psychologist known for his development of the concept of autosuggestion, famously prescribed, "every day in every way, I'm getting better and better," cannot single-handedly change reality or solve deep-rooted problems.[45] And they're right—to an extent.

The truth is affirmations aren't, to a full extent, magickal spells that can instantly alter the fabric of our lives. Instead, they're tools that can help orient our mindset and energy toward positive change. While it's crucial not to fall into the trap of denial about the realities of our life, affirmations offer a way to set an intention for transformation. For this reason, I do believe that they are an important and effective tool to introduce to you.

---

45 Coué, Émile, *Self Mastery Through Conscious Autosuggestion* (American Library Service, 1922)

Example Affirmations:

- *Things are being made better in this moment.*
- *Every day in every way, I'm getting better and better.*
- *I am a powerful creator; my intentions manifest reality.*
- *My intuition is a compass that leads me to truth and wisdom.*
- *I embrace change as a path to growth and learning.*
- *I am a conduit of positive energy, attracting abundance and joy.*
- *The energy I put into the world returns to me tenfold in positive ways.*
- *I trust my inner wisdom to lead me on my journey of self-discovery.*
- *I am constantly evolving, embracing each step of my transformation.*
- *My heart and mind are open to the endless possibilities of the universe.*

EXERCISE: WORKING WITH AFFIRMATIONS

In this exercise, we focus on using affirmations to foster a positive outlook. Affirmations are powerful tools for transforming your mindset and shaping your reality. This simple yet effective practice is about repeating empowering phrases to cultivate a mindset that aligns with your goals and aspirations, influencing both your conscious and subconscious thoughts.

Needs:
- A chosen affirmation (you can use one of the examples above)
- A quiet, peaceful space

Setup:
- Choose a tranquil area where you can concentrate without disturbances. This could be your special magickal spot or any calm environment that resonates with you.

The Path Within

- Prepare yourself for a moment of introspection and affirmation.

Instructions:
- Begin by selecting an affirmation. You can use one of my examples above or write your own.
- In your chosen quiet space, take a few deep breaths to relax and center your thoughts, releasing any stress or distractions.
- Repeat your chosen affirmation out loud. Say "things are being made better in this moment" in a clear, slow manner. As you articulate these words, visualize them actively shaping your reality, weaving a pattern of positive transformation.
- Fully engage with the affirmation. Feel its meaning and believe in its power to bring about positive changes.
- Incorporate this practice into your daily routine. Regular repetition of your affirmation reinforces its impact on your mindset.

Follow-Through:
- Practice this affirmation daily to deepen its influence on your consciousness.
- Reflect on your progress each night, noting any shifts in your attitude or challenges you've encountered.

Optional Adjustments:
- If you prefer, you can also integrate other affirmations that resonate with your personal goals and aspirations.
- Consider journaling your experience with this exercise to track your development and insights into your evolving thought patterns.

This exercise isn't about ignoring life's challenges, but about empowering yourself to face them with a mindset that's oriented towards growth and positive transformation. Regular practice of affirmations is a step towards aligning your energy with a flow of positivity, setting the stage for meaningful change and self-improvement.

Jake Kobrin

A SIMPLE PRACTICE TO DISCIPLINE YOUR MIND

A simple practice to discipline your mind was presented in a technical essay by Aleister Crowley called "Liber Jugorum."[46] Although the original technique was described as using a razor, it is safer—and the technique is just as effective—if you use a rubber band.

We've already established that there are thoughts that are in harmony and alignment with reaching the desired result, and others that lead away from it. This is a technique to be able to discipline the mind so that you are thinking the majority of the time in a way that is in alignment with the desired result. We used the example of the desired relationship and how some of those thoughts, such as thinking of yourself as desirable and loveable, are useful and resourceful, and some of those thoughts, such as seeing yourself as unlovable or the world as full of unavailable people, are unresourceful. Using this technique, you can discipline yourself so that you are only thinking resourceful thoughts.

It's really simple. You take a rubber band and put it on your wrist. Every time you catch yourself thinking an unresourceful thought, a thought that is not going to lead to you achieving your desired result, slap yourself on the wrist with the rubber band. It stings a little bit, but not very much. Immediately after you slap yourself on the wrist with the rubber band, you replace that thought with another thought that is more resourceful.

Here's an example. You notice yourself thinking "I am ugly, no wonder why I'm still single, I'm just not good enough to have a lover." The minute you hear that thought, slap yourself on the wrist with the rubber band. And then you immediately replace the thought with something like, "I have many loveable attributes, and I'm proud of the person I am. I know I've been through so much and I'm proud of my strength. I have a lot of

---

46   Crowley, Aleister, *Magick in Theory and Practice* (Samuel Weiser, 1997)

The Path Within

value to give to a partner in a relationship, and I fully trust that a relationship will materialize when it's the right time for that to happen."

You can do this for a specific goal, like the one I named as an example, or you can do this to eliminate negative thought patterns in general. If you practice this exercise consistently, ideally for twenty to thirty days minimum, your mind will become more and more positive until positive thoughts comprise the overwhelming majority of your thoughts.

EXERCISE: MIND DISCIPLINE WITH RUBBER BAND TECHNIQUE

This exercise, adapted from Aleister Crowley's "Liber Jugorum," is a simple yet effective method to discipline your mind and align your thoughts with your desired outcomes. It involves using a rubber band as a tool to train yourself to focus on resourceful, positive thoughts, thereby fostering a mindset conducive to achieving your goals.

Needs:
- A rubber band
- A quiet space for reflection

Setup:
- Select a comfortable and quiet place where you can reflect on your thoughts without distractions.
- Place a rubber band comfortably around your wrist.

Instructions:
- Start by identifying a specific goal or area of your life where you want to cultivate more positive thinking.
- Throughout the day, be mindful of your thoughts, especially those related to your goal.

Jake Kobrin

- Whenever you catch yourself having a negative or unresourceful thought—one that doesn't support your desired outcome—gently snap the rubber band against your wrist. This acts as a mild, physical reminder to shift your thinking.
- Immediately replace the negative thought with a positive, resourceful one. For example, if you think, "I am not good enough," snap the band and then replace that thought with, "I am capable and deserving of success."
- The key is to consistently practice this technique, ideally for at least twenty to thirty days, to instill a habit of positive thinking.

Follow Through:
- Keep the rubber band on your wrist throughout the day as a constant reminder.
- Reflect each night on the progress you've made and any challenges you encountered.

Optional:
- If you're uncomfortable with the physical aspect of the rubber band snap, consider a non-physical cue like a deep breath or a positive affirmation. However, I really do suggest the use of the rubber band, as without the small snap the exercise will not be as effective.
- You can apply this technique to various aspects of your life, not just the initially chosen goal.
- Journaling your experiences with this exercise can provide insights into your thought patterns and progress.

The Path Within

NEW THOUGHT

New Thought, also known as Positive Mind Metaphysics, is well-known for its mainstream adaptation into *The Secret*, but there is much more to this tradition, and it offers some simple but robust techniques for creating causation with your thought. Although it is not always associated with magick, for me the key definition of magick as "the science and art of creating change in accordance with your Will" is in alignment with the purposes of New Thought. There have been many writers on New Thought, including Norman Vincent Peale, William Walker Atkinson (who pseudonymously authored *The Kybalion*), Napoleon Hill, author of *Think and Grow Rich*, which is actually very much worth reading and offers some good magickal techniques, and the great mystic Neville Goddard. Compared to many complex magickal rituals, these practices might seem trite, overly simplistic, and superficial. Sometimes you just don't have the time or energy for complex magickal rituals. I use these New Thought techniques in my own practice alongside my ritual magick operations.

Creative Visualization

The most common exercise related to New Thought is Creative Visualization. This technique was especially proliferated by the mystic teacher Neville Goddard. Neville Goddard was a great twentieth-century mystic and pioneer in the New Thought movement. He was a student of Qabalah and a friend of Israel Regardie's, who was a pivotal figure in the world of occultism, renowned for his crucial role in preserving and democratizing the teachings of the Hermetic Order of the Golden Dawn. Goddard's teachings are simple: everything you experience is a reflection of your level of consciousness. "Experience in your imagination what you would want to be in reality. Do this and you will achieve your goal, whatever it may be."[47]

---

47 Goddard, Neville, *The Power of Awareness* (DeVorss & Company, 1952)

Many thoughts and techniques are at the core of Neville's philosophy, but these are the most common and powerful:

1. Vivid imagination, coupled with a feeling of the wish fulfilled, creates reality. In NLP, they say to emphasize seeing what you would see, feeling what you would feel, and hearing what you would hear, as well as smell and taste and a variety of other sub-modalities.
2. Revise your day, imagine it made perfect, as you are falling asleep.
3. According to Neville, the most powerful time to do these practices is right when you first wake up and right before you fall asleep. There are many official Neville audiotapes and many videos on YouTube to guide you through these practices.[48]

Creative visualization, which is, put simply, imagining the experience of something that you want to have happen, generally while in an altered, expanded, or deeply relaxed state. I have found it to be an effective technique on its own and also useful in combination with other magickal techniques.

EXERCISE: MASTERING CREATIVE VISUALIZATION

This practice involves vividly imagining your goals as already achieved, thus aligning your consciousness to make them a reality. It is particularly effective when practiced at specific times of the day and can be enhanced through emotional engagement.

Needs:
- Paper and pen for writing your goal
- A quiet, comfortable space for visualization

---

48 Goddard, Neville, *Feeling Is the Secret* (DeVorss & Company, 1944)

The Path Within

- Materials for creating a Treasure Map (optional), such as magazines, scissors, glue, and cardboard

Setup:
- Find a quiet time and place where you can focus without interruptions.
- Have your writing materials and Treasure Map supplies ready if you choose to use this method.

Instructions:
- **Defining Your Goal:** Write a clear, concise statement of your goal. Begin with: "It is my will to use all of my abilities to obtain the following goal: _____." Fill in the blank with your specific aspiration. Be precise in defining your goal. Consider the ultimate outcome you desire rather than just a means to an end.
- **Visualization:** Close your eyes and vividly imagine achieving your goal. Involve all your senses in this mental image. If visualization is challenging, remember that the key is belief in its existence on the astral plane, not necessarily clear visual imagery. Optionally, create a Treasure Map to aid your visualization. This collage of images representing your goal should centrally feature yourself or the word "me." We will examine this in the next exercise.
- **Daily Practice:** Twice daily, once upon waking and once before sleeping, spend five minutes repeating your written goal statement. Follow this with five minutes of visualization or examining your Treasure Map. If negative thoughts arise during the day, counter them immediately by repeating your goal statement.
- **Silence and Release:** After completing your daily visualization, release the goal from your immediate thoughts. Avoid discussing your practice or the goal itself with others to maintain the energy directed toward manifestation. Trust in the process without doubting or constantly reviewing your methods.
- **Emotional Engagement:** Invest emotional energy into your goal. The stronger your emotional connection, the more effective the visualization

process. Continue this practice consistently until your goal is achieved, then proceed with a new objective.

Follow Through:
Store your written goals and any materials used for the Treasure Map in a private place. Regularly review and update your goals as needed. Document your progress and any successes in your ritual or magickal journal.

Optional:
If you prefer digital methods, consider creating a digital Treasure Map or goal list. Adapt the visualization to fit your personal style and needs. If certain aspects of the technique resonate more with you, focus on those.

EXERCISE: CREATING A TREASURE MAP FOR VISUALIZATION

The Treasure Map exercise is an imaginative and effective tool, acting as a visual representation of your goals and aspirations. This practice involves creating a collage of images, symbols, and affirmations that represent what you desire to manifest in your life. Central to this collage is your own image or the word "me," anchoring the focus on your personal desires.

Needs:
- A board or large piece of paper
- Magazines or printed images
- Scissors and glue
- Markers or pens for writing
- A photo of yourself or the word "me" printed out
- A quiet space for creative work

The Path Within

Setup:
- Choose a comfortable space where you can work undisturbed.
- Gather all your materials, including a variety of images and symbols that align with your goals.

Creating the Map:
- Start by placing your photo or the word "me" at the center of your board.
- Surround this central element with images and symbols that represent your goals. These can include pictures of places you want to visit, items you wish to acquire, or activities you desire to experience.

Personalizing Your Map:
- Add affirmations, inspirational quotes, or specific words that resonate with your aspirations.
- Arrange everything in a way that feels visually appealing and meaningful to you.

Daily Engagement:
- Place your completed Treasure Map in a spot where you'll see it every day.
- Spend time each day looking at your map, allowing the images and words to reinforce your intentions and desires.

Follow Through:
- Regularly meditate on your Treasure Map, envisioning yourself achieving the goals depicted.
- Update your map as your goals evolve or as you reach certain milestones.

Optional:
- If you prefer, use digital tools to create an electronic version of your Treasure Map.

- Consider keeping a journal to document your thoughts and feelings as you engage with your map and observe the manifestations in your life.

Creating a Treasure Map is a creative and deeply personal way to connect with your goals and amplify your manifestation efforts. By regularly interacting with your map, you reinforce your intentions and align your energy with your desired outcomes.

THE "DEAR UNIVERSE" LETTER

A Dear Universe letter is a form of New Thought magick. I'm not sure where I learned it from, but it is something I began to practice intuitively when I was young. It is when you write a letter thanking the universe for exactly what you want, in as much detail as you can provide, for giving you exactly the thing you desire. Strangely enough, it works!

The Dear Universe letter should be charged in some way, which basically means associating an expanded, euphoric, or altered state of consciousness with the contents of the letter. This could look like you playing very uplifting and high-energy music, and dancing and jumping up and down in a very joyful state of mind while reading the letter out loud. You can do this as many times as you'd like, even reading the same letter every day for many days to strengthen your intention.

Here is a short example I made up for a Dear Universe letter:

Dear Universe,

Thank you so much for providing me the exact support I have been needing and looking for. You always provide me with so much, and sometimes I feel silly for doubting your beneficent and generous love, support, and presence. I was elated when I looked at my bank

The Path Within

account and saw a very generous amount of money there, enough for all of my living expenses, leisure, and luxury for many, many months! It feels so good to know that you've helped guide me to this abundant and secure place in which I am living now, even though a few months ago I felt like I was struggling. Thank you again so much for helping me get to a place of abundance, security, ease, and financial prosperity through the fun and lucrative and inspiring opportunities you sent my way, which are also deeply aligned with my values, purpose, and True Will. I love making such an abundant amount of money doing exactly what it is I love! I can go on and on with flattery and gratitude, but I just wanted to write this letter to really thank and appreciate you.

Thank you again!

Love,
Jake

If it feels better, you can replace the word *Universe* with *God* or any other name that describes your perception of spiritual power or deity.

EXERCISE: CRAFTING A "DEAR UNIVERSE" LETTER

Needs:
- Paper and pen for writing your letter
- A comfortable and quiet space for writing and visualization
- Optional: uplifting music to enhance your emotional state

Setup:
- Choose a peaceful area where you can write undisturbed.

- Prepare your writing materials.
- If you plan to use music, select tracks that evoke joy and positivity.

Instructions:
- **Writing the Letter:** Begin your letter with "Dear Universe" (or substitute with "God" or any name that resonates with your spiritual beliefs). Express heartfelt gratitude for the fulfillment of your desires. Write as though what you wish for has already occurred, detailing your thanks with as much specificity as possible.
- **Charging the Letter:** Create a euphoric and expanded state of consciousness while reading your letter. This can be achieved by playing high-energy, uplifting music and dancing or engaging in joyful movement. Read your letter out loud in this state, allowing the positive emotions to charge the intentions within your letter.
- **Repetition for Strengthening Intentions:** You may read the same letter multiple times, even daily, to reinforce and strengthen your intention.

Follow Through:
- Keep your "Dear Universe" letter in a special place where you can return to it for repeated readings.
- Reflect on the feelings and intentions you've expressed and observe any changes or manifestations in your life related to your letter.

Optional:
- If you prefer a more meditative approach, consider reading your letter in a quiet, reflective state instead of an energetic one.
- You can write multiple letters for different aspects of your life or goals.
- Consider revisiting and updating your letter as your goals evolve or as you experience manifestations of your intentions.

NEW THOUGHT, DEITY WORSHIP, AND THE MAGICK OF MENTAL CAUSATION
BY GUEST TEACHER MITCH HOROWITZ

I have been involved for many years in what might be considered mind metaphysics, New Thought, or whatever you wish to call it. These terms are popular within the culture, and sometimes I don't use them, but they are helpful in giving people a general understanding of what is being discussed. Some people will say "the secret," "manifestation," "law of attraction," or "the power of positive thinking." None of these are my terms, but I think generality is useful. I learned years ago that resisting a term gets you nowhere. I felt much more relaxed when I decided to embrace the term "New Age" rather than run away from it. To me, New Age is simply therapeutic spirituality. It's a radically ecumenical culture of therapeutic spirituality. I realized that I was going to be called it anyway, and I felt a great sense of relaxation when I stopped seeing it as an epithet and decided to embrace it in its highest iteration.

I don't get excessively distracted by certain terms because I think it's useful for people to communicate in generalities. I remember first encountering the New Thought thesis in my late twenties or early thirties. The basic contention is that thoughts are causative and that your emotionalized thoughts or psyche are an engine that replicates events in your life. Neville Goddard teaches that this concretizes into actuality, and one of my favorite expressions of his is that an assumption, though false, if persisted in will concretize into fact. I think very few people would disagree with this. Whether one's point of view is more psychological or spiritual, I think you can find something to agree with there. I felt a sense of a turning point in my life when I encountered this philosophy, and I felt excited about the idea that your thoughts are causative. I liked the self-sufficiency of it, and the idea that there was nothing to join.

Jake Kobrin

At this point in my life and in my writing, I'm working to be frank and upfront about the problems I have with this philosophy. I'm still very dedicated to it, but I need to be direct about the problems I have. I think this philosophy has done a better job of popularizing than refining itself. I think Neville was the last hugely wonderful, innovative voice in the philosophy. While it has great power and truth within its folds, it gets repeated a lot.

One of the things that gets repeated is that you have to assume the feeling state of the wish fulfilled. This has its basis in Western scripture, and many of the early New Thought pioneers grew up in rural circumstances with limited access to books. They took certain parabolic and universal human lessons from scripture and combined the insight of mesmerism. They thought of this unseen vital force as the subconscious or psyche. It is my belief that they combined these ideas to form the New Thought philosophy.

They embarked on some of their own private spiritual adventures, and they arrived at, I believe, an extraordinary understanding of the power of human thought, the power of the psyche, which I see as a combination of your thoughts and emotions to manifest experience, to heal the body, to bring things into your life, and to remake your world in concrete ways. Their method was foresightful of many things that are a part of our world today, including some of the more advanced placebo studies, studies in psychic research (which is personally very important to me), interpretations of quantum theory, and neuroplasticity. In fact, I think Neville really is the finest mystical analogue to quantum theory. He was saying and exploring things that would not become accepted within interpretations of quantum theory until maybe ten years after he said them, and well before they had become popularized to the general public.

At this point in my search, I find myself in a fitful place regarding New Thought, a philosophy that I have experimented with, written about, studied, and worked with as a seeker for many years. By nature, I am an anxious person. I experience anxiety and have all my life. I don't think I have been depressed a day in my life, but I do catastrophize and look at the future, near future, and enumerate all the things that could possibly go wrong. This is probably something that pushed me in the direction of studying New Thought. I believe there is a huge practical

The Path Within

problem in New Thought that has never been addressed from within the folds of the philosophy. I am making my own effort to address it with my new book, *Daydream Believer*, where I spend a lot of time on this idea.

The issue is the formula that has become popular and foundational with New Thought that you must assume the feeling of the wish fulfilled. I think it has utility and I think it works. At the same time, many individuals—myself included—find themselves unable to access that formula when they are in a state of suffering or deepest need. If you are experiencing grief, depression, anxiety, addiction, or anguish, that formula can be very cold comfort.

I have found that within New Thought culture, if you make the effort to talk about this, essentially what you're being told is, "well, try again." It starts to enter into the territory of catechism, where it's almost like being part of a very strict religious system where you're being told, "well, you know, say ten Hail Mary's and see what happens. Fast on Yom Kippur and you're good, you're in the book of life."

We in the alternative spiritual culture are no more immune from orthodoxy than anybody else, and we have to really watch out for that. If a seeker is earnestly saying, "hey, look, I'm having a problem here," the answer is not just, "well, try again," because otherwise I wind up just defending a dogma. Although I often speak in terms of the psyche, I primarily refer to the connection between thought and emotion.

It's important to note that our thoughts and our intellect run on their own tracks. Our emotions run on their own track. Our bodies run on their own track. If this wasn't the case, then, for example, nobody would suffer from addiction. If somebody was experiencing addiction, they would say, "well, you know, I realize this has become destructive, so I'm going to stop." But of course, life does not work that way. The body has its demands, and those demands are to be honored. We owe something to them. Likewise, our emotions have their own demands. If emotions were subservient to the mind, for example, then one could say, "Well, you know, I won't get angry at so and so when they say the predictable thing." But very often, we do find ourselves getting angry, we go to therapy, and we get cognitive-behavioral exercises, which may or may not work for the therapist themself. We make an effort to harmonize, but emotions and

Jake Kobrin

intellect each follow their own distinct paths, and we owe something to both. These forces, along with others, shape our lives. So, when an individual is in pain, it isn't enough to simply say, "I'll cultivate the feeling of the wish fulfilled, and that will unlock my psychical energies." Such an approach, while valuable, doesn't fully address the complexities of our inner struggles.

These forces, among others, make up our lives. So, when the individual is in pain, it's not enough to say, "well, you know, I'll cultivate the feeling of the wish fulfilled and that will be sufficient to sort of unlock my psychic energies." Neville, whom I hold in the highest regard—no intellectual figure has shaped my thinking more deeply, and I dedicated *Daydream Believer* to him—was a master of both metaphysics and an actor, a thespian by trade. This theatrical training gave him an extraordinary command over his body and psyche. His graceful presence and ability to embody feeling were, in many ways, a natural extension of his theatrical background. Yet, while I deeply admire and cherish his approach, I've often found that the cultivation of feeling states, which Neville emphasized as central to his method, does not come as easily to everyone, myself included. My analytical mind tends to dominate, which may explain my fascination with ESP research. Though I've had powerful moments where I've successfully conjured the emotional depth Neville described, those moments are rare. As much as I value his philosophy, I sometimes struggle with the feeling-centered focus, finding it difficult to fully integrate into my own experience.

So, I have begun to think about what could help me access this metaphysical quality of thought at times when I'm experiencing suffering. I don't know if it's necessary for me to defend the notion that the mind has metaphysical properties. I could certainly do so, and there are a lot of things that back up that point of view, such as psychic research, interpretations of quantum theory, some of the outer reaches of placebo research, neuroplasticity, and, of course, perhaps more important than any of these, the experience of the individual seeker and the testimony of the seeker over the course of millennia.

As a group of friends and co-seekers, I think we're probably in agreement with the idea that we lead an extra-physical life in addition to our physical existence. When I say spiritual, I mean extra-physical. So, my

The Path Within

challenge is how do I access the spiritual or the extra-physical powers of the psyche when I'm in a state of suffering, whatever it may be. I'll share the approach I've come up with and invite you to experiment with it and see if it's useful to you.

My first approach, and I feel this is very important, is to listen with fresh ears, even if something sounds familiar. We fail to recognize the contradictions within ourselves, so we assume things are familiar, but we don't truly understand them because we've never made the effort to explore them deeply. I believe that magick is still real, even if it takes a long time to work. One of the principles I abide by—and it can take a long time, or it can actually be very sudden—is to ask yourself in a very fresh and new way, without any moral embarrassment whatsoever, what you really want in life and strip away everything you know.

I often encourage people to go back to their memories of when they were three or four years old, before peer pressure had its grip on them. We all harbor memories from infancy and feel these things in our bodies and emotions, but we're not often able to recall them. There might be methods we can use to recall them, such as hypnosis or past life regression. Ages three and four are especially valuable because we form cognizant long-term memories, including of fantasies and dreams—things that we really want in life. Very young kids can be very clear about what they want in life, but this can get bled out of us by peer pressure, which can come from surprising places. I'm always trying to be cognizant that we all occupy our own subcultures, and we may occupy subcultures that on the surface are dedicated to heterodoxy, overturning things as they are and busting up orthodoxy. But lo and behold, human nature is human nature. Those subcultures have within them their own forms of peer pressure that can be really heavy and can get inside you and separate you from what you want.

Even within the private confines of your own psyche, there are certain rote thoughts and brakes that you put on yourself. You might think you want something, but that desire can be superficial. You may feel the need to reframe it, like saying, "I want this so I can help others." Now, if your genuine intention is to help people, that's admirable, but you need to be honest with yourself about your true motivations. These kinds of ortho-

Jake Kobrin

doxies can really get inside us, and we can be shamed by them. There are people in the spiritual culture who may yearn for very materialistic definitions of success. I'm speaking generally, of course. Even the very term "materialism" has a negative connotation, and I think options get closed off to us all the time because of peer pressure coming in ways that can really be sideways. It can hit us in very surprising ways, so I invite you to an experiment: be absolutely unembarrassed. This is private; you don't have to share this with anyone. You don't have to tell your significant other, your best friend, or your therapist. Just keep it to yourself.

What do you really want? Because I personally believe that we are terribly alienated from that. It's ironic because many of us live in societies that are very oriented towards pleasure and gratification or consumer pleasure, but no one can tell you what you want. I invite you to embark on this exercise with a total absence of embarrassment. Don't worry if the thing that comes to you seems off-key in terms of how you perceive your life, your identity group, your peers, or what's supposed to be right, deep, or altruistic.

I just asked you to use language that is entirely your own to tap into that wish. And I would also suggest that you write it down on a piece of paper (I'm a big believer in that) and not on a computer if you can avoid it. When you write that wish down on a piece of paper, you have created something tangible that was not there before. You should feel a sense of joy. It may be a piece of paper that you're carrying in your pocket for the time being, but it is a step. Even if you write down this wish and feel distant from it, you may be surprised at how it can subtly alter who you spend your time with. There may be certain groups of people who you may like or have an emotional attachment to, but some of them may not be facilitating what you really want in the world. Maybe they're deterring it, and you might start to see subtle but real changes in your life.

At this stage of my life, I'm living out things that I dreamt of when I was three or four years old, although it took me a long time to get there. I always like to point out to people that I didn't write my first book until I was well past the age of forty. My first book, *Occult America*, came out in 2009 when I was forty-three going on forty-four. Honestly, I thought I had left writing behind. When I was in my thirties, I was a publishing

The Path Within

executive, and I was not that happy. I felt like I didn't stand for anything and I wasn't doing anything of real value in the world. I had friends who said to me that wasn't true, but I knew there was a gap in my life. I didn't rediscover myself as a writer until I was thirty-six or thirty-seven, a time when a lot of societies tell you it's time to get serious and settle down. When I was in my early forties and I got my first book contract, I cried tears of joy. I never take it for granted because I didn't think this was going to come back to me. If you had spoken to me in my mid-thirties, I would have come up with some way of defending the choices I had made, but I was not a writer and I was not doing what I'm doing today.

It dawned on me that the stuff I had dreamt of when I was three or four years old, fantasies I had while I was playing with my friends, had emerged within my life. The philosopher Goethe said something to the effect of "what you wish for when you're very young will come upon you in waves when you're old, so be careful." A lot of people immediately want to argue with that statement and say there are things they wanted that they don't have. I can only invite you to peel back the layers of your life and see if you don't detect a congruity between what you wished for when you were very young and what you might be living out now or what you might live out later. It's critically important to identify that wish, which belongs to you exclusively. Personally speaking, I would keep it private and not feel the need to tell your boyfriend, girlfriend, spouse, or whomever.

I mean, again, this is entirely up to you, but I think holding that wish privately is uniquely important because other people have a way of detracting from what we're about. You might tell somebody something that you really wish for yourself in life, and that person might make some goofy joke or something like that, and it is depleting. It truly is depleting. I think there is a great power in silence. So, I invite you to do that because I think a clarified wish, which we rarely do with absolute lack of embarrassment, absolute personal candor, whatever it may be, is powerful.

That will bring you power; it may unfold eventually; it may unfold more quickly. In some cases, you may be quite surprised, but it will bring you power. Another thing I believe, and that I've been experimenting with, is a kind of continuation of this theme of a wish, but I guess it's more

Jake Kobrin

circumstantial or situational. Let's say you find yourself in a tough spot, whatever it may be. Might be somebody that you love has profoundly let you down or any number of things. This is the kind of situation where I think people find it difficult to access and use the classic new thought method, which is again, assuming the feeling state of the wish fulfilled.

I came to wonder whether the enunciation of a wish in and of itself, and it doesn't necessarily have to be a life wish, you know, it could be something very circumstantial, can be extremely important in your life. I began to wonder if the wish itself might be sufficient to enact the metaphysical energies of your psyche. Simply wishing. The critique of "just wishing" often points to those born into deeply oppressive circumstances, whose entire lives may be spent yearning for something better. What about their wishes? I think the point is that wishing is the starting point—it's the most basic, foundational act of magick, but it's only the first step. That distinction needs to be made clear.

I had a circumstance where somebody I knew did something that was very, very disappointing. I felt terribly eager to have some communication with this person, but I didn't know how to broach it. And I laid down on my bed and I experimented with this method of just wishing, wishing for deliverance from this situation. It didn't feel futile. It didn't feel like it was just some idle random thought that I was running through the exterior of my psyche. I wish that with all my guts, it was a totalizing experience. And you know, when you have those totalizing experiences, they're not altogether common, but you do feel intellect, emotion, and body almost right there, unified on the same track. I got the resolution that I was looking for.

I'll tell you another story. It's perhaps more dramatic. I was in the town of Waltham, Massachusetts, and on the Charles River in Waltham is this weird, late Victorian-era stone tower called NorAm Bega Tower that was built in 1899. It was what the Victorians used to call a "folly," meant to be an echo of an ancient Celtic tower. Supposedly, the Viking explorer Leif Erikson had a settlement on the Charles River, though it is uncertain whether this is true. Some local Viking enthusiasts decided to build this tower in 1899, and it has a beautiful, Gothic staircase leading to the top.

The Path Within

The windows are barred to keep out beer-drinking, heavy metal-listening high school students, but I managed to slip through and reach the top.

It was a crisp, bright winter day, cold but sunny. I was around forty years old and had not yet written my first book. From the top of the tower, I ventured a wish to be a successful, productive, working, and recognized author. It was a totalizing experience, as the wish was so sincere and unencumbered by other concerns. I felt authentic progress in my life after that time, and I believe passion is necessary. Emotion cannot be dispensed with, and these experiences of wishing were passionate, deeply emotional, intellectual, and physical. We avail ourselves of magick and spiritual methods because we have needs, and the wish can be a possible trigger of the psyche's powers. I have been experimenting with that. I invite you to experiment with a simple wish. There may be extraordinary power hidden within that seemingly familiar practice.

I'll share a third method with you that I use, and that is deity worship and prayer. Another of the issues I have with New Thought is that it's frequently heard—and again, Neville will say this in many lectures and talks—if you locate this thing called God outside yourself, you've missed the mark. Neville would say, "the only God is your own wonderful human imagination." I'm not sure that that division is helpful or, in fact, true.

From time immemorial, people all over this world, from Polynesia to Siberia, have engaged in deity worship. They identified certain energies, personified them, and then sought petitionary relationships with those personified energies.

I remember learning years ago that an archaeologist discovered an altar to moon worship in the Negev Desert that was estimated to be about 25,000 years old. I wept when I learned this because I felt it's so extraordinary. I'm not trying to be overly dramatic, but you are attached to a chain of seekers that goes back to that. These primeval people are our ancestors, and once they got past the needs of survival, procreation, and gathering food in whatever form, they turned to seeking a relationship with something extra-physical, something greater. They saw themselves as connected to the cosmos: "as above, so below." And so, it seems to me

Jake Kobrin

that I simply cannot fathom that for the vast majority of human history, our ancestors all over the world were just wrong.

I understand how compelling it is to make that argument and say that what is ultimately true is that it is just the energy of the mind. Well, I'm not saying that it's not the energies of the mind, but I don't think that believing in the energies of the mind requires that I discount or draw a line that says everything else is somehow a decoy. There is a fluidity. How would I know where personality melts into essence? Higher melts into lower, an act that is thought to be materialistic melts into an act that is thought to be immaterialist. These are all just concepts. I mean, there's not even such a thing as up and down. I could point up and it's meaningless to somebody who's watching from Australia, New Zealand, or Papua New Guinea. I'm pointing toward their down. It's all conceptual. There's this thing called gravity that keeps us here; it seems to be mass attracted to itself. We don't know exactly what it is, so up and down are just concepts, linearity is a concept, all these things are conceptual and conditional.

I'm hesitant to believe that the only power is my own imagination. It doesn't mean that that's not the case, as above, so below, but I don't think it means that I have to divorce myself from the idea that I can have a relationship with an energy, with a deified and personified energy.

Years ago, I was taking a car ride with Dean Raden, who's a great psychic researcher. I was telling him that I was reading this graphic novel, *The Death of Superman*. I said to him, the most extraordinary thing in this graphic novel is that Superman, at a certain point in the story, loses his powers. But he continues to try to do his thing, he continues to try to save people even though he's just an ordinary flesh and blood mortal. I thought that it was his superpower that's extraordinary. Dean asked me, "Does he have super emotions?"

I said, "No, he has super ethics."

Dean said, "Well, ethics come from the emotions."

I thought, "Yes, you're correct. Ethics come from the emotions. What are ethics? It's the ability to feel empathy, the ability to put myself in the position of another individual." So, it is emotional.

The Path Within

If our ancient ancestors were right, that these energies could be personified and deified, these energies could be sought in terms of relationship, in terms of petitioning, and that these energies were, in a sense, intelligences, then wouldn't it stand to reason that if there are these extra-physical intellects, they too must have emotions?

Many of the ancients in the Celtic world and Africa depicted the gods as very human. They felt rage, jealousy, and envy, much like us. So, wouldn't it stand to reason that if these extra-physical intellects exist, they have emotions, and possibly the old gods are lonely for human company and hunger for human veneration? This could give us an extraordinary opportunity to forge a relationship with one of these deities. We can identify a deity from the pantheon of ancient gods from whatever culture we resonate with, whatever figure we feel empathy for. The gods in all the ancient parables are racked by the same issues we are: they have lovers, they lose lovers, they go to war, they are jealous, they hate, they lose, they win, they disobey. Prometheus disobeyed and stole fire from the gods and was supposedly freed by Hercules. There is friction, love, passion, betrayal, and loyalty in all these stories.

If there is a figure we resonate with, we should make an appeal. We should throw out all orthodoxy and liturgy and see what happens. It could be one of the most extraordinary turning points of our lives. If there is an extra-physical energy, a deity that was once the center of a geographical world, we can imagine the anguish we could relieve by reaching out to this figure. Petitioning such a figure is a perfectly fine thing to do, as the ancients petitioned their gods all the time. Scripture is like a deal-making book. It's filled with the matriarchs and patriarchs saying, "you do this for me, God, and I'll do this in return." The ancients in Western scripture would argue with God. God punished Cain and Cain said, "The punishment you gave me, it's too much. I can't bear it."

And so God said, "All right, well, I'll amend it and I'll put the mark of the so-called mark of Cain on you. And anybody who lays a hand on you, who hurts you, will be punished multiple times."

Jake Kobrin

The ancients made deals with the gods or a God all the time. They had a relationship. What is necessary in a relationship? Affinity. Certainly loyalty, honesty, maturity, not losing your temper if something goes wrong, or at least not losing control. I'm not trying to be flippant, but a relationship with the gods might work in a similar way. Imagine the anguish you could relieve if my theory is right—and if it is, you're well within your rights to ask for a favor. That favor could be the turning point of your life.

To reiterate, I feel certain at this stage of my search for various reasons that the mind has causative powers. That the pioneers of New Thought were right in so many ways. But I think that the New Thought outlook became calcified pretty quickly as religions and spiritual systems frequently do. It didn't grow a great deal it did a better job of popularizing itself than it did of refining itself.

One of the great gaps in New Thought is the question of suffering on a mass scale. I don't think it responds well to real agonized suffering on an intimate scale. The global scale is a whole other question and a worthy one. But when the individual feels grief or anxiety or is experiencing addiction or depression, cultivating that feeling state can be a very cold comfort.

My approach at this point in my search is to come up with an absolutely clarified wish, because I think a clarified wish with a complete lack of embarrassment is powerful. It enacts the energy of the psyche. When you're in a situation that feels critical and you're having a hard time, whatever it may be, avail yourself of the power to feel a wish and try. I don't think you'll have to try very hard if it's something that you really want. Maybe there's friction in a relationship that needs to be dealt with. Maybe there's a wish for something in your work, in your work as an artist, or in some other walk of life, whatever it may be. Allow yourself to really feel and enunciate that wish with totality. If you find yourself in a public place, don't be embarrassed. Do it anyway. I've done this in the rotunda of the New York Public Library and an old girlfriend of mine from college, whom I hadn't seen in God knows how long, came up to me and said, "I didn't want to interrupt you. You looked like you were praying." So, you have to just let go of embarrassment sometimes. If you feel that passion within you, act on it. Act on it; it doesn't mean you have to jump up on a table or get thrown out

The Path Within

or anything, but act. That moment is precious, and it may not come back anytime soon.

Third and finally, seek a relationship with a deity if you wish. I have lived with this for a long time, and I don't feel like there is any problem or disparity or dividing line between enlisting the energies of your mind and also praying to a deity. We spend too much time drawing lines of demarcation that are just conceptual. If that feels like a paradox, that's okay too, because someone once said to me that one of the things you'll need on the spiritual path is a tolerance for paradox. You have to accept the presence of paradoxes; you'll twist yourself into knots if you refuse to. Availing yourself of a relationship to a deity of your choosing is an experiment, but it could become one of the most extraordinary turning points of your life.

CHAPTER FIVE

MAGICKAL MEDITATION

Meditation is arguably the crux of magick. Everything you do in magick is a form of meditation to some extent. The skills you will learn through formal meditation practice—to control your nervous system, develop single-pointed concentration of the mind, develop an ability to endure discipline and strengthen the Will, and uphold clear and vivid visualizations for long periods of time—are all extremely useful, and arguably essential, abilities to have when practicing magick.

Although various forms of meditation (and there are many different types of meditation) are commonly found in all types of magickal practice now. This was not always the case and, in fact, to my knowledge, classical Western magick, such as that found in the Grimoires, has no meditation within it at all.

It wasn't until the late nineteenth century that meditation became commonplace within occultism. This was largely due to the impact of H.

Jake Kobrin

P. Blavatsky, the founder of the Theosophical Society, and her role of popularizing eastern spiritual traditions such as Hinduism, Yoga, Tantra, Vedanta, and Buddhism. Blavatsky spent time studying Yoga and Buddhism in Ceylon, India, Tibet, and other places where there was a tradition of Eastern mysticism, and then popularized those practices within her syncretic Theosophical system.

Aleister Crowley visited India, Burma, Sri Lanka, and many other countries in the early twentieth century, and was one of the first Europeans to study, teach, and perhaps master Raja Yoga and meditation. Raja Yoga directly translates to "The Royal Yoga" —meaning "vehicle for Union" —and is different from the bendy, acrobatic Yoga that you find in most modern studios. It is more concerned with extreme states of mental concentration. Crowley was highly influenced by his mentor Alan Bennett, who was his main teacher in the Hermetic Order of the Golden Dawn where Crowley received his education in Magick and Esotericism, and who was later ordained as a Theravadan Buddhist Monk and practiced Buddhism in Ceylon. Crowley studied Raja Yoga, meditation, and other Theravada Buddhist practices in Ceylon, now Sri Lanka, under the tutelage of the Guru Sir Ponnambalam Ramanathan, a prominent Ceylonese (Sri Lankan) lawyer, politician, dignitary, and Hindu educationalist in the late nineteenth and early twentieth centuries.[49]

Blavatsky, Bennett, and Crowley were largely responsible for the spread of Eastern religion and spiritual practices in the nineteenth and twentieth centuries. Mahatma Gandhi even credited Blavatsky as a major influence and source of inspiration. This eventually resulted in the huge boom in popularity of Yoga, Buddhism, and Eastern Spirituality through the New Age movement of the 1960s and continuing through the present day.[50]

After his experiences with meditation in Ceylon and India, Crowley made meditation practice in the style of Raja Yoga foundational to his system of ceremonial magick and mysticism.

---

49   For more on Crowley's history, see Skinner, Stephen, "Crowley Chronology" in Aleister Crowley's *Four Books of Magick* (Watkins, 2021) and Kaczynski, Richard, "Chapter Four: The Mountain Holds a Dagger" in *Perdurabo* (North Atlantic Books, 2002)

50   Horowitz, Mitch, *Occult America: The Secret History of How Mysticism Shaped Our Nation* (Bantam Books, 2009)

The Path Within

FUNDAMENTAL MINDFULNESS PRACTICES

I want to introduce to you some basic and fundamental mindfulness practices. Variations of these basic mindfulness practices can be undertaken at any time while doing any activity, such as walking your dog, working out, or washing the dishes. I cannot overstate the enormous benefit of doing these practices, and I guarantee they will enhance all areas of your life like a wave that comes to wash and clean and balance out everything, including your magickal practice. In fact, as you do these practices, and become more and more content and present with life as it is, you might find that you need to do practical magick less and less.

First sit quietly, with your back straight, in any posture that is comfortable, in a place that is reasonably quiet. You can have your feet crossed on a pillow on the floor, or you can be sitting in a chair. Anywhere you sit and however you sit is fine, but make sure that you are not so relaxed that you will fall asleep. (If you do fall asleep, maybe just let yourself sleep. You are probably fatigued and actually need it!) Tibetan Buddhists practice with their eyes half-closed, and Zen Buddhists meditate while staring at a blank white wall to avoid succumbing to sleep or reverie.

Next try to relax any obvious areas of tension in your body, loosen any clothes (such as if your belt is tight), and start by taking a few deep breaths to signal to your body that it's time to be centered and relaxed.

Then just sit there. As you sit, don't feel like you need to do anything, just observe the sensations as they arise in your perception. The feeling of your butt on the pillow, your legs against the floor, thoughts of what you need to do today, worry, sleepiness, the warmth of the sun on your face, heat, coolness, the tickle of breath in the nose—whatever you observe, it's all fine. Take it all in, in an impartial and radically open way. Sit like this for five or ten minutes.

Then when you notice your body and mind begin to calm down, set an intention to focus on the sensation of your breathing. You don't have to breathe in any special kind of way. Just breathe normally and naturally. As you breathe in and out, notice where you feel the sensations most prominently. You might feel the coolness in the nostrils, warmth in the back of the throat, or the rise and fall of your chest or your belly. As you experience yourself breathing in, note very gently in your mind "breathing in," as you experience yourself breathing out, note very gently "breathing out." Your mind will inevitably wander, and you will likely catch yourself losing your concentration as waves of thoughts carry you away. That is totally fine and normal. When you notice that you've lost your concentration on your breath, simply notice and label it in your mind "thinking, thinking" and then bring yourself back to observing your breath.

You can start out by doing this practice for maybe five to fifteen minutes per day, ideally in the morning, but any time you can practice is good. As you become more comfortable with the practice, you may want to increase the amount of time you practice to thirty minutes, or forty-five minutes, or even an hour per day. This simple meditation exercise is the foundation of having a clear, calm, and balanced mind, and will perhaps benefit you more than any other practice in this book. Do not discount this practice because of its apparent simplicity. It is harder than it sounds.

EXERCISE: FOUNDATIONAL MINDFULNESS TECHNIQUES

In personal and magickal development, mindfulness practices stand as fundamental tools. These practices, simple yet profound, are designed to cultivate a sense of presence and awareness, enhancing every aspect of life, including your magick. As you engage more deeply in these practices, you may find your reliance on practical magick diminishing, replaced by a contentment and attunement with life as it unfolds.

The Path Within

Needs:
- A quiet, comfortable place for sitting
- Optional: A cushion or chair for sitting

Setup:
- Choose a calm environment where you won't be disturbed.
- Sit comfortably with your back straight—on a cushion on the floor or in a chair.
- Ensure you are alert enough to avoid falling asleep. (Tibetan and Zen Buddhist practices can offer guidance on posture.)

Instructions:
- Begin by loosening any tight clothing.
- Take several deep breaths to signal your body to relax and center.
- Let your body settle into a relaxed yet alert state.

Observation Phase:
- Simply sit and observe without judgment.
- Notice sensations, thoughts, and feelings as they arise, accepting them openly.
- Aim for five to ten minutes in this phase, gradually extending the duration.

Focus on Breathing:
- Shift your attention to your breath.
- Observe the breath's natural rhythm—the sensations of coolness, warmth, and movement.
- Mentally note "breathing in" and "breathing out" with each breath.

Handling Distractions:
- When thoughts arise and distract you, label them as "thinking" and gently return focus to your breath.

Duration and Regularity:
- Start with ten to fifteen minutes daily, ideally in the morning.
- Gradually increase the duration to thirty or forty-five minutes, or even an hour as you become more accustomed to the practice.

Follow Through:
- Consider keeping a journal to note your experiences and insights gained through these practices.
- Be consistent with your practice, as its benefits are cumulative.

Optional:
Remember the words of Aleister Crowley, summarizing the essence of meditation: "Sit still. Stop thinking. Shut up. Get out." These words underscore the simplicity yet depth of mindfulness practice.

By integrating these fundamental mindfulness practices into your daily routine, you cultivate a foundation for a clear, calm, and balanced mind, enhancing both your personal growth and your magickal pursuits.

THE RELAXATION RITUAL

The first and most important step to doing magick is being able to regulate your nervous system, calm, and center yourself. This ritual is designed to help you do this.

Begin by finding a place where you will not be disturbed for at least five minutes and eliminate any distractions, such as your cell phone. Get comfortable, ensuring that your back is straight if you are sitting, and that your legs and arms are not crossed. If sitting, allow your hands to rest, palms down, in your lap, and close your eyes.

The Path Within

Visualize a golden ball of beautiful, warm light surrounding your feet. Even if you cannot *see* the ball of light when you visualize it, know that it is there, and that if your powers of visualization were different, you would be able to see it. Allow this ball of light to rise up your legs and up your torso, then down your arms to your fingers, and finally up your neck and into your head until you are completely surrounded by the warm, golden glow. Imagine the feeling of total peace and relaxation and the disappearance of all tension. If you notice any tension anywhere, send the ball of light there and the tension will vanish.

Stay in this state of deep relaxation for a few moments, knowing that you can return to this state whenever you like by doing the relaxation ritual. If you are having trouble sleeping, you can try this ritual when you lay down at night instead of suffering or taking dangerous pills. Allow yourself to be at one with yourself.

When you are ready to come out of this state of deep relaxation, take three deep breaths and feel fresh life and energy coming into your body with each breath. Be sure to record your experience in your ritual diary.

By regularly practicing the Relaxation Ritual, you create a solid foundation for all your magickal practices, ensuring that you approach each ritual or spellwork from a place of inner calm and centeredness. Use this technique as a preparatory step before engaging in more complex magickal workings to enhance focus and efficacy.

GROUNDING PRACTICES

There is nothing more important in magickal practice than staying clear, centered, and grounded. It is the biggest risk to the magician that you can fly off into la-la land, or otherwise become an eccentric and paranoid wreck. Drug use usually fuels this type of descent, but it can happen to the best of us if we are not careful.

Jake Kobrin

Crowley urged students to practice meditation as the foundation for magickal work, and I agree. Some types of meditation can be heady, mental, and ungrounding. Your roots must grow deep before you can rise to the heavens.

I am by nature a very mental person, and so I know what it is to be ungrounded and to be "all in my head." If I'm not careful, intense magickal practice or study can make this worse. And so, I wanted to introduce from experiences some of the things that have helped me stay grounded during my explorations as both a psychonaut (explorer of psychedelic states of consciousness) and as a magician.

What does it mean to be grounded? The ground corresponds to the Element of Earth, and the Element of Earth corresponds to our physical lives and bodies. To be grounded means to be embodied, to be present and alive within our own physical vessels, to be fully here in the material world.

The first and most important thing is to be physically active and take excellent care of your health. This is a much higher priority than your magickal practice and should always be treated as such. During the process of working through this book, I want you to commit to taking excellent care of yourself, eating wholesome and nutritious foods that contribute to the health and wellness of your body, showing love to your body through movement and exercise, getting adequate rest and enough sleep, and drinking plenty of water. You also need to take care of your other material needs, such as making sure you have ways to earn income and establishing a degree of safety both financially and in your home. If you don't have these things at least rudimentarily under control, set an intention to put energy into these things before moving forward. You can use the practice of magick to supplement the vitality of these other areas of your life, but chances are these areas need to be reckoned with on their own plane, meaning you just have to do the mundane work to get your act together. There's no shame if you are currently struggling in these areas, and we all go through pitfalls and misfortunes. In this case, the regularity of your magickal practice might be a good fallback to the chaos that can at times beseech our lives.

Meditation and grounding are practices that help individuals connect more deeply with themselves and the present moment, often leading to increased mindfulness and tranquility. Grounding specifically involves techniques that bring one's attention and energy back to the physical body and the immediate environment, which can be particularly beneficial in managing stress and achieving a state of mental and emotional balance.

WALKING MEDITATION

Next, we will explore walking meditation. Walking meditation is an excellent embodiment of these practices. Unlike traditional seated meditation, it combines the mindfulness aspect of meditation with physical movement, offering a dynamic way to engage both the mind and body. As you walk slowly and deliberately, paying close attention to the sensation of each step, the rhythm of your breath, and the environment around you, you become more grounded in your physical experience. This form of meditation not only calms the mind but also creates a harmonious connection between the body and the surrounding world, making it a holistic practice for those seeking a more integrated approach to mindfulness and presence.

EXERCISE: WALKING MEDITATION

To begin, find a place to practice your walking meditation: a clean and quiet path where you will not be disturbed, about six meters in length. Then, determine the amount of time you will practice, maybe twenty minutes or so to begin, and decide that you will not disrupt your practice for this length of time. You can set a timer on your phone using the many available meditation bell and timer apps that are available before you

Jake Kobrin

begin, but put your phone on airplane mode and somewhere out of sight where it will not distract you. As you become more comfortable with this practice, you can practice anywhere, even on a busy city street, but at the beginning, it is better to practice somewhere calm and tranquil. It might be best to practice somewhere in nature, where the forest or the jungle can assist you in a deeper sense of connection with the web of life. Keep your eyes open during this practice to avoid tripping, falling, or any other kind of mistake.

Begin first by standing still at the beginning of your walking path. Notice the sensations of standing still, the stability, the feeling of the breeze on your skin, the sensations of your feet on the floor, and the sensations of your breath in your nostrils or your belly. As you are standing still, note gently in your mind, "standing, standing." Notice how it feels to be still.

Now begin to walk very slowly on your path, concentrating on the movement and sensations of your feet and legs. As you raise your foot to move forward, note "moving" and, as you place your foot down on the ground, note "placing." Do not lift your other leg until after you've placed your foot on the floor. Keep your gaze about a meter or two in front of you so that your neck is relaxed and not strained. The slower you can walk, the more concentration you will be able to cultivate.

Continue walking like this, slowly and with concentration, until you reach the end of your path. If you find yourself lost to thoughts, notice again that you are thinking by noting "thinking, thinking" and then return back to the sensations of walking, noting "moving... placing...."

When you reach the end of your path stand still again, feeling the sensations and noting "standing, standing..." and then turn back around again, noting in your mind the sensations of turning and noting "turning...turning...."

Then, begin to walk back again. The point is not to go anywhere. This is not a walk to the beach or a hike to the top of the mountain—although that can also be a beneficial experience—but rather an exercise and invitation to deeper presence. As you get used to this practice, you can instead break up the mindfulness into additional stages, noticing when you lift your heel by noting "lifting my heel," then noting when you are lifting your toe by noting "lifting my toe," noticing when you are moving your foot by noting

The Path Within

"moving my foot," and finally noticing when you are placing your foot by noting "placing my foot." This four-fold structure can be very balanced and result in a very deep and subtle level of concentration.

When you finish with your designated time, take a moment to thank yourself for this practice. You can also choose to dedicate the merits of your practice to the benefit of other beings, or to a specific cause or person, to continue strengthening a sense of altruism.

Either of these practices are available to you at any time that you need them, when you find yourself stressed out at work or ungrounded by a ritual practice or magickal operation that took you further from your body and into more numinous territory than you are used to. I suggest practicing both of these meditations regularly, not only as a prerequisite to more advanced magickal practice but as a sort of daily mental and spiritual hygiene as essential as brushing your teeth or showering.

ADVANCED MEDITATION: PART ONE, ASANA

The word *asana* means "posture." You may know this term from Hatha Yoga (the acrobatic and athletic Yoga popular in the west), but here the word means "how you sit for meditation." The only way to master asana is to practice, practice, practice. Meditation is a way of focusing your attention and calming your mind. The first step in learning how to meditate is learning how to control your body and sit still for a long period of time. There are four different meditation postures that you can try: the Ibis, the God, the Thunderbolt, and the Dragon.[51]

All of these postures are done with the eyes closed. The Dragon position is my personal favorite. Your buttocks rests on the heels of your feet, toes turned back, spine and head straight, hands on thighs. This is best

---

51 Shoemaker, David, *Living Thelema: A Practical Guide to Attainment in Aleister Crowley's System of Magick* (Anima Solis Books, 2013)

Jake Kobrin

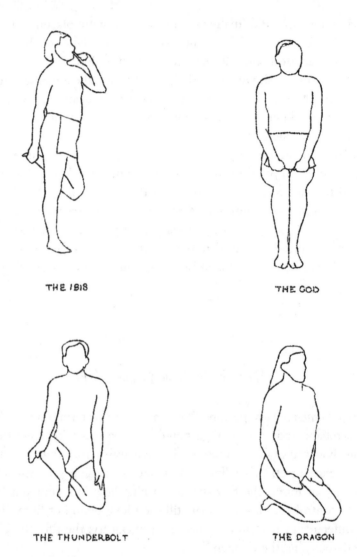

THE IBIS

THE GOD

THE THUNDERBOLT

THE DRAGON

done with a meditation bench, or a meditation cushion (possibly propped up by a Yoga block). Although the God posture may be simpler than the Dragon position, it does require the use of a chair, which may not always

The Path Within

be readily available. In the Dragon position, you sit with your butt slightly off the edge of a chair with your feet flat on the floor, your back straight, and hands on your knees.

You can also just sit cross-legged on a meditation cushion, and not even in full lotus posture. I often sit half-lotus, in which my left leg is flat on the floor, and my right foot is tucked on top of my left leg, with hands on my knees and back straight. I find it's helpful to sit on a bench or a cushion in which my pelvis is slightly higher than my knees. It is important to have good posture when you meditate. This means that your back is straight, your shoulders are back, and your chest is open. Your posture should reflect an attitude of nobility, strength, and courage. Your posture is a kind of anchor, and you should begin to feel the posture sync to a mental familiarity with the state of meditation as you practice more.

The first exercise is to choose one posture and practice sitting in it without moving. Once you have mastered one posture, you can try others. For this week, pick one posture and meditate for at least fifteen minutes every morning. You can gradually work up to longer meditation periods. Really give a good attempt with determination to not move throughout the duration of your sit.

EXERCISE: MASTERING ASANA FOR MEDITATION

Mastering asana is essential for focusing attention and achieving a calm state of mind. This exercise is designed to help you practice and become comfortable with various meditation postures.

Needs List:
- A quiet and comfortable space for meditation.
- Optional: Meditation cushion, bench, or chair.

Jake Kobrin

Setup:

- Choose a meditation posture: the Ibis, the God, the Thunderbolt, or the Dragon. Sitting cross-legged, in half- or full-lotus posture, is also fine.
- Arrange your space to accommodate your chosen posture, using cushions, benches, or chairs as needed.

Instructions:

- Adopt your chosen posture, ensuring your back is straight, shoulders are back, and chest is open. Maintain a noble, strong, and courageous posture.
- **For the Dragon:** Sit with buttocks resting on heels, toes turned back, spine straight, hands on thighs. Use a meditation bench or cushion for support.
- **For the God:** Sit on the edge of a chair with feet flat on the floor, back straight, and hands on knees.
- **For a simpler posture:** Sit cross-legged (half lotus or full lotus) with one leg flat on the floor and the other foot on the opposite leg, hands on knees, back straight. Elevate the pelvis slightly higher than the knees for comfort.
- Close your eyes (or keep them slightly open if following certain traditions).
- Focus on maintaining the posture without moving for the duration of the meditation.

Duration:

- Start with a fifteen-minute meditation session each morning, gradually increasing the duration as you become more comfortable with the posture.

Follow Through:

- Conclude each session with a moment of gratitude for your practice. Record any observations or experiences in your meditation journal.

Alternative Options:
- Experiment with different postures to find which suits you best.
- Adjust your cushioning or seating arrangement for optimal comfort and posture alignment.

Note: Your posture serves as an anchor for your meditation practice. As you become more familiar with a particular posture, it will naturally sync with your mental state of meditation, enhancing your focus and calmness.

ADVANCED MEDITATION: PART TWO, PRANAYAMA

Pranayama is the practice of controlling our breath—of understanding how to breathe in a way that calms the nervous system. Box breathing is a technique used to do this: inhaling for a count of four, holding for a count of four, exhaling for a count of four, and then holding again for a count of four. Using a metronome or a metronome app can help keep your breath consistent, but it's not necessary. The key to mastering pranayama is finding a way to make your breath last longer and longer, slower and slower, which also steadies and calms your nervous system. Remember, the key to effective practice lies in patience and gradual progression, ensuring comfort and ease in your breathing exercises.

Aleister Crowley suggested that practicing pranayama after using cannabis may be beneficial, although this should be approached with discretion and awareness of individual responses to such practices (and local laws).[52]

The type of breathing I most often undergo during meditation is a normal pattern of breathing, but with an acute awareness of the inhale and the exhale. This is what I was taught in Vipassana meditation retreats and what I have practiced most thoroughly. This is called *Anapana*. Its roots are in the Theravada tradition of Buddhism. Simply breathe in and breathe out,

---

52 Crowley, Aleister, *Magick in Theory and Practice* (Samuel Weiser, 1997)

without straining to control the breath, but notice the physical sensations of the breath. You might notice these sensations as a subtle coolness in the nostrils, or as a tickle in the very tip of the nose, or underneath the nose between the nose and mouth. You might also feel the sensations more deeply as a rising and falling of the chest, or belly. Wherever you notice the breath most prominently, maintain your attention there for a while. Then pick a more concentrated spot to focus on, where the sensations are very light or subtle, perhaps just underneath the nostrils where the air is tickling the area above the lips. This will concentrate and deepen your meditation. Focus on this spot until the end of the session. This is harder to do than it sounds!

After you have undergone a period of time of working with your chosen asana until it is comfortable and easy to maintain the posture for extended periods of time, begin to experiment both with the practice of regulated breathing and breath awareness exercises. Record your results in your magickal diary.

EXERCISE: PRANAYAMA, THE ART OF BREATH CONTROL

Pranayama is an advanced meditation technique focused on controlling the breath to calm and steady the nervous system. This practice encompasses various breathing exercises, including box breathing and breath awareness, to deepen your meditative state and enhance focus.

Needs:
- A quiet space for meditation
- Optional: Metronome or metronome app for breath timing

Setup:
- Choose a comfortable meditation posture.
- Prepare your space to ensure no interruptions during the exercise.

The Path Within

Instructions:

- Start with box breathing: inhale for four counts, hold for four counts, exhale for four counts, and hold again for four counts.
- Progress to alternate nostril breathing: Place your right thumb on your right nostril, exhale slowly through your left nostril for twenty seconds, then inhale for ten seconds. Switch and repeat with the other nostril.
- As you become more comfortable with the initial breathing pattern, aim to slowly extend the length of both your exhalations and inhalations. Start by increasing the exhalation and inhalation times by a few seconds each, ensuring you do so without causing any strain or discomfort.
- Practice maintaining a breath cycle of thirty seconds of exhalation and fifteen seconds of inhalation for an hour. Practice this thirty-second exhalation and fifteen-second inhalation cycle continuously for the duration of your sit. Focus on achieving this extended breathing pattern consistently, while maintaining a relaxed and steady rhythm.
- For a less controlled approach, practice breath awareness as taught in Vipassana meditation: simply observe the natural inhale and exhale, focusing on the sensations of the breath in various parts of the body. After a while of familiarizing yourself with the sensations, choose a spot where the sensations are subtle, like under the nostrils, and focus there to deepen your meditation.

Duration:

- Start with a session of around thirty minutes to one-hour, but even starting with fifteen minutes is okay, gradually increasing the length as you become more comfortable with the techniques.

Follow Through:

- Conclude each session with a moment of reflection and gratitude. Record your experiences and progress in your magickal diary.

Alternative Options:
- Experiment with different breathing patterns and rhythms to find what works best for you.
- Use a metronome or app to maintain consistent breath cycles if needed.

Note: Pranayama is a powerful practice that can significantly enhance your meditative experience. Regular practice will lead to improved control over your breath and a deeper, more focused meditative state. Remember, the goal is not to strain but to find a rhythm that brings depth, fullness, and regularity to your breathing.

ADVANCED MEDITATION: PART THREE, DHARANA

Dharana means "concentration." This is the third and final step of meditation practice, after you have mastered stabilizing your body for long periods of time, and the regulation of your breath is concentration or one-pointed focus. Dharana is the climax of the meditation practice.

There can be many different objects of concentration to use during a meditation session. Mantras, the use of repeated phrases, are very common, for example, but we will not use mantras here. For our practice, I will instruct you in two different practices, which will be most useful for the purposes of this book.

The first is a basic mindfulness meditation practice known as *Vipassana*. Get into your asana and begin to notice your breathing. Notice how the breath moves in and out of the body and the physical sensations associated with it, such as the rise and fall of your chest. Whenever you notice that you become distracted, become lost in a daydream or thought, or hear a strong noise or feel a strong sensation in the body, simply and compassionately note where your attention has gone to. You can say in your mind

The Path Within

"planning, planning," "sad, sad," "tightness, tightness," or whatever fits your situation, and then simply return your awareness back to the breath. You don't need to scold yourself for losing your concentration. This practice, although simple, is actually very difficult to do. The goal of this particular meditation practice, for the purposes of this book, is to hone and develop the faculties of single-pointed concentration. The achievement of this goal has very tangible benefits, such as a deeply relaxed sensation of clarity, ease, and spaciousness.

Perform body scans by becoming aware of the bodily sensations at the top of your head, and then moving down bit by bit, piece by piece, down to your toes, observing each and every part of your body. And then move your awareness back up again. Then, repeat for the entire duration of the sitting.

If you find yourself having visions, dreams, reveries, or other types of "astral experiences," do not fall prey to the seduction of such experiences! These experiences will come, and can be both interesting and pleasant, but are not the point of this practice. In fact, they are distractions from your goal of achieving single-pointed concentration. If you have these experiences, simply and dispassionately note them, and return to your breath. It is the most common pitfall of meditation practice, especially in the occult, New Age, and psychedelic communities, to become so enamored with the content of your visions and experiences during meditation so as to lose the plot completely when it comes to the actual point of meditation, which is to achieve a clear and steady quality of relaxed concentration.

I recommend that you begin with this breath awareness meditation practice. After you have mastered your asana and your breath, and are beginning to see real progress with this breath-awareness practice, we can move to the next practice. This can take anywhere from a few weeks to a few months to see results. Attending a Vipassana meditation retreat, like those provided on donation by the Dhamma.org meditation center, founded by the Burmese meditation master S. N. Goenka, and which are available practically all over the world, can help accelerate your practice.

Another way to practice dharana is to focus your attention on any sensations of the point between your eyes, in the center of your forehead, often called the Third Eye. Focus on this part of your body while maintaining your pranayama as described in the last exercise. If at any point your attention wavers, return it back to the point at the third eye where your attention is held.

EXERCISE: DHARANA, CULTIVATING CONCENTRATION

Dharana, the art of concentration, represents the pinnacle of meditation practice. This exercise guides you through two distinct concentration techniques: the primary practice of Vipassana, or mindfulness meditation, and a secondary method focusing on the Third Eye, to be attempted after mastering Vipassana.

Needs:
- A tranquil space for meditation
- A comfortable seated position or asana

Setup:
- Designate a regular time for your meditation practice.
- Choose a quiet, distraction-free area.

Instructions:
- **Vipassana Meditation:**
  - Settle into your chosen asana and begin to observe your breathing.
  - Concentrate on the sensations associated with breathing, such as the chest's rise and fall.
  - When your mind wanders or external distractions occur, acknowledge them ("thinking, thinking" or "noise, noise") and gently redirect your focus back to your breath.
  - The goal here is to develop a single-pointed concentration, fostering clarity and relaxation.

The Path Within

Addressing Distractions:

- If you encounter visions, dreams, or other astral experiences, note them without attachment and refocus on your breath. These are merely distractions from your primary goal of achieving focused concentration.

Progression:

- Continue this practice regularly until significant progress is made. This may take weeks or even months.

Duration:

- Engage in this practice daily, starting with a comfortable duration and gradually extending as your concentration improves.

Follow-Through:

- After each session, take a moment to reflect on your experience. Keeping a journal can help track your progress and insights.

Alternative Practice:

- Once proficient in Vipassana, consider attending a retreat for deeper practice, such as those offered by Dhamma.org.
- As you advance, explore other concentration techniques, like focusing on the Third Eye while maintaining your pranayama practice. If your attention drifts, gently bring it back to the point between your eyebrows.
- Dharana is a profound and enriching practice that sharpens your mental focus and clarity. Patience and consistent effort are key, as mastery is a gradual process.

Optional: The Muse Headband and Other Meditation Devices

The Muse headband represents an innovative intersection of technology and meditation, offering a unique approach that "gamifies" the meditation experience. This personal EEG (electroencephalogram) device works by monitoring brain activity during meditation sessions. It translates these brainwaves into feedback through an accompanying app, allowing users to track and analyze their progress.

The gamification aspect comes into play with the app's interactive features. As you meditate, the app provides real-time auditory feedback based on your mental state. For instance, you might hear calming sounds when your mind is calm and focused, and the sounds intensify when your mind wanders. This immediate feedback helps users understand their meditation practice on a deeper level and encourages them to develop their focus and mindfulness skills.

The Muse headband effectively makes meditation more engaging, especially for those who appreciate a data-driven approach to personal development. By turning meditation into a more interactive and measurable experience, it appeals to a broader audience, potentially drawing in people who might not be inclined towards traditional meditation practices.

THE "WHO AM I?" MEDITATION

The contemplative practice popularized by spiritual master Ramana Maharshi holds profound significance in the tradition of meditation and self-inquiry. Maharshi, a revered Indian sage known for his teachings on self-inquiry and spiritual awakening, emphasized a method called Samadhi, an integral component of the eight-fold path of Yoga. This technique involves deep, focused contemplation, particularly on the introspective question: "who am I?"

Ramana Maharshi's approach to self-inquiry invites individuals to engage in single-pointed concentration, directing their entire focus to unravel the essence of their true self. This practice involves sitting quietly and repeatedly asking oneself "who am I?" with genuine sincerity and openness. As various superficial answers surface—identifying oneself with nationality, gender, profession, or other worldly roles—the practitioner observes these responses dispassionately and returns to the central question.

The profoundness of this exercise lies not in finding a concrete answer but in the exploration it entails. It's common to reach a stage where no distinct answer arises, which is a critical point in the practice. The objective is to cultivate a quality of deep concentration and awareness, leading to the realization that the true answer to "who am I?" is beyond mere intellectual grasp. This process sharpens one's faculty of discrimination or Viveka, enhancing the ability to discern the real from the unreal, the eternal from the transient.

This specific form of concentration, dharana, evolves into a state of being where concentration and awareness merge, resulting in a profound and unwavering focus. Such a state is the ultimate goal of concentration practices in meditation and a significant milestone in self-realization and magickal practice. The "Who Am I?" meditation, as advocated by Ramana Maharshi, thus serves as a powerful tool in delving into the depths of one's consciousness and uncovering the essence of the self.

EXERCISE: "WHO AM I?" MEDITATION, SELF-INQUIRY

Needs:
- A quiet, comfortable space for meditation
- An open, curious mindset

Setup:
- Schedule a regular time for this meditation.
- Find a peaceful spot where you can sit undisturbed.

Instructions:
- Begin by sitting in a comfortable position.

Jake Kobrin

- Pose the question to yourself: "Who am I?"
- As answers arise (e.g., "I am a student"), observe them dispassionately, then return to the question.
- If a moment comes where no answer surfaces, note this silence and return to the question.
- The aim is not to find a definitive answer but to cultivate single-pointed focus and understand the elusive nature of self-identity.
- Through repeated practice, develop the ability to differentiate between what is real and unreal, between the eternal and transient.

Duration:
- Practice daily for a comfortable duration, gradually extending as you progress.

Clean Up/Follow Through:
- Reflect on your experience after each session. Journaling can be helpful.

Alternative Options:
- If struggling with concentration, try shorter sessions initially.
- As you progress, explore deeper levels of self-inquiry beyond surface-level identities.

The "Who Am I?" meditation is a profound tool for self-discovery and enhancing concentration. It requires patience and persistence, and over time, it leads to a state where concentration and awareness merge into a unified state of being. This practice is a cornerstone towards deeper self-understanding and spiritual awakening.

By engaging with these basic mindfulness exercises, regularly reminding yourself of your ethical codes and aspirations, taking good physical care of yourself, reminding yourself to enjoy yourself and not take things so seriously, and observing a healthy sense of objectivity and skepticism, you are already going to be in better shape than ninety percent of magickal practitioners. You might even be in better shape than ninety percent of all people by consciously choosing to cultivate happiness and foster well-being every day of your life!

MEDITATION BY GUEST TEACHER SEAN FARGO

The term "meditation" can mean all sorts of things. There are many kinds of meditations. When I first started as a monk, I specialized in what are known as "the Jhanas," or being able to concentrate the mind on a single point at the exclusion of all other types of experience or phenomena. With concentration practice, we practice being able to focus on one thing and one thing only for an extended period of time. When the mind wanders, which it will, we just bring it back to one thing.

Some things that we can concentrate on could be a visual object, narrowing your visual scope down to a smaller and smaller point over time, and sticking with that for as long as you can. Counting breaths can be a wonderful concentration practice in which we count each inhale or exhale from, say, one to ten, then ten back down to one, then back up to ten, and if we lose track, we can start over at one without berating ourselves or judging ourselves. This can help us to stay concentrated on the breath.

Some people use a sound like a repeating bell or the sound of silence. Some people focus on a physical sensation such as the sensation of the belly rising and falling, or the breath as it enters and exits at the tips of the nostrils. This can be a wonderful concentration practice.

Over time, when we find ourselves concentrated, relaxed, and present with that one thing the mind can enter very advanced states of concentration called the Jhanas. This isn't a religious thing. This is more of a biological

Jake Kobrin

phenomenon where the mind and the brain enter different states of unity where the body dissolves. In our experience, we enter these states of bliss, peace, and equanimity, and they're quite pleasurable. Usually, it takes many days of practice to enter these states. Limiting our exposure to media, including phone screens, and limiting a lot of our interactivity allows us to stabilize the mind.

As an aside, the Buddha talked about the proximate cause of concentration being happiness. In order for the mind to feel, or in order for us to feel safe enough to be able to concentrate on one thing and one thing only, it's helpful to cultivate a sense of well-being. We can practice this by maybe opening to a sense of safety in this moment, like "right now I'm safe." Or maybe we can reflect on some things that have made us happy in the past such as a wholesome sense of happiness, a wholesome sense of gladness. We can maybe focus on things that were karmically positive, or states of gratitude, generosity, and care. Maybe we reflect on a moment when we said "I love you" to a family member, or someone told us that they love us. First, we find a sense of gladness and care, and then move into concentration practice with a little bit more tranquility and stability.

Mantras can also be a great way to concentrate through repetition of phrases, a word, or a sound. But it's principally the repetition that will help us to concentrate.

Concentration is the fuel for mindfulness; it's what allows us to stay present with this unfolding wave of "now," and the now is always changing. To stay present for this unfolding "now," the unfolding experience as it's happening, we need some stability of mind, some concentration, some focus to be able to stay with it as it unfolds. As mindfulness practitioners, it is helpful to also do some concentration practices on the side, as well.

I'll just offer a pithy definition of mindfulness for you to consider, which is non-judgmental, moment to moment awareness of this actual experience. Mindfulness isn't about changing our experience, although we're cultivating our ability to influence our experience. We're not going into the experience hoping to change it, per se. We're here to be with it, to notice it as it is without judging it. It's our ability to be present in our lives: with our emotions in the body, emotions in our thoughts, physical sensation, our perceptions, our

The Path Within

conversations. And so, we're learning how to be present, whether it's pleasant or not, whether we like it or not. We can be present with pain, anxiety, and stress, if we learn how to open to it.

Lately, I've really been exploring fear and opening to fear (getting a sense of that experience, especially in the body), as well as opening to judgment and reactivity, happiness, joy, gratitude, and compassion, being present for all the beauty of life and noticing the good.

Usually, the foundational way to build a sense of mindfulness is to sense into the physical sensations in the body. We start small, and we go in baby steps. The more we practice, the better we get at it, and the more we're able to sense our experiences.

We work with different levels of reactivity by opening to them with gentle awareness, caring curiosity, and being present with what's here, turning towards our experience. A mindfulness practice can be just sitting for a few minutes a day, maybe trying five or ten minutes, and just seeing what you can notice in your body—what kinds of physical sensations you can notice in a place in the body that feels like it's within your window of tolerance and not something too overwhelming.

If you know you have trauma, then that trauma will be in your body somewhere, and you probably don't want to wake the tiger by starting there. We can find an area of the body like the belly or the feet that feels safe enough to explore with your awareness. You can be curious about temperature, sensing coolness or warmth. Sensing into temperature in the body, sensing heaviness and lightness, density versus hollowness, or moistness or dryness. This is especially interesting to explore around the heart. You can notice a sense of movement versus stillness, for example, in the belly, the lungs, or the throat—pleasantness or unpleasantness. Are certain physical, visceral sensations pleasant or unpleasant? Sometimes on the surface we may think they're one way, but when we really sense into them, we may be surprised. This happens all the time. Sensing into these physical characteristics of the body can be a really nice way to ground our awareness into the body.

Get a sense for these types of sensations that are always present, and over time we'll start mapping these kinds of sensations onto emotions because emotions live in the body; they have a mental manifestation, but

Jake Kobrin

they also have physical characteristics. As we practice sensing into the body, we'll start noticing how different sensations map onto different emotions. "Anger feels like 'this,' physically and viscerally. Sadness feels like 'that.' Contentment feels like 'this.' Forgiveness feels like 'this.'" And we begin building a sense of intimacy with ourselves.

The more we discover or uncover ourselves, the more we're able to empathize with how others feel as well. We can tune into the emotional territory of how others may be feeling. And because we're sensing into our experience with this gentle awareness, this caring curiosity, we're disarming our judgments. We're opening our hearts to ourselves.

Sometimes people like Jack Kornfield or Ram Dass may refer to mindfulness as "loving awareness." Other people call it more of a non-judgmental moment-to-moment awareness. Some people like Gabor Mate might refer to it as something similar to "caring curiosity." People like Sharon Salzberg may refer to it, from time to time, as a gentle awareness of what is. All of these definitions point to the key characteristics of opening to what is without agenda, this sense of connection, and staying with that from moment to moment. This takes courage because as all of you know, being human is not easy. There are plenty of experiences that we all share which are difficult that we would rather not have.

Mindfulness is opening to what is. The mind is not the same thing as the brain, in my opinion. Mindfulness is not "brainfulness," nor is it "headfulness." Some people will say that the mind encapsulates our whole sensory apparatus, meaning that it envelops the heart, the body, and the brain, all of which are very valuable. When we talk about mindfulness, it's not this analytical knowing from the brain. It's not an assessment. It's an embodied presence that includes the heart. As we walk through life and sit here on our seats, we open to this experience of sound entering the ears, the sense of pressure of the body on the seat and on the ground.

You may notice thoughts of the future and past. This isn't just meditation; it's life. Can we stay connected? The more we open to our shadows, the clearer our paths will become. That helps us to unlock our truth and helps us to connect with our purpose.

The Path Within

There are additional practices that help us to open our hearts so that we can connect with our experience with a sense of courage. These heart practices encapsulate love, kindness, and compassion—which includes us. These are often the missing pieces for a lot of people in the West, and include opening to joy, practicing equanimity, and developing a caring perspective. It also includes forgiveness practice—asking for forgiveness, forgiving others, and forgiving ourselves—and gratitude practice—reflecting on what we value, and giving thanks. It also includes generosity, what can we share with the spirit of service, reciprocation, wisdom, of knowing that nothing is truly ours, anyway.

There are plenty of other practices like these heart practices that help us to have the courage to face the full experience. Concentration practices help us to stay present. Heart practices help us to open to what is with a sense of courage and connection. We can play with all sorts of different kinds of experiences. Sounds entering the ears, sights entering the eyeballs, tastes in the mouth, sensations of the bottoms of the feet as we walk, and the mindfulness of walking. You can scan around the body sensing into areas of it, noticing types of physical and visceral sensations, and acknowledging the sensations of the body as we breathe, which is probably the most common mindfulness practice taught.

As we practice, we'll be able to sense more nuance and discover parts of ourselves we didn't know were there. We'll be able to sense emotions as they're happening and oftentimes will be able to sense underlying energies behind the presenting emotion, energies closer to our core that may be not want to be seen. It's often fear or grief. Rather than talk these scary emotions away, can we invite them for a little picnic? Can I get to know them a little, bit by bit, in baby steps, in a way that feels safe and not too overwhelming?

The Buddhist tradition I come from is rather orthodox. It's the same tradition as Jack Kornfield when he was a monk, where you eat one meal a day and live in a little hut in the middle of the forest. Sometimes, in certain places, there are tigers roaming around. You own zero possessions other than a robe, an alms bowl, and a pair of sandals. You sleep on a hardwood

Jake Kobrin

floor, with no blankets or pillows. You walk around the local town with your begging bowl. If people put food in your bowl, then you have something to eat that day. There was a lot of meditation and a lot of silence. Ninety percent of the talking is about dharma or Buddhist teachings. My teachings aren't exactly Buddhist, per se, and I typically teach in a secular way. I don't even consider myself Buddhist, but I like a lot of these concepts and practices, so I have decided to share them.

The goal of the tradition that I was in is enlightenment. In other traditions, the goals may differ toward helping others get enlightened first, and I don't think there's a right or wrong here. I respect all major religions and spiritual traditions. These teachings are really just to help us to remember what we already know, to access our own wisdom, to remember the power of love, and to help us to unlock barriers of connecting to ourselves and to others and to the world. You can say that in a million different ways. These are a few practices that have been very helpful for me.

I think, in classical terms, we talk about ethics as being a core foundation before we get to the practices of mindfulness and concentration. I think that the power of self-care and the intention to cultivate our awareness, the heart, and the mind is important. Having wise speech, where we're not berating or demeaning others and we're engaged in wholesome conversation that's respectful of all parties, is important. We need to tend to our communication and be careful with what we put in our bodies. Ethics is a foundational area of life that we need to tend to so we can access fuller awareness. If our bodies are polluted, if our mind is polluted, if our speech is polluted, and if our actions are polluted, then it's going to be difficult to gain clarity.

When our mental states are a little polluted, it can be easy to find an excuse not to sit down and just be, because we feel like we have work at and fix things. But those of us who have been meditating regularly know that when we take that time and practice and extend the meditation a little bit longer, we can come out the other side with a whole new perspective.

If our ethics aren't that clean—if we have messes on our hands—this is all the more incentive to practice so that we're more present for our

The Path Within

actions, our words, and for what we're putting in our bodies. We can be curious without judgement: "How am I feeling before I do this thing? How am I feeling as I'm doing this thing? How am I doing after I do this thing?" I'm not saying don't do certain things, but can we bring awareness to our experience before, during, and after so that we can get a sense of, "is this serving me? Is this serving my connection with the universe, with myself, and with life?"

For some reason, I feel compelled to share one practice that isn't really spoken about much. The Buddha called it "the most powerful mindfulness practice," but it's really not talked about much for some reason. It's mindfulness of death. It's not macabre or dark, but mindfulness of death is: "I'm sensing into this breath that I'm inhaling right now and opening to the fact that this could be my last." This can be triggering and can bring up a lot of stuff. This is normal, especially for parents, but it's the truth. This isn't hypothetical: this very inhale *could* be my last. And when we really open to that truth, when we really open to this breath: "this breath entering my nostrils and going down into my lungs, is potentially the last one that sustains me for a few seconds." It can shift our whole paradigm and help us to realize what's important, realize how precious this moment is. Can we open to it more?

People who may already struggle with depression should be careful with this practice and may want to sandwich it with some gratitude practice or self-compassion practice. Some people will go into nihilism, or get stuck on the nothingness of the universe. Let us try fill it up with love, all the while knowing that this very breath could be our last.

Mindfulness of death is often said to be the most powerful mindfulness practice there is and, quite frankly, it was the reason I decided to become a monk. When I realized I could die at any moment, I decided to focus on what I valued most. I quickly gave away my belongings and embraced the idea of becoming a monk. (I was already losing my hair, so that part didn't bother me much.) After a few years at the monastery, though, I had a shift in perspective. Reading Joanna Macy made me realize the urgency of addressing climate change and helping both animals and

Jake Kobrin

humans. I felt a calling to leave the monastery and take these practices into the world, where I could make a more active impact. So, a mindfulness of death can really put things in perspective and can help us to focus on what's most important to us, what we most want to share, and what we most want to cultivate.

CHAPTER SIX

FUNDAMENTAL CONCEPTS

In this chapter, we will explore the bedrock principles that are indispensable for the effective practice of magick. Central to the art of magick are three fundamental elements that serve as the pillars of every powerful and meaningful ritual: the act of banishing, the process of casting a circle, and the art of crafting an altar. These components are not mere steps in a ritual; they are vital practices that imbue magickal work with its potency and profundity. Banishing clears the space of extraneous energies, setting a purified stage for the ritual. Casting a circle creates a sacred and protective boundary, allowing practitioners to work in a focused and consecrated environment. Finally, crafting an altar serves as a focal point of personal power and intention, anchoring the energies of the magickal work. Together, these practices form the cornerstone of effective magick, shaping the ritual experience to ensure its depth and efficacy. This chapter aims to provide a comprehensive understanding of these practices, exploring their significance and offering guidance on their implementation in your magickal endeavors.

BASIC PRACTICES IN MAGICK

Banishing stands as the first and vital step in any magickal undertaking. It involves cleansing the space and setting the stage for a sacred environment. This act is more than a mere formality; it's a profound preparation that guarantees the ritual unfolds in a space marked by respect, purity, and safety. This foundational act ensures that the energies and intentions involved are pure and focused, free from external disturbances.

The act of casting a circle is often executed with tools like a wand, sword, chalk, rope, or even salt, and transcends mere physicality. The circle acts as a spiritual boundary, a delineation between the ordinary world and the mystical realms. It's akin to a protective sphere, enveloping the practitioner in a forcefield that guards against negative influences. This boundary is not just protective but also enhances the potency of the magickal work. The circle often includes specific sigils, symbols, or potent words, each variant tailored to the nature of the magickal work at hand.

The creation of an altar constitutes the third fundamental step. This involves arranging items representing the four Elemental forces—Earth, Air, Fire, and Water—symbolizing the union of the physical and spiritual domains. The altar serves as a focal point where earthly Elements converge with spiritual energies, amplifying the ritual's power. While altars can vary in form, often dedicated to specific spirits or entities, it's important to distinguish between an altar and a shrine; the latter is specifically devoted to a deity, while the former is specifically for ritual work.

When these three elements—banishing, circle casting, and altar crafting—synergize, they set the stage for a magickal ritual replete with depth and potency. Each component amplifies the other, creating a harmonious and powerful environment for the magickal work. It's essential to remember the earlier advice about selecting a dedicated space for your magickal endeavors. This space becomes the sacred ground where the circle and altar are established, further enhancing the sanctity and effectiveness of your magickal practices.

THE FOUR ELEMENTS

There are many symbolic systems used in magick. The most fundamental symbolic system in magick is the Four Elements. There are really five Elements, not four, but the fifth Element, Spirit, is intangible and abstract, and therefore will not be a part of our exploration during this section. The Four Elements comprise the rudimentary ingredients for all things and experiences that come into manifestation in the Universe. They are, in no specific order, Fire, Water, Air, and Earth. These four primary Elements are regarded as realms, kingdoms, or divisions of Nature. They are the basic modes of existence and action—the building blocks of everything in the Universe. All that exists or has the potential to exist contains one or more of these energies.

Continuing our exploration of the Four Elements in magick, it's fascinating to recognize that these Elemental characteristics are not just external forces but are also intrinsic to our very being. Every individual embodies aspects of Fire, Water, Air, and Earth, with each Element manifesting unique personality traits and tendencies. Just as Fire may symbolize passion and drive, Water represents emotional depth and intuition, Air signifies intellect and communication, and Earth embodies stability and practicality. In each person, these Elements blend in varying degrees, creating a unique alchemy that defines one's temperament and approach to life. Similarly, all material entities, from the grandest mountains to the smallest pebbles, encompass these Elements in diverse combinations, contributing

Jake Kobrin

to their physical, emotional, and spiritual makeup. This universal application of the Elemental principles underscores the interconnectedness of all things, emphasizing that understanding and working with these Elements in magick is not just about external manipulation, but also about internal exploration and balance.

The Element of Fire

In our examination of the Elemental forces in magick, the Element of Fire stands out for its dynamic and transformative qualities. Central to understanding Fire is its association with Will and the energy of action within an individual. This Element embodies the force that initiates and drives actions, as well as the spiritual energies that catalyze personal transformation.

Fire represents more than just physical flames; it symbolizes the inner flame that propels us forward, ignites our passions, and fuels our determination. It's the spark of creativity and the warmth of enthusiasm. In terms of daily cycles, Fire is aligned with noon, the time of day when the sun is at its highest, mirroring the peak of energy and intensity that this Element represents.

Astrologically, Fire is linked to three zodiac signs: Aries, Sagittarius, and Leo. Each of these signs encompasses unique aspects of the Fire Element—Aries with its pioneering spirit, Sagittarius with its quest for knowledge and adventure, and Leo with its warmth and leadership. These astrological associations provide deeper insights into the varied expressions of the Fire Element in personalities and behaviors. As we delve further into magickal studies, we will explore these astrological archetypes in more detail, uncovering the intricate ways in which they interact with the Elemental energy of Fire.

The Path Within

The Element of Water

The Element of Water in magick and esoteric practices embodies character-istics that are intrinsically passive, feminine, and receptive. [53] It symbolizes the sustaining and creative forces that are deeply connected to the subcon-scious. Often associated with emotions, Water extends to encompass the broader psyche. On a physical level, water is a familiar liquid compound composed of hydrogen and oxygen. Esoterically, however, it represents all liquid materials, embodying fluidity and the potential for transformation.

This Element evokes the image of primeval Waters, a metaphorical representation of primal matter in its most undifferentiated state. Just like molten metal before solidifying into steel, or water before freezing into ice, the essence of Water in esoteric thought is that of potentiality: unformed, undefined, and infinitely malleable.

Psychologically, Water is interpreted as a symbol of the unconscious mind. It reflects the archetypal feminine aspect of the personality, often linked to the maternal archetype: the Great Mother. This symbolizes not only nurturing and sustenance but also the deep, mysterious well of wisdom that resides in the subconscious. Water, therefore, is seen as a vast expanse of possibilities, the limitless, immortal Waters of Creation from which all forms emerge.

Submersion in Water, within this symbolic framework, signifies a return to this primal, formless state. It suggests a transformative process, akin to the transformative nature of Fire. In astrology, the signs Cancer, Scorpio, and Pisces are attributed to the Element of Water, each sign contributing its own nuances to their Elemental qualities: Cancer with its nurturing instincts, Scorpio with its depth and intensity, and Pisces with its boundless imagination and sensitivity.

---

53   Note on terminology: In this book, the terms "masculine" and "feminine" are used to describe abstract and spiritual qualities as they have been traditionally understood in various spiritual traditions over thousands of years. These terms do not refer to or reflect physical sex, gender identity, or societal roles. They represent universal energies or arche-typal forces that exist beyond concepts of gender, and their usage here is intended in this broader, symbolic sense.

Jake Kobrin

The Element of Air

The Element of Air in magickal and esoteric traditions symbolizes the essence of life and creativity, closely linked with the breath of life and the power of speech. It embodies characteristics that are active, masculine,and intellectual, yet also ethereal, abstract, and communicative. Air represents lightness, flight, and the subtle qualities of scent and smell.

In a tangible sense, Air is the mixture of gases that envelop the Earth, forming its atmosphere. Symbolically, it stands for the invisible yet vital force that drives creation and life processes, a theme echoed across various mythologies. Air is often associated with the intellect, particularly the ability for discerning and analytical thought, playing a vital role in the processes of communication and understanding.

In astrology, the signs Gemini, Libra, and Aquarius are intimately connected to the Element of Air, each contributing distinct qualities that embody this Element's essence. Gemini, represented by the twins, brings a duality that manifests in versatile communication and a curiosity-driven intellect, often leading to a multifaceted understanding of the world. Libra, symbolized by the scales, contributes balance and harmony to Air, emphasizing diplomacy, fairness, and a keen sense for relationships and aesthetics. Aquarius, depicted as the water-bearer, infuses Air with a sense of innovation and unconventionality, often leading to revolutionary ideas and a strong sense of individualism and humanitarianism. Together, these signs exemplify the Air Element's attributes of intellect, communication, and progressive thinking.

The Element of Earth

The Element of Earth in esoteric traditions is characterized by its passive, feminine nature, symbolizing solidity, materialization, and stability. It represents the physical, material universe—the tangible world that surrounds us, encompassing everything we can touch and feel. This Element is closely associated with the physical body, the concept of shelter, and financial aspects of life. In the Tarot, Earth is symbolized by the suit of Coins or Pentacles, highlighting its connection to material wealth and physical substance; Fire is symbolized by the suit of Wands, representing passion, creativity, and the driving force of action and willpower; Water is symbolized by the suit of Cups, emphasizing emotional depth, intuition, and the flow of relationships and inner feelings; and Air is symbolized by the suit of Swords, reflecting the qualities of intellect, communication, and the clarity of thought and reason.

Earth is deeply tied to qualities of productivity, fertility, growth, and regeneration. It embodies the dense, three-dimensional aspects of existence, grounding us in the world of appearances and form. Assigned to the cardinal direction North, Earth's influence is evident in the practical, grounded aspects of life.

Astrologically, Earth is linked to the signs Taurus, Virgo, and Capricorn. Taurus brings a focus on sensuality and stability, Virgo emphasizes meticulousness and practicality, and Capricorn is associated with structure and ambition. Together, these signs exemplify Earth's attributes of steadiness, pragmatism, and tangible achievements.

EXERCISE: EXPERIENCING THE FOUR ELEMENTS

This exercise is designed to deepen your connection with the four classical Elements and to experientially understand their unique qualities. By engaging with each Element, you can gain insights into their influence on your personality, environment, and spiritual practice.

Needs:
- A candle (Fire)
- A bowl of water (Water)
- A feather or incense (Air)
- A stone or a plant (Earth)

Jake Kobrin

Setup:
- Find a quiet and comfortable space where you won't be disturbed.
- Place the materials representing each Element in front of you.

Instructions:
- **Connecting with Earth:** Begin by holding the stone or touching the plant. Close your eyes and feel the weight, texture, and stability of Earth. Reflect on the qualities of Earth—stability, pragmatism, and materiality. Contemplate how these qualities manifest in your life and the world around you.
- **Engaging with Air:** Hold the feather or light the incense. Feel the lightness and observe the movement of air around you. Consider Air's qualities of intellect, communication, and abstract thought. Reflect on how these aspects are present in your interactions and thoughts.
- **Experiencing Fire:** Light the candle and watch the flame. Feel the warmth and observe its dynamic, transformative nature. Meditate on Fire's qualities of energy, passion, and drive. Think about how these qualities burn within you and fuel your actions.
- **Embracing Water:** Touch the water in the bowl. Feel its fluidity and adaptability. Ponder Water's qualities of emotion, intuition, and depth. Reflect on how these aspects flow through your emotions and subconscious.
- **Integration:** After connecting with each Element, sit quietly for a few minutes. Contemplate how all these Elements are interwoven within you and the natural world. Recognize the balance they bring to your life and spiritual practice.
-

Conclusion:
- Conclude the exercise with a few deep breaths, acknowledging the unity of these Elemental forces within you and around you. Journal your experiences and insights to track your evolving understanding and connection with each Element.

The Path Within

THE PENTAGRAM AND THE HEXAGRAM

The Pentagram is a powerful symbol that has been found throughout many cultures and religions and is often misunderstood as an evil representation of Satanism. However, it is a reminder of the ultimate unity of all things, and of the interconnectedness of all aspects of life. Each point of the star is thought to represent a different Element: Fire, Water, Air, Earth, and Spirit. Together, these Elements make up the cycle of life and remind us of the essential interconnectedness of all things. The Pentagram is a potent symbol of balance and harmony, representing the essential unity of life. It is a reminder that all life is part of a greater whole, and that all things are connected.

Furthermore, the pentagram, associated with the number five as a five-pointed star, is a representation of the microcosm, or any distinct and separable thing in the universe. It represents the human being as a microcosm, with the five points of the star being attributed to the head, the two arms, and two legs.

The hexagram, associated with the number six, is a six-pointed star found within Judaism and many other religious and spiritual traditions. It is a powerful and important symbol within magick, representing the unity of contrary things ("as above, so below"), including the marriage of polar energies and of soul and matter. The hexagram represents the macrocosm, or the totality of existence, whereas the pentagram represents the microcosm.

When one performs the Lesser Banishing Ritual of the Pentagram, which we will soon go over, it is a symbolic ritual that represents the unification of the microcosm with that of the macrocosm. The ritual is a reminder that we are all part of a greater whole and that we are inseparable from the whole. It is a reminder that we are all part of a larger, interconnected universe, and that we are all connected in some way.

Jake Kobrin

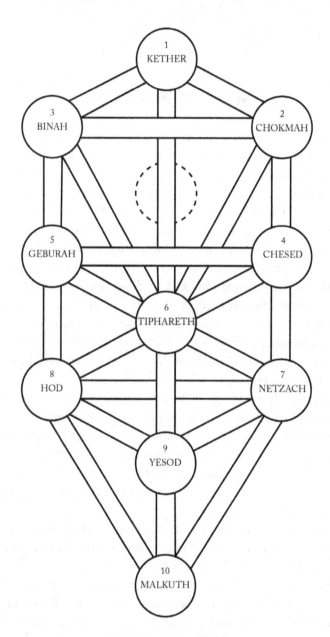

TREE OF LIFE

The Path Within

THE QABALISTIC TREE OF LIFE

The Qabalistic, or sometimes spelled Kabbalistic, Tree of Life is a symbol of profound significance in many systems of ceremonial magick. It is a reminder of our ultimate quest through life, our descent through existence, and our ultimate connection to something much greater than ourselves. The Tree of Life, as represented by the Hebrew Kabbalah's ten sephirot, offers us a way to understand the lessons of the path of descent into manifestation. Typically, Qabalah, sometimes abbreviated as QBL, relates to the non-denominational magickal Tree of Life, whereas the spelling Kabbalah often designates traditional Hebrew/Jewish spiritual practices.

Kether: The Crown
Kether, the first and highest sphere on the Tree of Life, represents the ultimate unity of all existence. It's a dimension where the concept of individuality and separation dissolves into the realization that everything is part of a singular, undivided entity. This understanding transcends the physical appearances and distinctions that are prevalent in the material world.

Kether symbolizes the beginning of all things, harkening back to the moment of the Big Bang, where the universe in its entirety was a unified singularity. From this point of singularity, the universe has expanded, evolved, and diversified. Despite these changes and the illusion of separation, Kether teaches that everything remains intrinsically connected, part of the same cosmic fabric.

Engaging with the essence of Kether brings about a profound spiritual experience. It offers a sense of peace, comfort, and enlightenment, as one recognizes and surrenders to this all-encompassing divine unity. This sphere is closely associated with the Monad, a term signifying the totality of existence or the universe in its most fundamental state.

Jake Kobrin

In Kether, we embark on understanding the interconnectedness of all life and existence, setting the foundational tone for the exploration of the subsequent Sephiroth on the Tree of Life. This sphere invites us to embrace the cosmic unity that underpins our existence, guiding us toward a deeper comprehension of the spiritual and material universe.

Hokmah: Wisdom

Following Kether on the Tree of Life is the sphere of Hokmah, representing the initial differentiation within the unified cosmos. As the second sephirah, Hokmah symbolizes the "other"—it is where the singular cosmic unity of Kether divides, giving rise to duality and relational existence. This division is not one of separation but of extension, where the oneness begins to interact with itself in various forms.

Hokmah embodies the concept of wisdom through connection. It is akin to seeing the face of a beloved or encountering the "other" in its many manifestations. This sphere explores the dynamics of relationships—the interconnectedness with different aspects of the cosmos, including parts of ourselves, our loved ones, and even the divine. In Hokmah, the universe is no longer solitary; it becomes a shared experience with the multitude of existence's facets.

This sephirah is an archetypal realm where profound lessons of love are learned, alongside the inevitable experiences of loss and grief. Such emotional depths contribute to the wisdom of Hokmah, as they are integral to understanding the nature of relationships and interconnectivity.

Astrologically, Hokmah is associated with the zodiac, reflecting the diversity and range of experiences and personalities found within the cosmos. Just as the zodiac encompasses a spectrum of archetypes and energies, Hokmah represents the vast potential and variety that emerge from the original unity. It invites exploration of how these diverse elements interact and contribute to the grand unfolding of the universe.

Binah: Understanding

Ascending from Hokmah in the Tree of Life, we encounter Binah, the third sephirah, a sphere where the potential for manifestation unfolds. Binah

The Path Within

represents the continuation of the cosmic division initiated in Hokmah, but here, it evolves into the formation of distinct, individual forms. It is the domain where the initial spark of creation multiplies, giving rise to the diverse and manifold expressions of existence.

In Binah, the abstract oneness of Kether and the duality of Hokmah translate into tangible reality. This sephirah is akin to a cosmic womb, where the raw materials of the universe—like stardust and cosmic energy—coalesce to form galaxies, stars, and planets. Binah symbolizes the process of creation in its most primal form: the emergence of life and matter from the void.

This sphere is where the principle of "three" becomes significant—every union of two elements brings forth a third entity. This can be seen in the birth of a child from two parents, the creation of a community from individual relationships, or the synthesis of new ideas from merging concepts. Binah, therefore, embodies the idea of creation not as a singular event but as an ongoing, dynamic process.

Astrologically, Binah is associated with Saturn, reflecting the structure, form, and discipline necessary for manifestation. Saturn's influence in this sphere emphasizes the boundaries and frameworks that shape and define the physical universe.

Da'ath: Knowledge

Da'ath occupies an enigmatic position. Located between the third sephirah, Binah, and the fourth, it resides within the Abyss—a vast, metaphysical chasm that separates the supernal, more abstract sephirot from the more manifest, concrete ones.

Da'ath is often referred to as the "invisible" or "unrealized" sephirah, a concept rather than a definitive sphere like the others on the Tree. It represents the threshold of the unknown and unknowable aspects of existence. In the ascent and descent through the Tree of Life, Da'ath is the point where the divine sparks of creation plunge from the higher, more ethereal planes into the denser, material planes.

This non-sephirah embodies the mysteries that lie beyond human comprehension—the vastness of black holes, the possibilities of alternate universes, and the enigmas of dark matter and dark energy. Da'ath serves as

Jake Kobrin

a reminder of the limits of human understanding and the vast, unexplored territories of the cosmos and consciousness. Its presence on the Tree of Life encourages seekers to embrace both knowledge and mystery, recognizing that some aspects of existence remain hidden, inviting continual exploration and wonder.

Chesed: Mercy

As we cross the enigmatic Abyss on the Tree of Life, we arrive at Chesed, the fourth sephirah. This sphere represents the initial emergence from the ethereal planes into a state of expansion and manifestation. Chesed is often visualized as an abundant, overflowing fountain of creation, where the universe's raw potential begins to take form.

In Chesed, the abstract concepts and divine energies start their journey toward materialization. This sephirah is likened to a vast, cosmic river or an ocean, symbolizing the unending flow of atoms, energy, and possibilities. It embodies the concept of mercy in its most expansive form–a benevolent, nurturing force that supports and sustains all of creation.

This sphere is where we encounter the essence of love in its most universal aspect. Chesed teaches us about the nature of giving and receiving, urging us to embrace the ebb and flow of love and life. It's a domain where we learn to trust in life's inherent goodness, to surrender to the currents of existence, and to embrace the risks and rewards that come with being part of the vast universe.

Astrologically, Chesed is associated with Jupiter, reflecting the planet's qualities of growth, expansion, and abundance. Jupiter's influence in Chesed highlights the joyous and generous aspects of this sephirah, emphasizing the themes of prosperity, optimism, and the boundless nature of love and light. In the adventure through the Tree of Life, Chesed marks a transition from the formless to the form, from potential to actuality, encouraging us to open our hearts to the infinite possibilities that life offers.

The Path Within

Geburah: Strength

Geburah, the fifth sephirah on the Tree of Life, stands as a counterbalance to the expansive nature of Chesed. While Chesed represents the boundless flow and abundance of creation, Geburah introduces the concept of limitation, discipline, and strength. This sphere embodies the necessary constraints and structures that give shape and form to existence.

In Geburah, we encounter the challenging but essential aspects of life—its limitations, endings, and the need for discernment. This sephirah teaches us that the infinite love and potential represented in Chesed must be tempered with understanding and acceptance of life's inherent boundaries. Geburah is about recognizing the value of restraint, the importance of making choices, and the significance of endings as part of the natural cycle of life.

Here, we learn the vital lessons of existence: that to live is to navigate a world of choices and consequences, to understand the balance between giving and withholding, and to acknowledge the finiteness of our physical form. Geburah reminds us that even in a universe composed of endless love and possibilities, practical realities such as self-care, sustenance, and rest are essential.

Astrologically associated with Mars, Geburah reflects the planet's qualities of courage, determination, and conflict. Mars' influence in this sphere highlights the themes of struggle, resilience, and the necessary confrontations that lead to growth and development. In the exploration of the Tree of Life, Geburah serves as a grounding force, teaching us the power of choice, the reality of limits, and the strength found in facing life's challenges head-on.

Tiphareth: Beauty

Nestled at the core of the Tree of Life is Tiphareth, the sixth sephirah, embodying the essence of harmony and beauty. Tiphareth is the symbolic heart of the Tree, where the dynamic flow of creation and the structures of form find equilibrium. This sephirah represents the perfect balance between the expansiveness of Chesed and the discipline of Geburah.

Jake Kobrin

In Tiphareth, we engage in the delicate act of balancing the boundless potential of the universe with the tangible realities of our existence. It is a sphere where the abstract and the concrete converge, teaching us to embrace and express our unique individuality within the broader context of the cosmos. Tiphareth encourages us to offer our best to the world while accepting the limits of what can be given and received.

This sephirah also explores the deeper emotional aspects of the heart. It is the archetypal plane of profound love and the vulnerability that comes with it. In Tiphareth, we experience the joys and sorrows of love, the opening and breaking of the heart, and the resilience that follows. It teaches us that to love is to be truly alive, to embrace the risks and rewards of emotional connection, and to continually find strength in our capacity to love and be loved.

Astrologically associated with Sol (the Sun), Tiphareth resonates with the qualities of radiance, warmth, and illumination. The Sun's influence in this sphere underscores the themes of vitality, clarity, and the life-giving energy that sustains all existence. In the expedition through the Tree of Life, Tiphareth serves as a guiding light, helping us to find balance in our lives and reminding us of the beauty and strength inherent in our open hearts.

Netzach: Victory

Ascending further along the Tree of Life, we arrive at Netzach, the seventh sephirah, often likened to the mythical Garden of Eden. Netzach represents a realm of primal, unspoiled beauty and eternal victory, symbolizing the vibrant, flourishing aspects of existence. It is a sphere where the natural world is not just observed but deeply experienced and appreciated.

In Netzach, we connect with the pure, unfettered essence of life and creation. This sephirah invites us to immerse ourselves in the wonders of the natural world, to recognize our integral role within it as caretakers and participants. It's a place of emotional and spiritual abundance, where we can indulge in the joys of existence, savoring the beauty and richness of life.

This sphere also encompasses the concept of innocence and the pure, unadulterated joy of being. In Netzach, we engage with life in its most genuine form, unburdened by complexities and free to explore the depths

The Path Within

of our emotions and connections. Here, we encounter the "Other" in its most natural state, embracing the transformative experiences that such encounters bring, and unveiling the deeper mysteries of existence.

Astrologically aligned with Venus, Netzach resonates with the qualities of love, harmony, and pleasure. Venus' influence in this sphere accentuates the themes of attraction, aesthetic appreciation, and the celebration of sensory and emotional experiences. Netzach, in the exploration through the Tree of Life, serves as a reminder of the beauty and vitality inherent in the world around us and within ourselves, urging us to partake in and contribute to the ongoing creation and appreciation of life's wonders.

Hod: Glory

Descending deeper into the Tree of Life, we encounter Hod, the eighth sephirah, embodying the essence of understanding and intellect. In Hod, the experiential knowledge gained in the preceding spheres is transformed into intellectual understanding and analysis. This sphere encourages a deeper exploration of knowledge, where experience alone is no longer sufficient; instead, there is a profound desire to comprehend, analyze, and internalize the lessons of existence.

In the sphere of Hod, we engage in the intellectual processes of categorization, comparison, and critical thinking. It is a space where the mind's capacity to discern, question, and understand is celebrated and honed. Hod represents the pursuit of wisdom through structured thought and logical reasoning, inviting us to delve into the complexities of knowledge and the intricacies of the mind.

However, Hod also teaches us about the limitations of intellectual understanding. As we analyze and categorize, we often come to realize how vast and unknowable the universe truly is. This realization instills in us a sense of humility and awe, reminding us that the pursuit of knowledge is an endless quest marked by both discovery and mystery.

Astrologically, Hod corresponds to Mercury, the planet associated with communication, intellect, and analytical thought. Mercury's influence in this sphere highlights the importance of clear thinking, effective communication, and the quest for understanding. In the exploration through the

Jake Kobrin

Tree of Life, Hod serves as a reminder of the glory and power of the mind, as well as the need to balance our intellectual pursuits with an appreciation for the unfathomable and wondrous aspects of existence.

Yesod: Foundation

Progressing further into the mystical depths of the Tree of Life, we arrive at Yesod, the ninth sephirah. Yesod serves as a crucial nexus point, a dimension where the collective unconscious and the world of mythos converge. This sphere is the foundation upon which the higher, more abstract aspects of the Tree find expression in symbols, dreams, and archetypes that resonate deeply across cultures and time.

In Yesod, the ephemeral and intangible aspects of our psyche—our dreams, symbols, and collective myths are given form. This sephirah acts as a mirror, reflecting the inner workings of our subconscious minds and the shared narratives that define human experience. Yesod is where the unconscious undercurrents of our thoughts and feelings come to the surface, revealing the universal themes and stories that underpin our existence.

This sphere is also a gateway to altered states of consciousness. Through practices such as meditation, ritual, and trance, we can tap into the rich dimension of Yesod, exploring the symbolic and archetypal energies that flow through this realm. It is a place of deep introspection and spiritual exploration, where the boundaries between the individual and the collective blur, offering insights into the shared human experience.

Astrologically, Yesod corresponds to Luna (the Moon), reflecting the Moon's connection to intuition, emotion, and the subconscious. The Moon's influence in this sphere highlights the ebb and flow of psychic energies, the cycles of introspection and revelation, and the powerful pull of our innermost desires and fears.

In the expedition through the Tree of Life, Yesod serves as a reminder of the importance of our inner worlds and the subconscious drivers of our actions and beliefs. It invites us to delve into the depths of our psyche, uncover the hidden forces that shape our lives, and connect with the universal narratives that bind us all.

The Path Within

Malkuth: Kingdom

At the base of the Tree of Life rests Malkuth, the tenth sephirah, embodying the culmination of the quest down the Tree. Malkuth represents the final grounding point, the domain where the celestial transforms into the terrestrial, where the ethereal energies of creation manifest into tangible, physical forms. It is the sphere of earthly existence, the material world in all its diverse and magnificent expressions.

In Malkuth, the cosmic journey from the primordial moment of the Big Bang reaches its destination. The atoms and divine energies that have traversed the Tree of Life culminate here, crystallizing into the physical universe. These sparks of divine light have taken form as the mountains, rivers, trees, and all living creatures—from the tiniest insects to the vastest oceans and including humanity itself. Malkuth is where the unmanifest becomes manifest, where the intangible essence of creation materializes into the concrete reality we perceive and interact with daily.

This sephirah symbolizes the interconnectedness of all physical forms. It shows us that everything from the celestial bodies to the minute cellular structures shares a common origin. Here, we humans find our place in the grand cosmic narrative—emerging from the gods, stars, and the very womb of creation. Malkuth invites us to recognize and honor our quest through existence, to embrace life with grace and joy, and to acknowledge our role as both creations of and participants in this universal dance.

Astrologically, Malkuth corresponds to the Earth, reinforcing its association with the physical, tangible aspects of our world. In the context of the Tree of Life, Malkuth is not merely an endpoint but a vital connector that loops back to the highest dimensions, symbolizing the cyclical nature of existence and the continuous interplay between the spiritual and the material.

In Malkuth, we are reminded of our physicality and our spiritual origins, encouraging us to live with an awareness of our place within the broader whole of existence. It beckons us to engage with life in all its facets, to find beauty and meaning in the everyday, and to see ourselves as an integral part of the cosmic whole.

Connecting the Spheres: The Pillars and Triads

In addition to the ten spheres (and eleventh invisible sphere) of the Tree of Life, there are twenty-two paths that connect the spheres. These are representative of transitional energies between any two connected spheres and are symbolized by the twenty-two Major Arcana cards of the Tarot, which offer further exploration into the mysteries of the Tree of Life.

THE THREE PILLARS: BALANCING DUALITIES

The Qabalistic Tree of Life is structured around three fundamental pillars, each symbolizing different but interconnected cosmic principles and forces. These pillars are essential in understanding the Tree's representation of the universe and our travels within it.

Pillar of Severity (Left Pillar)
Comprising the spheres of Binah, Geburah, and Hod, the Pillar of Severity embodies the passive, structuring elements of nature. It is the foundation of form, order, and discipline, imposing necessary boundaries and constraints. This pillar represents the universe's formative aspects, providing structure and definition to the boundless energy of creation. It symbolizes the necessary restraint that shapes chaos into order, reflecting the principle that creation requires limits to become manifest.

Pillar of Mercy (Right Pillar)
In contrast, the Pillar of Mercy, which includes Chokmah, Chesed, and Netzach, stands for the active, expansive forces of the cosmos. This pillar is the embodiment of growth, generosity, and dynamic action. It represents the

The Path Within

universe's benevolent and nurturing qualities, fostering expansion, evolution, and the boundless potential of life. The energies of this pillar fuel the creative process, driving the forward momentum of existence and evolution.

Middle Pillar

The Middle Pillar, also known as the Pillar of Equilibrium, Consciousness, and Initiation, balances between the Pillars of Mercy and Severity. It includes Kether, Tiphareth, Yesod, Malkuth, and the unseen Da'ath. This central pillar represents the Tao, the unifying and harmonious force that integrates the universe's dualistic aspects. It symbolizes the balance between expansion and contraction, action and restraint. The Middle Pillar is key to understanding the Tree's profound mysteries, as it embodies the harmonious interplay of all existence and the balance necessary for spiritual and psychological growth.

The Middle Pillar is a representation of the mystical Tao, the overarching principle that pervades and unifies the entire universe. It includes the Sephiroth that represent the highest ideals (Kether), the balanced human consciousness (Tiphareth), the foundation of collective unconsciousness (Yesod), and the physical world (Malkuth), along with the bridge of knowledge and the unseen (Da'ath). This pillar symbolizes the transmutation down the Tree from the divine to the earthly, embodying the interconnectedness of all things and the path of harmonious existence.

In Qabalistic studies, these pillars offer a framework for understanding the balance and interaction between various spiritual and psychological forces. The Pillar of Severity and the Pillar of Mercy represent the extremes of nature's dualities, akin to the concepts found in Jungian psychology, Taoist philosophy, and other metaphysical systems. The Middle Pillar unites these dualities, symbolizing the path of harmony and the integration of opposites. This understanding is crucial for navigating the Tree of Life, as it illuminates the interconnectedness and balance essential for spiritual growth and enlightenment.

THE TRIADS: LAYERS OF INFLUENCE

The Qabalistic Tree of Life is also composed of three triads, each composed of three spheres. At its zenith, the Celestial Triad—Kether, Chokmah, and Binah—radiates the creative genesis of the cosmos. Descending into the dimensions of balance and morality, the Ethical Triad—Chessed, Geburah, and Tiphereth—melds divine inspiration with life's pragmatic forces. Further down, the Magickal Triad—Hod, Netzach, and Yesod—immerses in the profound depths of emotion and instinct. Anchoring this celestial structure is Malkuth, our tangible, physical world, influenced by all yet part of none. This intricate arrangement, a harmonious interplay of opposites, encapsulates the dynamic unity of existence, inviting us to perceive the duality of the universe not as conflicting forces but as complementary halves of a greater whole.

Supernal Triad (Upper Triangle)
At the apex of the Tree lies the Supernal Triad, consisting of Kether, Chokmah, and Binah. This triad, forming an upward-pointing triangle, embodies the highest creative forces of the universe. It represents the purest form of divine energy and the initial stages of manifestation.

- **Kether (The Crown):** The topmost sphere, symbolizing the unity and source of all creation.
- **Chokmah (Wisdom):** The second sphere, representing the dynamic force of creation and the beginning of differentiation.
- **Binah (Understanding):** The third sphere, embodying the receptive and formative aspects that give structure to the universe's creative energies.

The Path Within

Ethical Triad (Middle Triangle)

The middle triangle, pointing downward, comprises Chessed, Geburah, and Tiphereth. This triad symbolizes the moral and ethical dimensions of the universe and the equilibrium of forces that govern life's evolution.

- **Chessed (Mercy):** The fourth sphere, symbolizing benevolence, growth, and expansion.
- **Geburah (Strength):** The fifth sphere, representing discipline, limitation, and the necessary boundaries of existence.
- **Tiphereth (Beauty):** The sixth sphere, positioned at the heart of the Tree, embodies harmony and balance, integrating the energies of Chessed and Geburah.

Magickal Triangle (Lower Triangle)

The lower triangle, made up of Hod, Netzach, and Yesod, deals with the tangible, experiential aspects of existence, such as emotions, instincts, and the subconscious.

- **Netzach (Victory):** The seventh sphere, associated with the enduring aspects of nature and the emotional forces that underpin existence.
- **Hod (Glory):** The eighth sphere, representing the intellect and the analytical understanding of the world.
- **Yesod (Foundation):** The ninth sphere, symbolizing the collective unconscious and the shared archetypes and dreams of humanity.

Malkuth, the tenth and final sphere, stands alone, representing the physical universe and material reality. Though not part of any triad, Malkuth is influenced by all and symbolizes the culmination of the divine energies as they manifest in the material world.

In the study of the Qabalistic Tree of Life, understanding these triads is crucial. They represent different stages and aspects of the cosmic process, from the inception of divine will in the Supernal Triad to the materialization of these energies in Malkuth. To fully grasp the Tree's wisdom, one must recognize the importance of balancing and integrating these various aspects, seeing them not as separate entities but as interconnected parts of a whole. This holistic view encourages a deeper understanding of the universe and our place within it, guiding us towards spiritual and personal harmony.

THE FOUR QABALISTIC WORLDS

In the mystical tradition of Qabalah, the concept of the Four Worlds offers a profound framework for understanding the process of creation and manifestation. This intricate system is closely aligned with the Tetragrammaton, YHVH—the sacred, ineffable name of God in the Hebrew Bible. Each letter in YHVH corresponds to one of the Four Worlds, representing different stages or "magical notes" of existence, from the highest spiritual planes to the physical world. The adventure begins in Atziluth, the divine world of pure archetypal existence and God's thoughts, akin to the initial spark of inspiration. It then descends into Briah, the creative world where ideas take shape. The process continues through Yetzirah, the formative world of the Astral Plane where these ideas gain structure, and finally culminates in Assiah, the tangible world of physical manifestation. This layered structure of the universe, though complex, unfolds naturally, allowing us to experientially grasp the beauty and intricacy of the cosmic descent from divine thought to material form.

Atziluth, The World of Emanation (Yod, י):
Atziluth is the highest and most sublime of the four worlds. Associated with the first letter of the Tetragrammaton, Yod (י), this dimension is purely spiritual, representing the divine will and the archetypal essence

The Path Within

of existence. It is the world closest to the divine source, characterized by unmanifest potential and pure godly thought. Here, the divine plan begins, untouched and unaltered by material influence.

Briah, The World of Creation (Heh, ה):

The second world, Briah, corresponds to the first Heh (ה) in the Tetragrammaton. This is the domain where the divine blueprint begins to take conceptual form. It is the world of creation in the broader sense, where abstract ideas and divine intellect manifest. Briah is less about physical creation and more about the development and maturation of the divine thought originated in Atziluth.

Yetzirah, The World of Formation (Vav, ו):

Yetzirah, aligned with the letter Vav (ו), is the third world. Here, the initial ideas and concepts from Briah start to gain shape and definition. Often referred to as the Astral Plane, Yetzirah is where planning and design take place, leading to the formation of structures and systems that will eventually materialize in the physical world. It's a world rich in symbols and archetypes, forming the blueprint for physical existence.

Assiah, The World of Action (Final Heh, ה):

The final world, Assiah, corresponds to the final Heh (ה) in the Tetragrammaton. This is the world of physicality and action, where the plans and forms from Yetzirah become tangible reality. Assiah represents the material universe in all its diversity and complexity. It is the culmination of the creative process, where spiritual energies are fully expressed in physical form.

These four worlds provide a framework for understanding the process of creation from the initial spark of divine inspiration to the concrete manifestation in the physical world. Each world plays a crucial role in the cosmic scheme, reflecting a different aspect of divine emanation and providing a unique perspective on the descent from the spiritual to the material.

Jake Kobrin

SUMMARY AND OVERVIEW OF THE QABALISTIC TREE OF LIFE

The Qabalistic Tree of Life is a central symbol in ceremonial magick and various esoteric traditions. It represents the ultimate quest of existence and serves as a guide to understanding the cosmos and our place within it. It represents both the descent and the ascent of consciousness into various stages of spiritual and material existence.

Structure of the Tree of Life

- **Kether (Crown):** At the Tree's summit, Kether symbolizes cosmic unity and the interconnectedness of all beings, akin to a monad or the entirety of existence.
- **Chokmah (Wisdom):** This sphere represents the first division within the oneness, embodying duality, love, and the complexities of existence. Corresponds to the entire zodiac, the fixed stars.
- **Binah (Understanding):** Binah is where manifestation begins, signifying the emergence of multiplicity and creation. Corresponds to the classical planet Saturn.
- **Chesed (Mercy):** This sphere is associated with abundance, flow, and the surrender to life's goodness. Corresponds to the classical planet Jupiter.
- **Geburah (Severity):** Geburah contrasts Chesed, teaching about life's limitations, resilience, and the necessity of making choices. Corresponds to the classical planet Mars.
- **Tiphareth (Beauty):** At the heart of the Tree, Tiphareth balances mercy and severity, symbolizing open-heartedness, acceptance, and love. Corresponds to the classical planet Sol (the Sun).
- **Netzach (Victory):** This sephira embodies the natural world and innocence, emphasizing our connection to and role in nature. Corresponds to the classical planet Venus.

The Path Within

- **Hod (Splendor):** Hod is the realm of intellect, where understanding and the pursuit of knowledge are central themes. Corresponds to the classical planet Mercury.
- **Yesod (Foundation):** Representing the collective unconscious, Yesod connects us with shared myths and human experiences. Corresponds to the classical planet Luna (the Moon).
- **Malkuth (Kingdom):** The final sephira, Malkuth, grounds the Tree in the physical world, signifying the culmination of the spiritual descent into the material world. Corresponds to the manifest world, the Earth.
- **Da'ath (Knowledge):** An invisible non-sephira, Da'ath represents the unknowable aspects of existence, like the concept of dark matter and alternate universes. It lies between spheres four (Chesed) and three (Binah), and has no classical planetary attributions.

The Pillars and Paths

The Tree comprises three pillars: the Middle Pillar of Equilibrium, the Pillar of Severity, and the Pillar of Mercy, each representing different aspects of nature and consciousness.

Twenty-two paths connect the sephirot, symbolized by the Tarot's Major Arcana, representing transitional energies and life lessons.

The Qabalistic Worlds

The Tree of Life also encompasses the concept of Four Worlds: Atziluth (archetypal realm), Briah (creation), Yetzirah (formation), and Assiah (physical manifestation). Each world corresponds to a different aspect of the creative process and the Elements.

Each world corresponds to a letter in the Tetragrammaton, YHVH (יהוה), the sacred name of God in the Hebrew tradition: Atziluth, The World of Emanation (Yod, י); Briah, The World of Creation (Heh, ה); Yetzirah, The World of Formation (Vav, ו); and Assiah, The World of Action (Final Heh, ה).

Jake Kobrin

Significance and Application
The Tree of Life is more than a symbol; it's a framework for understanding the spiritual path and the universe's structure. It guides individuals in exploring their spiritual path, offering insights into the balance of dualities, the process of creation, and the interconnectedness of all existence.

In summary, the Qabbalistic Tree of Life serves as a profound and multifaceted map of the cosmos, offering a unique lens through which to explore spiritual growth, universal connections, and the nature of existence.

LIBER 777

When I first began to explore the world of magick and Aleister Crowley, I came across *Liber 777*.[54] It was always on the shelf in the Occult section at bookstores—even the mainstream ones like Barnes and Noble—so I assumed it was his most famous and important work. But when I tried to read it, I was completely lost! What were these tables, Hebrew letters, and words I had never seen before?

What I quickly came to realize is that *Liber 777* is a reference book, not a book to be read cover to cover. It is meant to be consulted when preparing to do a ritual. It contains tables of correspondences, which are used to design rituals by identifying practical correspondences.

For example, say you want to do a ritual for love. You would look up Venus and find that it corresponds to the number seven in the first column. Anything that is listed next to the number seven corresponds to the goddess Venus. This can give you a lot of information to use in your ritual, from

---

54   Crowley, Aleister, *Liber 777* (Samuel Weiser, 1977).

The Path Within

other Goddesses that correspond (Hathoor or Aphrodite), to Archangels (Haniel), to the Sephirah on the Tree of Life (Netzach), to practical details like colors, plants, precious stones, scents, Tarot cards, and much more.

So, when designing a practical magick ritual, *Liber 777* is the place to start. Once you know your purpose, you can use the correspondences to design a meaningful and powerful ceremony. We will explore using *Liber 777* to design your own rituals in later chapters.

CHAPTER SEVEN

ESSENTIAL RITUALS

When exploring and mastering the art of magick, certain rituals stand out as essential and fundamental, forming the bedrock of practice for both novice and seasoned practitioners alike. This chapter is dedicated to unravelling these pivotal rites, providing a comprehensive guide to the ceremonies and practices that are fundamental to the magickal path.

Rituals are more than mere routines; they are potent acts of transformation and communion. Each ritual, steeped in symbolism and intention, serves as a bridge between the mundane and the mystical, allowing the practitioner to tap into deeper dimensions of consciousness and universal energies. Through these rituals, one can manifest desires, seek spiritual insights, and forge a deeper connection with the unseen forces that permeate our world.

This chapter delves into a variety of essential rituals, each with its unique purpose and methodology. We begin by exploring the foundational rituals that every practitioner should know. These include the Lesser Banishing Ritual of the Pentagram, a staple in creating sacred space and warding off negative influences, and the Middle Pillar Ritual, which aids in balancing and aligning the spiritual energies within.

UNDERSTANDING CASTING, BANISHING, AND INVOKING

Magickal practice typically involves three primary steps: casting, banishing, and invoking. Each has a unique purpose and plays a crucial role in preparing for your rituals. The following exercise focuses primarily on casting a circle, but let's first understand the differences between these three aspects:

- **Casting:** Casting a circle establishes a protected space for your magickal work. This sacred boundary serves as a shield against negative energy and a concentrator of your magickal intent.
- **Banishing:** Banishing involves expelling negative energies or unwanted influences from your space, allowing for a purified environment. This process often follows the casting of the circle to ensure that the sanctified space is clear and ready for the invocation.
- **Invoking:** The invocation is the process of calling upon desired energies, deities, or spirits into your ritual space. This action allows you to draw on these powers or presences to aid in your magickal workings.

With these definitions in mind, let's proceed with the exercise for casting a circle.

The Path Within

EXERCISE: CASTING A CIRCLE

As we discussed previously, the casting of a circle is a foundational practice in esoteric and magickal traditions. It serves to create a sacred, protected space for spiritual work, enhancing focus, and establishing a barrier against external negative energies. This exercise is particularly beneficial before engaging in deeper magickal practices or rituals.

Needs:
- A quiet, comfortable space
- Willingness to visualize and focus

Setup:
- Choose a quiet area where you won't be disturbed.
- Sit or lie down in a comfortable position.
- Ready yourself for a period of uninterrupted meditation.

Instructions:
- **Preparation:** Begin by calming your mind. Take deep, slow breaths, allowing your body to relax fully.
- **Visualizing Divine Light:** Imagine a vast, infinite space. Envision a brilliant point of light descending upon you, infusing your being with tranquility and peace.
- **Creating the Circle:** Visualize a circle of radiant light emerging from within you. With each breath, see this circle becoming brighter and more robust, creating a luminous shield around you.
- **Empowering the Circle:** Deepen this visualization. Feel the light forming a protective barrier, securing your space from negative influences.

- **Affirming the Circle's Power:** Recognize the strength of this circle. Trust in its ability to protect you and enhance your magickal capabilities.

Follow Through:
- As you conclude the meditation, gently bring your awareness back to your physical surroundings. Open your eyes slowly, maintaining the sense of peace and protection. The circle remains a metaphysical shield even after the meditation.

Optional:
- You may incorporate specific symbols or personal elements into the circle for a more personalized experience.
- This practice can be done at any time to reinforce your sense of spiritual protection, not just before magickal work.

BANISHING

Banishing rituals are a crucial part of magickal practice, serving as forms of spiritual containment. They are designed to remove or keep out unwanted spiritual entities or energies, thus creating a purified and sacred space for the practitioner. It's a way of demarcating the spiritual realm and the physical world and maintaining order during the practice. Banishing is an ancient and powerful form of magick that has been used throughout the ages to create and maintain boundaries, as well as to energetically cleanse a space. When done correctly, it can help to create a powerful forcefield of protective energy around you and your environment. It can also remove any unwanted energies, entities, or spirits that may be lingering in the space. This can be quite useful before or after any magickal ritual, depending on your practice. While some prefer to banish before casting the circle

The Path Within

to ensure the space is clear, others choose to do so afterward as part of closing the ritual and solidifying the work.

Lighting herbs or incense is a common form of banishing, and it can be used to energetically purify a space. Smudging is practiced by most religious and spiritual traditions of the world and originates in ancient indigenous shamanism. White sage or frankincense and sometimes palo santo are burned as a form of banishing and cleansing a space. In magick, many incenses have associations with specific energies and specific uses, but these three incenses are universal for cleansing. This is nuanced, however, as some of these smudges are indigenous to cultures that see them as sacred, and the proliferation of their use and the resulting endangerment of these plants is a controversial subject. I recommend using smudges that do not offend traditional indigenous cultures or result in the endangerment of any plants.

However, there are more powerful forms of banishing rituals that can be used to achieve a deeper level of cleansing. These powerful rituals can be found in many ancient texts and can be used to create strong boundaries, remove any unwanted energies, and cleanse a space in preparation for magickal work.

In chaos magick, laughter is seen as being a powerful form of banishing, and there are many other methods used historically for banishing including the clanging and clattering of swords, the use of holy water, and the use of certain Latin prayers such as those from the Catholic Mass. We will be exploring a fundamental magickal ritual from The Order of the Golden Dawn known as The Lesser Banishing Ritual of the Pentagram, or the LBRP for short.

There are also many banishing rituals that we will not be exploring in this book. For example, the Star Ruby is a banishing ritual that has its origins in Thelemic magick. The Banishing Ritual of the Hexagram is another ritual of a similar nature, but it is used to banish planetary influences rather than Elemental ones. This distinction may be too complicated to cover in this book, and so we will not be learning about it here. Both of these rituals are widely available in many other sources.

The concept can be seen in something as mundane as a ring of peppermint oil deterring ants. Here where I live in Bali, there are many ants that will quickly find and subsume a cup of coffee or any food if you leave it out for more than five minutes. Enclosing the coffee in a

Jake Kobrin

ring of peppermint oil, even if it's dry and imperceptible to our human senses, deters the ants. Despite the boundary being virtually imperceptible to human senses, the ants perceive it and will not cross. Banishing rituals and circles, which are cast with specific symbols either physically or in one's imagination, work the same way. This highlights the essence of banishing rituals and containment in magick—creating an energy barrier that may be invisible to the ordinary eye but is very much present and active in the spiritual world.

Symbols also play a crucial role in the formation of these magickal spaces. Circles and triangles common in the ritual designs aren't just shapes; they carry a deeper, symbolic significance. A circle often represents wholeness, unity, and protection, while a triangle is associated with ideas of harmony, balance, and manifestation.

The use of Hebrew writing in the creation of these magickal diagrams further emphasizes their sacred nature. Hebrew is often associated with the divine language, and its characters are believed to carry potent mystical energies. Writing names or invocations in Hebrew around or within these shapes is a way of harnessing and directing these energies.

A classic example of this kind of containment is the traditional Triangle D'Art in evocation magic. The Triangle D'Art is a bounded space, usually delineated by lines drawn on a surface or in the air, within which a spirit or entity is evoked. It serves as a containment field, allowing the magician to communicate with the entity while keeping it separate from themselves and their environment.

Remember, though, that the power of these rituals and symbols lies not only in the actions and the designs themselves but also in the belief and intent of the practitioner. Magick is as much about the inner landscape of the magician as it is about the outer actions they perform.

THE LESSER BANISHING RITUAL OF THE PENTAGRAM

The Lesser Banishing Ritual of the Pentagram, or LBRP, is an essential part of ritual magick, it is used to clear the area of any unwanted energies and to create a sacred space for the practitioner. The ritual begins by drawing a pentagram in the air, and then calling on the four Archangels to guard the space. The practitioner then vibrates certain divine names such as Yahweh and Adonai, before reciting a prayer of protection. Finally, the practitioner invokes the pentagram, which is a powerful symbol of protection. The power of the LBRP lies in its ability to banish any unwanted energies that may be present in the area, and to create a space of protection and safety for the practitioner. It is a powerful tool that can be used to cleanse and protect the magickal space and is a valuable addition to any magick practice. It is one of the essential rituals in the system of ceremonial and ritual magick as formulated in the Golden Dawn and related organizations and is the first ritual to be learned and performed as part of any of these systems. A version of the pentagram ritual can be found in many magickal systems.

The LBRP is a banishing ritual with two purposes. It helps to center, calm, still, and concentrate the mind, banishing any psychic interference or mental chatter that might interfere with the magickal work. It also serves to clean the external space in which the ritual is performed, much like a chemist or surgeon sterilizing their lab and equipment. On an astral level, the LBRP does the same thing, allowing only those things that are desired to remain within the circle. There is both an Invoking and Banishing form to the Lesser Pentagram Ritual. The LBRP is known as the *Lesser* Banishing Ritual of the Pentagram, as there is also a greater form of the Pentagram Ritual. However, at this time, we will not be exploring this ritual.

On a basic level, "astral level" means that the dimension of the psyche and imagination is not separate from the external world, and that it is

Jake Kobrin

possible to create changes in a collective field of the imagination. In magick, there is an idea that certain places have an astral atmosphere, distinct and yet overlapping the physical environment, and in these astral environments there can be energies or entities that only exist in that realm of perception. These things may not be material in nature, but this does not make them any less real. The comic book series *Promethea*, written by Alan Moore, does an excellent job of conveying this concept and is recommended reading for those who are interested in magick.[55]

The Lesser Banishing Ritual of the Pentagram (LBRP) is a powerful tool for creating a protective forcefield of divine light, similar to the casting of a circle in Witchcraft. This razor-thin, diamond-strong boundary shields the magician from external influences, allowing magickal energy to build up and charge within a contained space. Banishing rituals like the LBRP also serve to purify both the space and the magician, clearing away Elemental and microcosmic energies, as well as any "astral nasties" —harmless yet unsettling entities that reside on the astral plane. According to Donald Michael Kraig's *Modern Magick,* the LBRP also removes "negative" energies, leaving the space clean and neutral for magickal work. For these reasons, it is recommended to perform the LBRP before and after any magickal ritual to ensure a purified and protected environment.

When it comes to the Lesser Pentagram Ritual, the process of invoking is much like the clearing and banishing of Elemental energies, but instead of ridding yourself of them, you are calling upon the pure and clean Elemental energies. This is helpful if you need extra power when doing ritual work. Different forms of Elemental energies (Earth, Air, Fire, Water, and Spirit) can be invoked, but we'll get to that later. For now, just start practicing and learning the ritual.

If done correctly, you should feel a sense of lightness and clarity after banishing. After invoking, you should feel a sense of holiness and energy. This ritual also helps to balance and harmonize the four Elemental energies in your life, on all planes of existence. This is the first step for the aspiring magician and why the ritual is an important part of the magickal path.

---

55   Moore, Alan, and J. H. Williams III, *Promethea* (DC Comics, 1999)

The Path Within

If done on a regular basis, this ritual can help to bring Earth, Air, Fire, and Water into harmony. This means that one should begin to feel a balancing of the different aspects of their life and its circumstances. It may help to bring into balance the financial or material aspects of life, the thinking and intellectual side of life, the will and passion of life as well as one's spirituality and sexuality and drive, and the deep waters of one's psyche, one's feelings, dreams, and emotions.

Considering that this ritual is a banishing ritual and its aim is to clear, one should not be surprised if heavy or unprocessed psychic material rises to the surface to be felt and purged. This is a natural part of the process, and although it can be uncomfortable, it is ultimately temporary and for one's benefit. It is helping to bring one into greater harmony and balance. The ancient saying of "as above, so below" can be useful to remember here, so when one banishes a space and equilibrates the Elements in that space, one is also doing this to themselves.

When it comes to magick, the Lesser Pentagram Ritual or some other form of banishing is an absolute must and a prerequisite for safe and controlled magickal operations. I find that if I invoke it in the morning, I have more energy for the day, and then banishing it at night before I go to bed helps me drift off to sleep easily with a feeling of safety and calm. Even in times when insomnia strikes, performing the LBRP has been the perfect remedy for a peaceful slumber. Now, if you want to perform the invoking form right before bedtime, don't be surprised if you have difficulty sleeping—it's like you just drank a caffeinated beverage. However, be careful not to rely too much on the banishing form only without balancing it out with the invoking rituals, as you might eventually feel drained or depleted. That is why both forms are highly recommended for regular, daily practice. Memorizing it should not take too long either. Once memorized, the ritual should take just three or four minutes, but the longer you build up energy while performing the ritual, the more powerful it will be. There are many good demonstrations of these rituals available online.

PERFORMING THE LBRP

Before learning and practicing this ritual, it is important to remember that there are many different forms of it, with some minor and some more substantial changes. This is the version I have come to know and practice daily; however, this is my way of doing it, not the only way. If you ever find a variation that works better for you, then go ahead and stick with that one.

To begin, face east and stand behind your altar. Allow yourself to relax deeply into the present moment. You may refer to the Relaxation Ritual, take some deep breaths, or do a round of four-fold breathing to become calm and centered. Give yourself the time to sink into the serenity of the moment, and when you are ready, you can begin.

Step One: Perform the Qabalistic Cross

Stand still and allow your breathing to take you deeper into stillness. Feel your feet firmly rooted to the earth. Now imagine that the earth is a tiny ball beneath you. As you breathe and relax, feel yourself growing larger and larger, until even the Milky Way galaxy is a small sphere of light beneath you.

Now, visualize a ball of radiant white light above your head. This ball is only a sliver of the full glory of Divine Light, but it is your conduit to connect with a higher power. Reach your hand up and make contact with the sphere of light, then bring it down and make a line of light from the sphere into your forehead. As you do, intone the name "Ateh." Touch your chest and point your fingers down towards your feet, at your groin, and intone "Malkuth." Visualize a line of light going down infinitely through your feet as you do this.

Touch your chest again, then your right shoulder, and intone "Ve-Geburah," visualizing a line of light flowing infinitely out through your right side.

The Path Within

Touch your left shoulder and intone "Ve-Gedulah," visualizing a line of light infinitely to your left side.

Finally, clasp your hands before you and intone "Le-Olam Amen," visualizing a glowing ball of light at your heart center. Allow the power of this simple ritual to fill you with a feeling of centeredness.

The translation of the Hebrew words used in the Qabalistic Cross ritual are as follows:

- **Ateh (התא):** This translates to "you are" or "thou art." It is a recognition of the Divine presence.
- **Malkuth (תוכלמ):** This means "kingdom." It represents the material world, the earthly world, and the manifestation of the Divine in the physical.
- **Ve-Geburah (הרובגו):** This translates to "and Power." It is associated with strength, judgment, and severity in Kabbalistic tradition.
- **Ve-Gedulah (הלודגו):** This means "and Glory." It's also known as "Ve-Gedulah" or "Ve-chesed," referring to the attributes of mercy, loving-kindness, and greatness.
- **Le-Olam (םלועל):** This translates to "forever."
- **Amen (ןמא):** A word of affirmation, often translated as "so be it" or "truth."

The Qabalistic Cross is a ritual that symbolizes the connection and alignment of the individual with the Divine. By invoking these Hebrew words, the practitioner acknowledges the presence of the Divine ("Ateh"), connects with the earthly and material reality ("Malkuth"), balances the forces of power and judgment ("Ve-Geburah") with those of mercy and greatness ("Ve-Gedulah"), and affirms the eternal nature of this connection ("Le-Olam Amen"). This ritual serves as a grounding and centering practice, bringing a sense of holiness and balance between the spiritual and material aspects of existence. It's a way to align oneself with the higher powers and to bring that sacred energy into one's life, fostering a sense of peace, centeredness, and spiritual alignment.

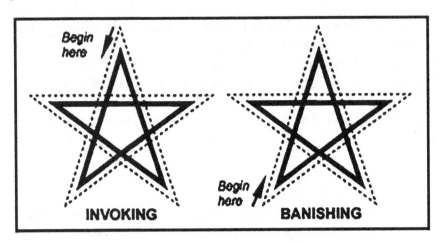

Step Two: Formulation of the Pentagrams

Begin by using the Air Dagger as your tool for drawing the pentagrams in the Banishing form of the ritual. Though some may opt for using a separate Banishing Dagger, any dagger will suffice. In the event that you do not have access to a dagger or are performing the ritual in a space where a dagger is not available, you may use the *sword mudra* by extending two fingers outwards, as if you were imitating the holding of a gun.

Draw the pentagrams, beginning from the bottom left-hand corner by your hip, in an upward motion. Visualize the pentagrams being drawn with bright blue flames, like the color of the fire on a gas stove-top but much brighter.

Step to the East and use your dagger to draw the pentagram. Then make the Sign of the Enterer, which is a traditional magickal body posture (as if you are diving into the pentagram hand and headfirst with your left foot forwards), and charge it with as much light and energy as you can.

Intone the divine name YHVH (*yeh-hoh-wah*), inhaling as much air as you can and exhaling the air completely as you say the name, so that the name is vibrated, almost like Tibetan or Tuvan throat singing. Imagine that you are charging the pentagram with the divine name.

The Path Within

Finish with your first finger touching your lip, as if you are shushing someone, and stomp your foot to seal the energy into the pentagram—the Sign of Harpocrates, or the Sign of Silence. Harpocrates, pronounced *hahr-paw-kroh-teez*, was the god of silence in the Hellenistic religion, adapted by the Greeks from the god Horus, who in Egypt represented the rising sun. He is one of the many forms of Horus and represents potential, as he is often depicted as a baby in a lotus flower with his finger on his mouth like a fetus does in the womb.

Next, draw a line to the South and the pentagram in the same manner. This time, make the Sign of the Enterer and intone ADNI, which is pronounced *ah-doh-noy*. Make again the Sign of Silence.

Now draw a line to the West and draw the pentagram again. This time make the Sign of the Enterer and intone the name AHIH, which is pronounced *eh-hee-yay*. Make again the Sign of Silence.

Finally, draw a line to the North and draw the pentagram again. Make the Sign of the Enterer, and this time when you dive towards the pentagram, chant the divine name AGLA, pronounced *ah-gee-lah*. (Some pronounce this simply as *ah-glah*.) This word AGLA is a notarikon (a Qabalistic code) for Atah Gibor Le-Olahm Adonai, which means "thou, O Lord, art mighty forever." Make the Sign of Silence again.

Finish drawing the line to the center of the first pentagram in the East, then holding your tool at your chest return to the center of the circle in a clockwise direction, standing behind your altar.

Step Three: Evoking the Archangels
Having drawn the four pentagrams and intoned the four god names of the Four Elements within the four directions, we now stand in the center of the circle and evoke the Four Cardinal Archangels.

After you have returned to the center of your circle, visualize the four glowing blue pentagrams and a line of light surrounding you. Each of the Archangels should have a massive and mighty presence.

Jake Kobrin

Hold your arms outstretched and say: "Before me, Raphael" (pronounced *raw-phy-ehl*). Imagine a great Archangel with wings outstretched in robes of yellow, holding a caduceus wand looming in front of you beyond the perimeter of your pentagram. Imagine feeling a calm breeze coming from behind the figure, and other symbolic correspondences to the Element of Air.

Next, say: "Behind me Gabriel" (pronounced *gah-bree-ehl*). Imagine a female Archangel dressed in blue flowing robes and holding a chalice. Imagine feeling moisture emanating from behind her, and other symbolic correspondences to the Element of Water.

Next, say: "To my right hand, Michael" (pronounced *mee-chai-ehl;* the "ch" sound is a guttural sound like in the Scottish "loch"). Imagine a powerful male Archangel in flowing red robes holding a great flaming sword. Imagine heat coming from the south behind the Archangel, and other symbolic correspondences to the Element of Fire.

Next, say: "To my left hand, Uriel" (pronounced *ohr-ree-ehl*). Imagine an Archangel with green robes, holding a pentacle, to your left hand. Imagine the smell of fertile soil, fresh wheat, or imagine other symbolic associations with the Element of Earth coming from the North.

Optional (adopted from Damien Echols):[56]

Next, say: "Above me, Metatron" (pronounced *meh-tah-tron*). Imagine a great, pure Archangel of made of glowing white light looming above you. I often imagine Metatron as a kind of geometric form rather than as a humanoid Archangel. Metatron is stationed at Keter and represents the highest forces on the Qabalistic Tree of Life.

Finally, say: "And below me, Sandalphon" (pronounced *san-dal-phohn*). Imagine an Archangel in brown robes and holding a cornucopia overflowing with bread and fruits below your feet. Sandalphon is stationed at Malkuth and represents the manifestation of the material forces of the Tree of Life.

---

56   Echols, Damien, *High Magick: A Guide to the Spiritual Practices That Saved My Life on Death Row* (Sounds True, 2018)

The Path Within

Step Four: Enclosing the Sphere

Close your eyes and visualize the great scene you have created: four luminous blue pentagrams of flame, a bright blue line enclosing a circle around you, and the imposing presence of four (or six) Archangels looming all around you. As you stand in the center of this powerful formation, take at least one full, deep breath and imagine that you are charging your being with divine light with every inhalation. As you exhale, lift your arms above your head and envision a great sphere of light forming around you, engulfing you in a cocoon of energizing light. Finally, imagine a glowing yellow hexagram, the Jewish Star of David, hovering above your head and below your feet. Feel the divine power of this sacred space.

Say: "For about me flames the pentagrams, and within the column shines the six-rayed star."

Step Five: The Qabalistic Cross

Finally, perform the Qabalistic Cross again, in the exact same manner as before. Congratulations, you have now just performed the Lesser Banishing Ritual of the Pentagram!

The invoking form of the ritual is performed in the exact same way, only using the wand (or wand mudra) instead of the dagger (or sword mudra). When performing the invoking form of the ritual, you draw the pentagrams in a downward left motion starting from the top of the pentagram. To clarify, while the Archangels are always evoked, the purposes of the banishing or the invoking rituals are different. The invoking pentagrams bring in new and more powerful divine light energy, whereas the banishing pentagrams seek to clear out any stagnant or malignant energies from the space.

If you take the time to incorporate the Lesser Pentagram Ritual into your daily practice, you can reap a multitude of benefits. You will have more energy, a more balanced or relaxed energy, and a stronger and more attractive aura. This can help you to attract more positive experiences into your life without even trying. It's okay to use a cheat sheet or a similar page to read from while performing the ritual before you've committed it to memory, but eventually it must be memorized—and usually only takes a few minutes to perform once you have it down.

It is essential that one become competent in banishing rituals before they can be successful in exploring the more advanced forms of magick. The LBRP is a great place to start, but it is by no means the only banishing ritual out there. If you find something else that resonates more with you, then, by all means, use it. And even if you stick to the LBRP, you can experiment by making minor adjustments to it and observe the effects. Ultimately, however, safety must always come first, and banishing is an essential part of performing magick safely.

GENERAL INVOCATION

Drawing a circle and doing a banishing ritual are ways to form a protected vessel of energy in which our magickal work can be done. We can then open ourselves up to a greater source of power, which we may call the divine, or by many other names such as the Headless or Bornless One or IAO. IAO is a Gnostic name that alludes to Isis, Apophis, and Osiris—three Egyptian deities that represent the cycles of creation, destruction, and renewal that are inherent in the natural order of the universe. To access this power, we can use a general invocation, which is a way of raising energy. This often takes the form of reciting certain magickal verses that serve as prayers and supplications. Through this ritual, we can commune with the divine and be empowered and guarded by its strength.

Sometimes, general invocations can also be performed as energetic practices that help to build and raise energy. This can be done through intoning divine names, chanting mantras, and using vibration to increase the energy. Breathing and Taoist practices, such as the Microcosmic Orbit, can also be used to create and circulate energy. The Middle Pillar is a practice from the Hermetic Order of the Golden Dawn that is specifically used to build and circulate energy.

The Path Within

In ceremonial magick, specific invocations are used to open portals and channel particular energies. For example, one may seek to access the energy of a certain deity, such as Thoth, or the energy of a planet like Mercury, or the energy of a sphere of the Tree of Life like Hod. Thoth was the Egyptian god of symbols, the intellect, and communication. Mercury, like Thoth, is a planetary energy in astrology used to illustrate the principle of communication and the intellect. Hod, the eighth sphere on the Qabalistic Tree of Life, is also associated with Mercury and faculties of the mind. Through these invocations, we are able to tap into a special frequency of consciousness, which helps us to carry out our magickal work. These specific invocations also offer us a way to meet with certain energies, spirits, and deities that can only be accessed through the right channels. This all makes sense when seen in the context of a greater magickal system, such as the one taught by the Order of the Golden Dawn; however, it may be too much for someone just starting out on their magickal practice. For now, let us focus on general invocations.

An Example of a General Invocation

One of the most popular ways to begin a magickal ritual is to invoke energies that are conducive to the goal of the ritual. For this purpose, I have written a general invocation that I use when I begin my rituals. After casting and banishing my circle, I stand behind my altar facing east and recite this invocation in a passionate way, connecting with the words and the energies behind them. Though my invocation can be used by others, I recommend writing your own or collecting other general invocations that you feel a deeper connection to. One of the most well-known general invocations is the Bornless One ritual,[57] which is found in the Goetia, a grimoire famously translated by Aleister Crowley. This ritual, however, originally comes from the Ancient Greek Papyri, also known as the PGM, and has nothing to do with the original grimoire from which the Goetia is derived.[58] Below is my

---

57   Crowley, Aleister, and S. L. MacGregor Mathers, eds., *The Goetia: The Lesser Key of Solomon the King* (Weiser, 1995)

58   Skinner, Stephen, *Techniques of Graeco-Egyptian Magic* (Golden Hoard Press, 2014)

Jake Kobrin

own general invocation. Parts of this invocation are inspired by the Bornless One ritual and other invocations, including the Analysis of the Keyword from the Golden Dawn's Hexagram Ritual.

My Personal General Invocation

In the wilderness of the world, where the edges of the earth meet sky, I call to the spirits that dwell here. To the unseen forces that lie in wait in the land, the air, the water, and the fire. In this place, where the veil between what's here and what's beyond is thin, I stand still. My will is set to work within the unseen.

I reach out to the arbiters of fate, their unseen hands guiding from the shadows. At the threshold of the unknown, I accept the forces of chance and destiny. I am here, a seeker at life's crossroads, a guardian of deeper truths. With each breath, I draw in the secrets of the world, and with each breath out, I set forth my will.

I remember the old ways, the lessons passed down through blood and time. I'll take up the tools I need, shape my path with them. I call to the old gods, to the forces of nature, asking for their aid. Virgo, Isis, mother of all; Scorpio, Apophis, the destroyer; Sol, Osiris, dead and risen; I invoke the trinity of Isis, Apophis, Osiris, IAO. I arm myself with will and faith, ready to face what the gods will bring.

I stand alone against the vastness, a seeker of the unknown. My words go out to the powers that be, in the sky, in the earth, in the water, and in the flame. I ask them to listen, to heed my call.

The circle is drawn and cast. I await the signs. I ask for the strength to walk the path set before me, to carry the weight of my choices. May the powers that be grant me what I need to forge my own way, to carve my own destiny.

GUIDE: CRAFTING AND PERFORMING A GENERAL INVOCATION

Purpose:
General invocations in magick are rituals to connect with divine or cosmic forces, often symbolized by various names or concepts like the Headless One, IAO, or Elemental energies. They serve to raise and direct energy for magickal work.

Preparation:
- Ensure a quiet, undisturbed area for the ritual.

Process Overview:
- **Circle Casting and Banishing:** Start by creating a protective energy boundary, clearing the space of any external influences.
- **Invocation of Divine Forces:** Call upon higher powers using names or symbols meaningful to you, like IAO (Isis, Apophis, Osiris), representing archetypal forces and life cycles.

Detailed Steps:
- **Open the Ritual:** Face east, behind your altar if you have one, grounding yourself in the present.
- **Invoke Elemental Spirits:** Call upon the spirits of the Four Corners and the gods of the Elements.
- **Connect with Ancestral Wisdom:** Acknowledge ancestral spirits for guidance and empowerment.
- **Invoke the Deities of the Monad:** Specifically call upon deities that represent the Monad and the eternal powers of God such as Isis (creation), Apophis (destruction), and Osiris (renewal). Use their attributes to symbolize your intentions.

- **Declare Your Will:** Clearly state your intent, using powerful, resonant language.
- **Seek Divine Assistance:** Ask for the aid of gods, goddesses, and cosmic forces in your magickal work.
- **Affirmation of the Circle and Path:** Declare the space as sacred and affirm your readiness to walk your chosen path.

You can use my example invocation, or feel free to adapt or write your own.

Conclusion:
- Close the ritual by thanking the invoked entities and gently grounding yourself back into everyday consciousness.

Note: Tailor the invocation to your path and preferences. Feel free to explore other invocations like the Bornless One ritual for inspiration. As you grow in your practice, you may wish to create more personalized invocations. You can also use Psalms, such as Psalm 23, or passages from the Thelemic Mass as a general invocation for your rituals.

THE MIDDLE PILLAR

Performing the Middle Pillar ritual is a powerful way to draw upon the magickal force of the universe and to invoke and channel this energy through your body. This exercise, which originates from the Golden Dawn tradition, can help to strengthen the energies of balance, union, and harmony that are associated with the Middle Pillar of the Tree of Life. It is an important part of daily practice and can be used in ritual work to connect to and build magickal energy.

After reciting a general invocation, the Middle Pillar is an exercise that can help to further circulate energy in your sphere. By intoning the

The Path Within

Divine Names associated with the spheres of the central (Middle) pillar of the Tree of Life, it is possible to tap into the energies of this sacred symbol. By engaging in this practice, one can come to understand the magickal force of the universe and use it to achieve balance, union, and harmony.

First, perform the Lesser Banishing Ritual of the Pentagram (LBRP) or its invoking form. Now, be present in the moment and step behind your altar, if you have one, facing east with your hands down at your sides. Allow yourself to relax, closing your eyes and steadying your breathing. Find a place of stillness and calmness within your mind and let go of any thoughts or expectations that may be lingering.

Allow your awareness to drift above your head, to the point just beyond the top of your head. If you have recently performed the LBRP, then you should be able to behold a glowing sphere of white brilliance. If not, simply allow your mind to fill with the image of a brilliant white sphere. Spend a moment in contemplation of this sphere and let the awe of its presence wash over you. This sphere is the spatial representation of your higher self, of your connection to the divine. As you contemplate this, the brilliance of the sphere should grow brighter. Now, vibrate the divine name EH-HEH-YEH (היהא), and the sphere should become even brighter than before.

Next, visualize a slender beam of light streaming down from the divine brilliance above your head, flowing through the center of your head and stopping at the nape of your neck. Here, the beam widens, forming a ball of light that is not quite as big as the one above. In your mind's eye, take in both the brilliant sphere above your head, the smaller ball of light at the base of your neck, and the beam of light connecting them. Acknowledge this as the link between your conscious and your Higher Self, allowing the ball of light at your neck to grow in intensity and size. Then, vibrate the God name "YHVH (הוהי) (YUD-HEH-VAHV-HEH or YEH-HOH-WAH) EL-OH-HEEM."

Allow the power of your consciousness to travel from the ball of light at your neck to the solar plexus below your rib cage, manifesting as a sphere of luminosity. Feel the warmth of an internal sun as the brightness of the sphere increases and intensifies. Vibrate the God name "YHVH

(YUD-HEH-VAHV-HEH or YEH-HOH-WAH) EL-OH-AH VA-DAH-AHT (תעדו הולא הוהי)."

In the same way, observe the light trickle down to the area of the genitals and build into a sphere. Consider yourself as the ruler of your "lower" or bodily self. Intone the God name "SHAH-DAI EL CHAI (ידש לא יח)" (the "Ch" sound is again reminiscent of the Scottish "loch").

Summon the light once again. When the light is summoned, it should form a sphere that envelops both the feet and the ground. This sphere should be divided equally, half of it resting above the ground, embracing the feet, and half below the ground, connecting you to the world of the physical. Here, the name "AH-DOH-NYE HA-AHR-ETZ (ינדא האראי)" should be vibrated.

At this stage, one should envisage huge spheres of light hovering above the head, at the throat, at the solar plexus, at the groin, and at the feet; each sphere should be linked to the sphere above and below by a shimmering ray of light.

As you breathe in, envision the light radiating and growing stronger, with each sphere becoming full of vibrant energy. As you exhale, feel the energy rise up your back, all the way to the first energy center, the top of your head. Then, begin the Middle Pillar ritual anew, and with each round, imagine the energy centers becoming brighter and more alive with energy.

Once you have experienced the powerful effects of the Middle Pillar ritual, linger in its tranquility for as long as your heart desires. Then, take a deep breath and, as you exhale, imagine the images slowly fading away into the ether. Although they may no longer be visible, they still linger in the atmosphere. This is the final step in the Middle Pillar Ritual.

Finally, continue to perform the rest of your magickal working until finished. Or, if you have reached the end of your ritual, record the results, impressions, and experiences in your ritual diary, so that you may look back upon them in times to come.

Completing the Lesser Ritual of the Pentagram and Middle Pillar ritual is a great way to energize yourself on a daily basis. If you practice these rituals regularly and for a sustained period of time, you will begin to experience tangible shifts in your energy and feel the positive effects.

The Path Within

I recommend that you commit to doing the Middle Pillar ritual at least five to ten times daily, after you have finished the LBRP or the Lesser Invoking Ritual of the Pentagram (LIRP).

Translation and description of the Hebrew terms:
- **EH-HEH-YEH (אהיה)**: The Divine Name associated with the sphere above the head.
- **EH-HEH-YEH AH-SHER EH-HEH-YEH (אהיה אשר אהיה)**: This phrase from Exodus, often translated as "I am that I am."
- **YHVH (יהוה)**: The Tetragrammaton, often pronounced as "Yehowah" or "Yahweh."
- **YHVH EL-OH-HEEM (יהוה אלוהים)**: "LORD God," combining YHVH with Elohim.
- **HVH EL-OH-AH VA-DAH-AHT (יהוה אלוה ודעת)**: "LORD God of Knowledge," associated with the sphere of Tiphareth.
- **SHAH-DAI EL CHAI (שדי אל חי)**: "The Almighty Living God," associated with the sephirah Yesod.
- **AH-DOH-NYE HA-AHR-ETZ (אדני הארץ)**: "My Lord of Earth," associated with the sphere of Malkuth.

GUIDE: THE MIDDLE PILLAR RITUAL

The Middle Pillar Ritual, derived from the Golden Dawn tradition, is a potent practice designed to align and harmonize your energies with the cosmic forces. It focuses on the central pillar of the Kabbalistic Tree of Life, enhancing balance and unity within.

Preparation:
- **Set Your Environment:** Find a peaceful space, ideally with an altar, facing east.

Jake Kobrin

- **Relax and Center:** Close your eyes, breathe deeply, and attain a state of calm.

The Ritual Process:
- **Initiate with LBRP/LIRP:** Begin with the Lesser Banishing (or Invoking) Ritual of the Pentagram to purify and prepare your space.
- **Visualize the Upper Sphere:** Imagine a brilliant white sphere just above your head. This represents your higher self and connection to the divine. Intone *Eh-heh-yeh* to intensify its brightness. *Eh-heh-yeh*, from Exodus 3, means "I will be what I will be," a name of Kether, the highest sephirah, symbolizing infinite potential.
- **Connect to the Neck Center:** Envision a beam of light from the upper sphere descending to your neck, forming a smaller sphere. Vibrate "YHVH Elohim" here, focusing on the connection between consciousness and the Higher Self.
- **Solar Plexus Sphere:** Let the light move to your solar plexus, creating a bright sphere. Intone *YHVH Eloah Ve-Da'at* (Lord God of Knowledge), symbolizing Tiphareth, the center of balance.
- **Genital Sphere Activation:** Draw the light down to your genitals, forming another sphere. Use *Shaddai El Chai* (Almighty Living God) for Yesod, integrating your physical and spiritual selves.
- **Grounding at the Feet:** Finally, direct the light to encompass your feet and the ground. Chant *Adonai ha-Aretz* (My Lord of Earth) for Malkuth, ensuring grounding and physical connection.
- **Circulate the Energy:** As you breathe, see each sphere growing vibrant. On the exhale, visualize energy rising up your spine to the top sphere, cycling the energy through each center.
- **Closing the Ritual:** After completing the rounds, gently allow the imagery to fade, maintaining the energetic presence. Record any experiences or insights in your ritual diary.

Frequency and Commitment:
- Practice the Middle Pillar Ritual daily, following the LBRP or LIRP, for effective energy alignment.

The Path Within

- Regular practice enhances perceptible shifts in your energy field, fostering spiritual and physical well-being.

Conclusion:
- The Middle Pillar Ritual is a transformative exercise in the Golden Dawn tradition, offering a pathway to harmonize and channel cosmic energies. By integrating it into your daily routine, you can deepen your spiritual practice and achieve greater balance and unity in your life.

ESTABLISHING A CONSISTENT DAILY PRACTICE

After exploring key rituals and techniques, let's delve into establishing a steady daily routine that enhances the skills essential for efficacious magickal workings. My suggestion entails two dedicated periods of formal practice each day—one immediately upon rising in the morning and another just before retiring at night. These sessions could vary in length from a quarter of an hour to a full hour. Initially, we must identify our training goals—what specific skills are we aiming to develop? Which exercises will we select for our practice? What are our primary training aims?

First and foremost, we need to implement a set of exercises that serve as magickal cleanliness, akin to our daily physical hygiene rituals like teeth brushing. Learning to purify our energy field, whether we understand this psychologically or in a more mystical sense—often described as strengthening or energizing the aura—is crucial. It's vital to not only summon magickal energy but also to tolerate its escalating intensity in a healthy manner. Directing this energy towards our predefined goals is another key skill.

It's imperative to grasp the basics of Yoga and meditation, including posture and focus. This enhances our mental concentration. Without the ability to concentrate, channeling and steering energy during magickal rituals

Jake Kobrin

becomes a challenge. Equally important is initiating a magickal journal and cultivating the habit of regular, disciplined recording. This practice is a fundamental discipline vital for all these exercises and is a cornerstone of your future endeavors.

We should also familiarize ourselves with magickal symbols, such as the Tree of Life, the four Elements, and the Tarot. Work to memorize and understand the connections between the sephiroth and the paths on the Tree of Life. Having familiarized ourselves with these practices, let's develop a daily practice that utilizes them.

Consider this as a sample morning routine:
- **Record Dreams:** As dawn breaks or you wake up from your morning alarm, take a moment to write down any dreams in your dream journal.
- **Morning Basics and Beverage:** Get out of bed and do whatever you need to do. Go to the bathroom, shower, brush your teeth, et cetera. Enjoy a cup of tea or coffee, if you like. I recommend taking L-theanine which strengthens concentration, especially if you are drinking coffee. (L-Theanine is naturally occurring in black and green tea.) I do not recommend checking your phone before your practice.
- **Positioning at Altar:** Position yourself at your altar, facing east.
- **Relaxation Technique:** Engage in several cycles of fourfold breathing or any other relaxation technique of your choice.
- **Ritual Performance:** Perform the Lesser Invoking Ritual of the Pentagram, followed by the Middle Pillar Ritual for five to ten rounds.
- **Meditation:** Spend fifteen minutes to an hour meditating in your asana. Focus on your breathing, bodily sensations, or a chosen object of concentration.
- **Concluding Ritual:** Conclude your session with the Qabalistic Cross.
- **Documentation:** Record your practices and experiences in your magickal diary.

For the night-time routine:
- **Unwind from the Day:** As evening arrives, take some time to relax and detach from the day's activities.
- **Ritual Performance:** If you choose, perform the Lesser Banishing Ritual of the Pentagram (LBRP) to create a peaceful and secure environment.
- **Record Daily Experiences:** Make an entry in your diary noting your day's experiences and reflecting on your progress.
- **Meditation:** Consider including a session of meditation. Even a short session, even just fifteen minutes, can be helpful.

Note: It is recommended to limit practices like the Middle Pillar in the evening to avoid disturbing your sleep.

Rhythm in daily practice is crucial. It communicates with our subconscious through symbols and patterns. To maximize the benefits of your routine, adhere to a consistent schedule—same time and place, six days a week. Allow yourself a break occasionally. Setting unrealistic goals can lead to feelings of inadequacy and failure. Therefore, approach your practice with a gentle attitude and savor its rhythm.

THE QABALAH IN MAGICK: UNDERSTANDING THE COMPONENTS OF RITUAL
BY GUEST TEACHER DR. DAVID SHOEMAKER

I have been actively supervising magicians in their initiative work, magickal work, and work in Yoga for the past twenty-five years. This includes reviewing diaries, testing them on their knowledge, testing them on magickal and yogic procedures, and being engaged as a magician myself. This has given me a certain perspective on what works for people, what pitfalls come up

Jake Kobrin

for people, and the kinds of ways of talking about some of these concepts that seem to be most effective and sink in the best.

I primarily work in terms of supervisory work within formal initiative organizations, such as One Star In Sight and Temple of the Silver Star. Since I have been involved in these specific organizations, I am coming from a very specifically Thelemic perspective on magick, which has been hugely influenced by Crowley's work. I understand that everyone has to experiment and find not just the practical tools that work best for them, but also the spiritual home that is best for them.

From a Thelemic perspective, if you buy into the doctrine of True Will, you have a basic nature that is intrinsic to who you are as an incarnate human being. Knowledge of one's own True Will is the single greatest magickal tool you could have, because once you have defined that with some specificity, the choices you make about magickal operations will be framed by it. Aleister Crowley's initiatory systems suggest the method of coming to full awareness of the True Will is what he called the "Knowledge and Conversation of the Holy Guardian Angel." Crowley talked about it in different ways in different phases of his career, depending on who he was talking to.

The good news is you don't have to know what the HGA is. If you do the steps of this magickal and initiatory approach, you get all the answers you need because the practices work. Crowley's greatest contribution to the world of magick was this pragmatism, which I certainly align with in my work. Do what works. Grab stuff from places wherever you want, as long as it works, and as long as you can synthesize it and integrate it in a meaningful way. Don't get bogged down in the dogmas and doctrines of things. Focus on finding magickal tools that work for you and practice them.

So why then would we do something really esoteric like a magickal ritual when we want a job? Our magickal tools are probably the job application, the phone call, the interview, and the skills that are needed for that job. The answer is that the magickal ritual can help you to understand your True Will and to put that into some degree of conscious awareness so that you can carry it out.

The Path Within

Rituals are a method of focusing the Will and sustaining attention and focus for a magickal working. To use a metaphor, if someone's magickal goal was to write a poem, they must know the tools they need to use, such as the English alphabet, grammar, syntax, and rhyme. To do a good magickal ritual, one must use correspondences such as Hebrew, Greek, Latin, and other alphabets, as well as correspondences for colors, incenses, and animals. The Tree of Life is an incredibly rich set of symbols that can be used as a filing cabinet, where the idea of the Sephiroth is a place to store ideas and concepts that relate to a certain energy or transition of energies.

To speak the name of God in all the worlds is how one does magick: all four worlds simultaneously. This means that one must be able to have a language of symbols and an ability to work with symbols so that the idea of the magickal aim can be brought from its most ineffable, non-specific divine levels, down through layers of universal mind into one's own individual mind, and then into the practical physical world. This pretty much describes the four worlds of that divine being: Atziluth, the sort of archetypal symbol world; Briah, the universal symbols; Yetzirah, the world of the human mind and of the astral realm and the natural world of symbols; and Assiah, the fourth of the four worlds, which is the crystallized manifested universe, but also the crystallized manifested result of the ritual.

The Tree of Life and Qabalistic symbolism is set up in accordance with these principles. For example, if one wants to construct a ritual that's designed to bring down force through the four worlds, there are some handy symbols, names, and other correspondences that are already plugged into those four worlds that we can utilize. For example, in the Atziluthic world, the divine world, if you take any Sephira, there's a God name that goes with it; for the Briah world, there's an Archangel that goes with that sphere; for the Yetzirah world, there are the choirs of angels. And then there's the palaces of Assiah, the Heavens of Assiah.

Structuring a ritual and understanding the components of the ritual is important. There have already been some materials presented on the sort of

Jake Kobrin

the phases of ritual. I will pick an example later. I'll use Mars and Geburah from the Tree of Life as an example and walk you through the way the four worlds would fall into place, the names you would use, the colors, the incense, and all of that.

The components of an effective ritual are modular; there are certain types of components that need to be there, but what you plug in to those components can vary quite a bit, and that's the fun part of designing a ritual. That's the creative part.

The components of a ritual are the preliminaries, banishing, purifications, consecrations, general invocation, the oath or proclamation, the specific invocation, bringing down the magickal link, and then the closing. The preliminaries include things like considering if I really want to do this and if I really want the outcome that I think I want. Additionally, the preliminaries include things like choosing how I'm going to symbolize things, what the invocation will be, and most importantly, what sphere or path on the Tree of Life I'm going to use as my key for the correspondences and symbols I'm going to use.

Banishings can include the Lesser Banishing Ritual of the Pentagram, the Star Ruby, clattering swords, and laughter. Purifying and consecrating is an interesting concept. Purification is a symbolic gesture that says, "anything that's not part of this magick that I'm trying to do can get out." Purification is typically associated with Water, and consecration is usually associated with Fire. It's a way of sacralizing the pure thing that's been washed away of distracting stuff and now you're saying, "I am now aligning this with the highest divine forces that I have access to."

This follows a principle that is really important and perhaps under-emphasized in magickal practice: banish the general before you invoke the specific. If you're going to invoke an Element (let's say Fire), banish all Elemental influence from your sphere before you bring in the one Element you want in that session or portion of the ritual.

To use a practical example, performing a Lesser Banishing Ritual of the Pentagram is a great way to banish Elemental influence. After this, you can do a Greater Invoking Ritual of the Pentagram of Fire, which is the one thing you want. This is followed by all the stuff you are going

The Path Within

to do with it. Finally, you should do the Greater Banishing Ritual of the Pentagram of Fire at the end.

When performing a ritual, it is important to banish things at the end. This is when you have made the talisman, consumed the Eucharist, or done whatever inner transformation you wanted to do with it. You have described the astral region that you want to describe, whatever the aim was. To ensure that you don't leave the tap on, so to speak, you should banish the one force at the end of your session.

You can also look at this sort of like dosing. How much of a dose of fire do you want right now? Do you want to leave the tap on overnight and get more fire, or do you want to just get enough to consecrate the thing and then turn it off? You can use a physical talisman that's consecrated with that force and take it out of its protective covering. Look at it, hold it, or keep it on your person for the kind of dose you need, and then put it away when you've had enough.

The general invocation is like turning on power to the whole house. You want the current coming into the house so that you're ready with a specific invocation to put the power to whatever specific room you want. This is why things like the Middle Pillar Ritual, or some intense Kundalini work, are generally useful in this context. The oath or proclamation is a focus of the conscious intention of the magician. It is important to have some sort of statement of magickal intent.

We will reference *Liber 777* for our magickal correspondences such as what God names to chant, what incense to burn, and so on. *Liber 777* is a book that many magicians get early in their career. It is a catalogue—not necessarily something you're going to read and digest and hold in mind. It is something that you're going to gradually get acquainted with and perhaps gradually memorize parts of it (the most useful and practical components, usually).

Bringing down magickal force can be done in a variety of ways. For example, I described a ritual I did for Jupiter in a podcast episode. This ritual involved tracing out a flaming sword, like on the Tree of Life, on the floor of the temple with some tape. We kept walking down it and then went to the top and walked down it again, chanting the whole time. We were embodying

Jake Kobrin

the symbol we were using and chanting the various hierarchies of Jupiter. We brought the force down through the four worlds.

Another way to understand a magickal experience is that we become a talisman, an attractor for the force we're trying to embody. A good ritual will have that effect, that somehow the temple, the magicians, and the symbols, attitude, intention, and names all become an attractor for that force. The more you've trained yourself to associate certain ideas with certain colors, symbols, names, and so on, the more precise your control will be over the magick and how it works.

Once you've brought down the magickal force, you need to complete the magickal link by locking it in either in consciousness or in the physical world. If the whole point was to bring in an astral atmosphere, then you can banish it once you've done that. But if you want to create a talisman, then you need to have some sort of climax that locks it into the talisman. This might be a ritual climax where everyone is giving the Sign of the Enterer and aiming it at the talisman and projecting all the force that has been brought into the talisman. Or it might be a Eucharist, where what you are charging is some cakes of light from the Thelema tradition and a goblet of wine and, while you are consuming that, you are locking in the invoked force through consumption of those materials that have been charged one way or another.

Finally, you want to complete the magickal link either in consciousness or in physicality. To do this, you can do a banishing ritual, such as a Greater Pentagram Ritual of Fire to send home the one thing you have invoked. Then, you can give a license to depart, such as saying, "in the name of Ra Hour Kuit, I set free any spirits which may have been imprisoned by the ceremony. Go forth in peace under your abodes and habitations, and harm none in your passing. Be there a peace between us and be ready to come when called." Finally, you can give a single knock or something to seal the deal.

Let me talk about the kinds of aims one might have in doing a ritual. I will draw on Aleister Crowley's writing called the *Arte Magica,* which was originally a private instruction for OTO but was subsequently published. I am reading from an elaboration of this, which was presented in Jim Schuman's book called *776 and 1/2.* These are key to the Sephirot,

The Path Within

so remember what you know so far from the nature of the Sephirot on the Tree of Life and see how the magickal aim that is key to it sort of is in line with the nature of that sphere.

For Kether, which is undifferentiated spiritual source, the aim is to generate magickal force to ensure the continued and increasing capacity to practice this art. For Chokmah, which means "wisdom," the aim is to ensure the right performance of this art. For Binah, which means "understanding," the aim is prosperity and increase of the magickal order within which one works, or from which one has obtained training and of its leaders as a happy duty of gratitude and as a service to all seekers who will come after one on the path.

For the sphere of Jupiter, symbolizing plenitude, the aim might be ease of circumstances to perform the Great Work, and to ensure sufficient leisure and honor the pursuit of the Great Work. For Geburah and Mars, the aim is to establish a protective bodyguard of invisible warriors, to secure freedom from interruption during the practice of the magickal art. This may include specific protection such as preservation of physical health.

For Tiphareth, the spiritual center of the Tree, representing spiritual enlightenment and awakening in the conscious adept, the aim is the Knowledge and Conversation of the Holy Guardian Angel. For Netzach, the Venus sphere symbolizing devotion, the aim is devotion to the divine, Nuit, Babylon, and so on, or one's own nature as dictated. For Hod, the sphere of intellect, the aim is further insight into nature and her laws, such as science. For Yesod, the sphere of the subconscious and autonomic functions, the aim is the modification, purification, enhancement, equilibration, and correction of any characterological or other psychological aspects of oneself, as well as the fulfillment of the finite aspects of one's True Will. Finally, for Malkuth, which is the bottom tree on the sphere and relates to the physical world and manifest reality, and the physical body, the aim is the establishment of the Law of Thelema and the Kingdom of Ra Hour Kuit upon the earth, as well as diverse matters such as the rejuvenation of one's own body if desired, the powers of healing, and so on.

I've talked a lot about the different components of ritual and a lot about invocations and the various ways to use them. I want to give you some

Jake Kobrin

tips on creating effective magickal invocations, whether they be ritualized, poetic, dramatic, or otherwise. The point here is that whatever we're doing, we have to find a way to bring ourselves during the ritual to kind of a climax of energetic focus and intensity. A lot of the tips for good invocations are like tips for good sex, frankly. That might be a useful way to think about this. With sex, you want to be focused and generate a lot of energy to bring it up to a climax, but not have it be over too quickly and sustain your energy, making the power be in the room for a long time before you're done.

Before I go into specifics, let me give a few more comments from Crowley. One of the things that you may have noticed is a distinction between evocation and invocation. Evocation is calling this force outward, generally used for low yet erratic entities, such as Goetic spirits, planetary spirits, and intelligences. The magician commands and controls the spirit. Crowley says the magician soon discards evocation almost altogether, and only rare circumstances demand any action whatever on the material plane. The magician devotes themselves entirely to the invocation of a God. And as soon as their balance approaches perfection, they cease to invoke any partial God, only that God vertically above them in their path, which is essentially the Holy Guardian Angel.

So, a person who perhaps took up magick merely with the idea of acquiring knowledge, love, or wealth finds themselves irrevocably committed to the performance of the great work. I've seen this time and time and time again over the years. My teachers saw it for decades before that. People come in with all kinds of wild ideas about what they want to get from magick. And once they've trained enough to be good at and have the tools they need to get what they want, they realize that these wants are not that important. In the process, they discover that they are on a path of self-discovery and spiritual development, and some of those simple, mundane aims just don't seem as important anymore. Perhaps more importantly, as they are more in touch with their True Will, the stuff is happening anyway. They are working in harmony with the universe, and so the things they really need to execute their True Will are presented to them. These things tend to be given to you without having to ask because you are a talisman of your True Will, and the more you are out there living it out, the more that stuff is drawn to you.

The Path Within

Invocation, in contrast with evocation, is calling the force inward to you. Generally, for entities such as gods, Archangels and such, the rule of thumb is that if you want all of yourself to be more like the thing, invoke it. If you want it to be more like you, if you want it to do your bidding and to go be an extension of your Will in the world, evoke it. There are lots of things that would be good for evoking that you wouldn't necessarily want all of yourself to be more like, such as some little goetic spirit that does a special thing and has a special talent to bring you if you ask for it.

Many of us would not sign up to shape our entire being to be more like a spirit. We want them to be an extension of us. Therefore, the rule of thumb is to invoke it if you want all of yourself to be more like the entity and evoke it if you want it to be an extension of you and your Will.

To properly invoke a force, you must first personify it outwardly and then embody it. Describe the God you're trying to invoke and start to act as the God would speak and look. For example, begin the ritual with statements of admiration and list the attributes of the God. By the end, you should be speaking as if to the God. This will help you create yourself as a proper form to attract the force.

To address the multifaceted nature of the force you're trying to invoke, look at *Liber Astarte,* Crowley's writing on devotional magick. There is a sevenfold formula for coming up with good ritual worship statements for the God or Goddess you've chosen. Start with an implication as of a servant unto their Lord, then an oath as of a vessel to their lead, then a memorial as of a child to their parent, then an orison as of a priest unto their God, and so on. Think of all the ways you could describe the force you're trying to invoke and flesh it out. Look at it from all angles and fall in love with all the different aspects of it.

The most important thing is to inflame yourself in prayer. Crowley describes this as the whole secret of the process. Lose yourself in the frenzy of your adoration of the principle you're trying to invoke. The words, ideas, images, incense, dancing, music, and colors should make it intense. Fall in love with it and bring it up to a climax. Stop short of the climax repeatedly by strength of Will, then go back to it again and again until it doesn't even occur to you not to stop.

Jake Kobrin

Once you have decided on the force to be invoked for the purposes of the overall ceremony, focus only on invoking that force. Forget about the purpose of the ceremony. Crowley says that the failure to do so is the single most common source of error in invocation. So, once you know you have already decided all the stuff that is going to be in the ritual, then just do it. Just be in the flow of it, and don't go back into brain land where you're thinking, *should I have made that thing a different color?* Or just get out of that head space and into the intense flow of the ritual.

The course of a proper invocation mirrors the overall process of the aspirant toward union with the Holy Guardian Angel and the full discovery of the True Will. We inflame ourselves in prayer, making our whole life into a suitable invocation for our Holy Guardian Angel. We unite with the Holy Guardian Angel in ecstasy.

Just like in a ritual, you are uniting with the ritual aim. You go forth into the world as the prophet of your Holy Guardian Angel. Your thoughts and words embody the will of your angel, as they have always been one in essence. You have gone through an impassioned process of uniting with it and at the end, you go out a changed person. Your relationship to the force you've invoked is different.

To clarify some of the references that have been given in terms of books, *Magick in Theory* and *Practice is Part Three of the Four-Part Magick* book, which is also called *Liber ABA* or *Book Four*. The most fleshed-out, well-annotated version is the one that's been out since the early nineties. The following is from Aleister Crowley's *Magick in Theory and Practice*, Chapter XV, "Of the Invocation."

In the straightforward or "Protestant" system of magick, there is very little to add to what has already been said. The magician addresses a direct petition to the being invoked. But the secret of success in invocation has not been hitherto disclosed. It is an exceedingly simple one. It is of practically no importance whatsoever that the invocation is right. There are a thousand different ways of compassing the end proposed, so far as external things are concerned. The whole secret may be summarized in these four words: "Enflame thyself in praying."

The Path Within

The mind must be exalted until it loses consciousness of self. The magician must be carried forward blindly by a force which, though in them and of them, is by no means that which they in their normal state of consciousness calls "I." Just as the poet, the lover, the artist is carried out of themselves in a creative frenzy, so must it be for the magician.

It is impossible to lay down rules to the obtaining of this special stimulus. To one the mystery of the whole ceremony may appeal; another may be moved by the strangeness of the words, even by the fact that the "barbarous names" are unintelligible to them. Sometimes over the course of a ceremony, the true meaning of some barbarous name that has hitherto baffled their analysis may flash upon them, luminous and splendid, so that they are caught up into ecstasy. The smell of a particular incense may excite them effectively, or perhaps the physical ecstasy of the magick dance.

Every magician must compose their ceremony in such a manner as to produce a dramatic climax. At the moment when excitement becomes ungovernable, when the whole conscious being of the magician undergoes a spiritual spasm, at that moment must they utter the supreme adjuration.

One very effective method is to stop short, by a supreme effort of will, again and again, on the very brink of that spasm, until a time arrives when the idea of exercising that will fails to occur. Inhibition is no longer possible or even thinkable, and the whole being of the magician, no minutest atom saying nay, is irresistibly flung forth. In blinding light, amid the roar of ten thousand thunders, the Union of God and humanity is consummated.

If the magician is still standing in the Circle, quietly pursuing their invocations, it is that the conscious part of them has become detached from the true ego which lies behind that normal consciousness. But the circle is wholly filled with that divine essence; all else is but an accident and an illusion.

The subsequent invocations, the gradual development and materialization of the force, require no effort. It is one great mistake of the beginner to concentrate their force upon the actual stated purpose of the ceremony. This mistake is the most frequent cause of failure in invocation.

Jake Kobrin

A corollary of this theorem is that the magician soon discards evocation altogether—only rare circumstances demand any action whatsoever on the material plane. The magician devotes themselves entirely to the invocation of a god; as soon as their balance approaches perfection, they cease to invoke any partial god, only that god vertically above them in their path. And so, a person who perhaps took up magick merely with the idea of acquiring knowledge, love, or wealth, finds themselves irrevocably committed to the performance of The Great Work. It will now be apparent that there is no distinction between magick and meditation except of the most arbitrary and accidental kind.

On this point, I would just add that the whole point of Yoga and meditation generally is to still the mind, focus the mind, and train the ability of the mind to keep that focus. That is why Yoga training is so useful in the practice of ceremonial magick: the focus becomes one of the keys of success with practical magick.

Finally, I just want to close by giving a sample of a kind of assemblage of symbols that you might use for a particular ritual purpose. So, let's pretend we're going to do that ritual of Mars, or Geburah on the Tree of Life. This sphere relates to power and force and fiery energy and all of that. So that's our key set of symbols. We decide it's going to be Geburah—number five. So, you get out your copy of *Liber 777*, look at the column or line five, which is going to connect to all the Geburah stuff across the entire book.

What colors go with the fifth Sephira? Well, there are four of them. The four color scales are orange, scarlet, red, and black. These correspond to the four worlds. You could have an invocation where you visualize the God in orange, the Archangel in scarlet red, the angelic choir in bright scarlet, and the final name of the sealing of the talisman in red and black. You use the colors and the hierarchy of names to bring that force down through those worlds. If you have internalized the meanings, this can be very powerful.

The names for Mars in descending the four worlds are *Elohim Gibor* (Almighty God), the Atziluthic God name; Khamael, the Briatic Arch-

The Path Within

angel name; *Seraphim,* which means "fiery serpents" for the angels in the world of Yetzirah; and Madim is the name in Assiah. Your incense might be dragon's blood resin, and you might have deities keyed on, or symbols or invocations keyed to deities like Horus or the Greek Ares, the Roman Mars, and the Norse god Tyr. All of this comes from *Liber 777.*

Once you have decided on your key, you're going to turn to line five: Mars or Geburah. Follow it across and you will get more symbols than you can use in one ritual. But it will get your wheels turning. You will start thinking about what is meaningful to you. What pantheon do you most connect with? What ritual forms, what other sorts of symbols, gems, incense, or colors really speak to you?

I wanted to conclude with something more practical in terms of executing the construction of a ritual using the symbols from the Tree of Life and from *Liber 777,* as that is really the magician's primary sourcebook.

CHAPTER EIGHT

MAGICKAL ARTS

Exploring the mysteries of ritual magick has opened our eyes to the ability to cast and banish circles, meditate and focus our minds, and call on the powers of the universe through invocations. Now let us discover one of the most powerful yet simple techniques known to magick—sigilization.

Austin Osman Spare's modern sigil magick evolved from ancient forms of magick, and with it he believed we could access the depths of our subconscious during moments of ecstasy. We could craft symbols to psychologically affect ourselves and manifest our desires in the real world. Spare developed his own "alphabet of desire," using a process of redundancy to create symbols by removing all letters that were repeated and morphing the remaining letters into a new symbol. This can also be done with an image or several, or an automatically conceived image alone—it is an ever-evolving and creative process.

Jake Kobrin

Sigil magick is an incredibly potent practice and is one of the most efficient and effective methods known. It requires no faith, and so nothing to stand in opposition to. This form of magick is crafted to elude our inner guards and can be performed almost anywhere with just a pen and paper or a fingertip in the soil. Sigils can be thought of as a means of encoding information into a concentrated bundle that can be sent into the depths of our unconscious.

This quest of magickal initiation and transformation begins by exploring the field beyond the boundaries of our conscious minds, which I call the psychic sensor. This is the part of us that decides what is possible, and all too often it is tempted to maintain the existing order over the possibilities we yearn for. To access this part of us, sigil magick is a powerful tool that can bypass the psychic sensor and manifest our deepest desires through symbols the rational mind can't comprehend, but the deep mind can. With minimal effort, these symbols are a magickal equivalent to a lottery scratch card, providing us with a simple and effective way to create positive changes in our lives.

Sigil magick is a powerful and attractive practice, giving us a way to bring about new and unique experiences into our lives, regardless of whether they are traditionally seen as beautiful or not. It is a vehicle for us to go beyond the limits of our conscious minds, tapping into the depths of our unconscious, and encoding our wishes into symbols that the rational mind can't fathom, yet the deep mind can understand. With a sigil, we can grant ourselves the wishes we yearn for that can be achieved with minimal effort. This can be done with just a pen and paper, or even our fingertips in the soil. The psychic sensor within us can often be tempted to keep the world in its current state, stopping us from manifesting the changes we desire. However, a sigil can get around this, granting us a magickal ticket to make a change that is more effective than affirmations or other methods. So, in essence, a sigil is a wish-fulfilling squiggle, a simple and potent way to bring about the transformation we seek.

The great artist Austin Osmond Spare, the father or grandfather of sigil magick, wrote: "Oh ye, who are living other people's lives. Unless desire is subconscious, it is not fulfilled. No, not in this life. Then verily

The Path Within

Sleep is better than prayer."[59] Truer words have never been written. To bring about a change in our lives, we must make a shift in our perspectives and the hidden narratives that originate from our subconscious minds. Sigil magick can be used to do this, as it bypasses the conscious mind and instead plants a psychic seed in the subconscious. This is done through focusing on a symbol in a state of gnosis or altered consciousness, such as through exhaustion, mind-altering substances, or meditation.

One common and potent method to charge a sigil is through orgasm. While the topic of sex magick is vast and intricate, beyond the full scope of this book, we can still harness the creative and transformative power of sexual energy to effectively charge a sigil. The act of reaching orgasm generates intense energy and focus, making it a powerful moment for sigil activation. Through learning the theories and techniques of practical magick, understanding different kinds of sigils and their use and activation techniques, as well as how to create custom-tailored sigils, we can reprogram the brain and alter consciousness. This has the potential to impact and amplify our abilities and magickal workings, thus allowing us to achieve tangible shifts in reality.

A sigil is a symbol of a desired outcome, requiring a greater degree of focus to craft than simply writing it down. After creating the sigil, the magician charges and releases it, infusing it with emotion, intention, and conviction. The releasing is intended to move the desire from conscious thought into the depths of the unconscious. It is a symbol that is meant to bring about transformation. Once the desire is shaped into a sigil, the magician releases it from their mind and then performs an activation or charging. Finally, they await the manifestation of their wish.

Discovering what you truly want is the starting point of any magickal path. To truly understand this, we must learn to look within and ask ourselves what we desire, rather than what we think we should want or what society has taught us. Examine your desires list that you made earlier to familiarize yourself with your deepest desires. This is a lifelong process of deepening your relationship with yourself and uncovering why

---

59   Spare, Austin Osman, *The Book of Pleasure (Self-Love): The Psychology of Ecstasy* (IHO Books, 2001)

Jake Kobrin

you are here. You can start this process right now and continue to work on it for the rest of your life, as your desires will continue to evolve.

Once you have a deep, true, and heartfelt desire that you can feel in your body, write it out on a piece of paper as if it has already happened. For example, if your desire is to get free food every time you go out to eat, you would phrase it as, "every time I go out to eat, I get free food." This is the way to create a sigil that has the power to manifest your wish. You have to be open to the idea and not too clingy—almost as if you are forgetting about it. When it happens, you will be surprised and say, "oh yeah, I forgot I did that." Word them in such a way that they are already part of your life, like saying, "I'm so happy to live in my dream apartment," not "I want to get my dream apartment." The power of manifestation lies in the intention and clarity of your words.

When it comes to any form of magick, ethics are of the utmost importance. It can be easy to forget this, and you may find yourself using sigil magick in a way that can potentially do harm to yourself or others. We can explore ways to assess the potential risks of using sigil magick, but in general, it is wise to avoid using it to manipulate someone's free will. For example, if you have a love interest, then it is not wise to use sigil magick to make them fall in love with you. Although I have experimented with it in the past and can attest that it can work, I strongly advise against using sigil magick to manipulate someone's free will—such as making a love interest fall in love with you. While the results may seem appealing, interfering with another person's autonomy can have unintended consequences, both karmically and energetically. It may lead to superficial or short-lived outcomes that lack genuine connection and mutual respect. Magick is most powerful when it aligns with higher principles, such as respecting the free will of others. Attempting to control someone's emotions or actions not only undermines the natural flow of relationships but can also create an unhealthy dynamic that ultimately harms both parties involved.

Instead, it is better to use sigil magick to express an intention of being in a loving, healthy, and romantic relationship, leaving it open-ended. Furthermore, the sigil's manifestation will be done through natural means; what might seem like a coincidence or happenstance could be the

The Path Within

result of the sigil's power. For instance, you may write a sigil with the intention of manifesting ten thousand dollars, then end up in a café you don't normally visit, go in a certain direction as a result, meet someone, and before you know it, you have created a new income stream and made your ten thousand dollars. This may not feel overtly magickal if you had forgotten about creating and charging the sigil, but its power is very real.

CRAFTING YOUR SIGIL

To make and charge a sigil is to bring one's intent into action. To begin, form a statement of intent in the positive present tense, such as "I am deeply in love with my romantic partner." Remove the vowels, followed by the repeating letters. "I am deeply in love with my romantic partner" becomes "MDPLYNLVWTHMYRMNTCPRTNR," and then "MDPLYNVWTHRC." This leaves you with a set of characters that can be creatively combined into a magickal glyph. Play with drawing the forms of these letters, combining them together until it feels right and magickal. This is your sigil. To further amplify the power of this ritual, charge the sigil and then destroy or forget about it. We can embellish on this ritual form to add extra power and safety to our workings, but these are the core components. Through this, we make our intent real by taking action and creating something tangible, that can then be set free to make its own way in the world.

I had one student who was blind and liked to take the letters of a statement and create mantras out of them, obscuring them just enough so that the subconscious mind can still recognize them. For example, take the statement "I am deeply in love with my romantic partner," and turn it into "MDPLYNVWTHRC," which can be transformed into "Modo Polyno Vowo Toheric," creating a magickal mantra sigil that can be used in combination with visualizing the sigil in meditation.

I AM DEEPLY IN LOVE WITH
MY ROMANTIC PARTNER

I̶ AM D̶E̶E̶PLY I̶N L̶O̶V̶E̶ WITH
M̶Y̶ R̶O̶M̶A̶N̶T̶I̶C̶ P̶A̶R̶T̶N̶E̶R̶

MDPLYNVWTHRC

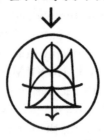

Remember, being an artist is not a requirement for this. What matters is your ability to express your intention through symbols in a way that resonates with you. As an artist, I often strive to create symbols that are aesthetically pleasing and reflect the intention in some way, whether that be through texture, flavor, emotion, or atmosphere. But it doesn't have to be complicated; sometimes it can be as simple as some squiggly lines on a piece of paper. This is not about making a grandiose art piece to show off to others; no one else needs to ever see it. This is simply for you, and whatever way you can get your intentions into your subconscious.

The Path Within

CHARGING YOUR SIGIL

When it comes to performing a sigil charging ritual, there is no one "right" way. Different practitioners have different methods, like a recipe with certain traditional attributes. One step that may be helpful is to do divination on it first. You want to make sure that whatever you are doing won't potentially harm yourself or another person. Intuition can be a guide, but it is also wise to use divination methods such as Tarot, I Ching, geomancy, or even muscle testing. If the divination shows that the ritual could be damaging, it's best to avoid it. We will dive deeper into divination in a later chapter.

It is important to ensure that the space is cleared of anything that may disrupt the ritual, and that you feel protected and safe. It doesn't have to be too complicated—simply light some incense and sit on your meditation pillow—but for those who are looking for something more, there are complex banishing and consecration rituals. All in all, it's a matter of personal preference.

Invoking the highest source of divinity within us and the universe can be done through a prayer or petition, or by calling on angels or deities. There are also specific practices to assist, like the Middle Pillar, Tantric Yoga, or Taoist exercises such as the Microcosmic Orbit which can help build energy. This is a practice to build and circulate energy, often used in tandem with sexual activity to concentrate the energy generated in arousal. We will not be exploring this practice in this book. (I suggest *Taoist Secrets of Love: Awakening Male Sexual Energy* by Mantak Chia to learn more about this practice.) If we have a presence and awareness of energy in our body, then this can be cultivated intentionally to have greater control over it, both alone and with a partner.

Jake Kobrin

Next, we seek gnosis, striving to reach an altered state of consciousness that is highly receptive and relaxed to effectively implant our sigil. Techniques like meditation and concentration can be instrumental in quieting the mind. Additionally, binaural beats can induce a trance-like state, aiding in focusing on the sigil. Binaural beats, created from two separate tones played in each ear, lead to brain entrainment in states like theta or beta waves. There are many free binaural beats available online for meditation or concentration, along with various apps designed for this purpose.

Chaos magicians often recommend the "death posture," a method of emptying oneself of all energy, to achieve gnosis. Another approach is OSHO's dynamic meditation, involving jumping, screaming, and then falling into stillness. Guided videos and audio tapes for these practices can be found online as well. Visualizing the sigil as one falls asleep is another effective method, as the brain becomes highly impressionable. While trance-inducing drugs are often illegal and should be approached with caution, they can be potent in achieving gnosis to charge a sigil. Creative methods like drawing the sigil in the sand, carving it into a candle and then burning it, also contribute to charging it. Finally, a sensory deprivation tank provides an optimal environment for deep relaxation and receptivity. Invented by Dr. John C. Lilly for psychedelic research in the 1960s, these soundproof, dark, and isolated chambers filled with extremely buoyant water facilitate a profound state of relaxation. Lilly's research into altered states of consciousness and the mind's nature provides invaluable insights into magick and self-transformation, highlighting the significant impact of internal exploration on personal and spiritual growth.

As we have seen throughout the ages, people have used various altered states of consciousness to access the power of their intentions. This is no different today, as we can charge sigils through a variety of techniques, such as adrenaline-filled activities, drumming and dancing, physical sensory overload, and pain. Even fear can be a powerful tool for charging a sigil if you focus on it while doing something that scares you.

The Path Within

DISPOSING OF YOUR SIGIL

Once you have charged the sigil with whatever means you wish to use, there are different ways to dispose of it. Burning it is one way, with the thought that by doing so, you are releasing your attachment to the outcome and allowing it to manifest in the unseen world. You can leave it at the crossroads, which have traditionally been believed to represent the intersection of time and space that we exist in, where anything is possible. You can also throw it into a river, or use low-attention processing, which is when you keep the sigil somewhere visible but don't pay too much attention to it. After disposal, close the ritual and banish again, thanking the spirits and telling them to leave. To end the ritual, you may choose to do something light such as watch something funny, eat some food, call a friend, or go for a walk. This helps to brush off the experience and start the process of forgetting.

It can be a challenge to not consciously hold onto a desire, especially when it is something that we really want. But there are ways to work around it. One such way is to create sigils and store them in a box, not remembering why you created them in the first place. This allows the desire to manifest in its own natural way, free from anxiety and desperation. It is important to have an open, relaxed energy and not be too attached to it, as this will increase the likelihood of it coming about. Additionally, breaking down a big goal into steps and creating sigils for each of those steps can also be effective. This technique is called *shoaling*. For an extra boost, Gordon White's "Robo Fish" technique from his book *The Chaos Protocols* can be used. The book is named after experiments done with schools of fish where they found that by introducing a robotic fish, and then changing its direction, that they could change the direction of the entire school of fish. This also applies to creating a sigil for something you know with certainty will happen, such as what you will eat for breakfast the next day. By including this sigil in the shoal, it increases the likelihood of the other sigils manifesting. Ultimately, the key to unlocking our desires is to relax and let go of conscious thinking. If we allow our subconscious to take over, we can manifest our desires more easily.

SIGILIZED WORKS OF ART

In magick, the art of sigilization stands out as a uniquely powerful practice, blending artistic expression with ritualistic intent. This process transcends the mere creation of symbols; it involves an intricate blend of formulation, design, aesthetics, and execution, tailored to each individual's artistic medium and mental framework. Whether through drawing, painting, writing, sculpting, or even filmmaking and music, sigilization allows creatives to manifest their innermost desires and intentions in physical or conceptual forms.

Sigils, as a cornerstone of magickal practice, are more than just visual representations; they are personalized artworks, be they drawings, collages, paintings, or even musical pieces, that resonate deeply with the creator. To imbue these sigils with power, one must align them with their "True Will" —a concept that can manifest as a word, symbol, ideal, lifestyle, or attitude unique to the individual. Traditional approaches to sigils, often seen as arbitrary and lacking in personal creativity, can be transcended by allowing one's imagination to dictate the shape and content of the sigil. This could involve experimenting with letters, runes, numbers, or other symbols to create a unique magickal language. Simplifying these symbols is key, as it aids in visualization and embedding them into the subconscious.

The Path Within

The expansive nature of sigil magick was explored in a discussion with Carl Abrahamsson, representative of Thee Temple ov Psychick Youth (TOPY).[60] TOPY was an influential organization founded in the 1980s, whose significance in the context of magick and self-transformation lies in its pioneering blend of contemporary culture, psychic exploration, and ceremonial magick, which inspired a generation of spiritual seekers and artists to explore unconventional paths toward personal enlightenment and creative expression. Abrahamsson emphasized that a sigil is not just a glyph but can manifest in any artistic medium. The process itself, he noted, is thematic and can be as varied as the artist's imagination, from collages to immaterial art forms. The intention behind the creation is what transforms an artwork into a sigil. He also highlighted the unique approaches to incorporating non-physical art forms, like films or songs, into magickal rituals, suggesting visualization techniques during the artwork's presentation.

TOPY's approach to sigil magick was not only about pushing creative boundaries but also about reclaiming art from traditional spaces like galleries, making it deeply personal and inherently magickal. Abrahamsson pointed out that the privacy of these creations, often destroyed to erase them from conscious memory, adds to their efficacy. This concept contrasts starkly with the contemporary trend of art being created for public consumption and validation on social media. He stressed the significance of creating art from a deeply personal space, infused with the creator's life force, and intended not for public display but as a sacred, personal object.

This exploration into sigil magick underscores the importance of personalization and creativity in magickal practices, demonstrating that the power of sigils lies not just in their visual form, but in the intent, process, and personal connection of the creator to their work.

---

60   This conversation took place during the Bali Art Magick retreat in Tabanan, Bali, Indonesia in December 2022.

EXERCISE: EXPANSIVE SIGILIZATION IN CREATIVE PRACTICE

Expansive sigilization embraces the idea that sigils, traditionally simple glyphs, can be any form of artwork, extending into various creative mediums. This exercise is designed to broaden the traditional approach to sigil creation, incorporating the personal creative processes of artists, writers, sculptors, and musicians. This method aligns with the belief that the power of a sigil lies not just in its form but in the intention and creative energy invested in it. It's about integrating your true will, your deepest intentions, and personal aesthetic into a tangible or intangible art form, making it a uniquely personal magickal act.

Needs:
- Your chosen artistic medium (canvas, clay, musical instrument, software, etc.)
- A private space conducive to creativity and magickal practice
- Tools specific to your chosen medium (paints, instruments, editing software, etc.)
- A journal or digital document for recording your process and reflections

Setup:
- **Creative Space Preparation:** Arrange your workspace to support focus and artistic flow.
- **Intention Setting:** Contemplate your true will or intention that you wish to manifest.
- **Material Gathering:** Assemble your artistic tools and materials relevant to your chosen medium.

The Path Within

Instructions:
- **Formulating Your Sigil:** Start by conceptualizing your sigil. It could be a piece of music, a sculpture, a painting, or any other form of art. Let this be guided by your intention.
- **Creative Process:** Engage in the creation of your sigil using your chosen medium. Allow your intuition and creativity to guide the process, infusing the artwork with your intention and energy.
- **Sigil Charging:** Once your artwork is complete, charge it with your intent. This can be through a ritual, meditation, or any personal method that symbolically activates the sigil's power.
- **Integration into Magickal Practice:** Use your charged sigil in your magickal workings. This could mean displaying the artwork, performing the piece of music, or incorporating the sculpture into your sacred space.
- **Reflective Recording:** Document the process, your feelings, insights, and the outcomes in your journal. This will help in understanding the effectiveness of your sigil and refining your practice.

Follow Through:
- After completing your sigil, engage in activities that ground you back into the mundane world. This could be as simple as tidying your workspace, taking a walk, or engaging in a hobby unrelated to your magickal practice.

Optional:
- **Non-Physical Sigils:** If your sigil is in a non-physical form (like a film or song), consider ways to integrate it into a ritual or meditative practice. This could involve visualizing the sigil during a significant moment or using it as a focal point in meditation.
- **Community Sharing:** While traditionally sigils are kept private, consider if sharing your artwork could amplify its power, especially if it aligns with your intention. This could be through a gallery, a performance, or even online, but always be mindful of the intention behind sharing.

- **Revisiting Sigils:** If you feel drawn to revisit a sigil you've created in the past, consider how reconnecting with it might reinforce or evolve the original intention. This can be particularly powerful for ongoing projects or long-term goals.

HYPERSIGILS

A *hypersigil* is another form of sigilized artwork. Grant Morrison, a chaos magician and comic-book writer re-envisioned the sigil and introduced the concept of the hypersigil. This concept takes the static image of the sigil and elevates it, incorporating elements such as characterization, drama, and plot to create a magickal narrative construction that weaves the story into a spell. The hypersigil imagines a transmedia story, inviting the reader to be part of a transformative experience.

The concept of a hypersigil is a powerful one—a feedback loop between an external persona and a primary self, capable of manifesting real changes in the world around us. Grant Morrison described hypersigils as a form of sigil extended into the fourth dimension, and his comic series *The Invisibles* is an example of such a creation. In the same vein, the internet offers us numerous opportunities to create our own hypersigils through blogging, social media updates, the choices we make defining our online persona, and more. These choices reflect and amplify our awareness of self and can have a profound impact on our lives in the real world.

I propose that you experiment and create your own hypersigil. This could take many forms—a poem, a story, a song, a dance—and requires a high level of absorption and concentration to be successful. The hypersigil is a dynamic model of the magician's universe, a hologram, or poppet which can be manipulated to bring about real changes. It is a powerful tool at our disposal—one that we should explore and experiment with.

The Path Within

This concept takes the static image of the sigil and elevates it, incorporating elements such as characterization, drama, and plot to create a magickal narrative, inviting the reader to be part of a transformative experience. Through blogging, social media updates, podcasts, and the choices we make defining our online persona, we can create our own hypersigils—a feedback loop between an external persona and a primary self. We can use symbols and archetypes to represent and bring about the desired change, creating a powerful visualization of what we desire to bring into our lives. By creating a powerful narrative artwork that represents our intentions, we can use the energy of the hypersigil to create positive changes in our life. The possibilities are endless—let us explore and experiment with this powerful tool.

EXERCISE: CRAFTING YOUR OWN HYPERSIGIL

This exercise draws inspiration from Grant Morrison's reinterpretation of sigils as narrative and story-based within a chaos magick framework. A hypersigil transforms a static symbol into a living story. It's an artistic and magickal process that creates a feedback loop between one's external persona and inner self, manifesting tangible changes in the external world. This exercise invites you to create your own hypersigil, harnessing the power of narrative and personal symbolism to catalyze change.

Needs:
- A creative medium of your choice (writing, drawing, music composition, etc.)
- Tools relevant to your chosen medium (pen and paper, musical instruments, digital software, etc.)
- A comfortable and inspiring environment for creative work
- A journal for planning and reflection

Jake Kobrin

Setup
- **Selection of Medium:** Choose a medium that resonates with you for crafting your hypersigil, such as storytelling, music, dance, or visual arts.
- **Space Preparation:** Arrange a conducive space for uninterrupted creative flow.
- **Conceptualization:** Think deeply about the intention or change you wish to manifest through your hypersigil.

Clear Instruction:
- **Narrative Development:** Begin by crafting a narrative or concept that embodies your intention. This could be a character's unfolding narrative in a story, a sequence in a dance, or a progression in a piece of music.
- **Artistic Creation:** Using your chosen medium, create the hypersigil. Let the narrative unfold, infusing it with personal symbols, emotions, and desires related to your intention.
- **Activation and Engagement:** Once your hypersigil is created, engage with it actively. If it's a story, read or tell it; if it's a song, sing or play it; if it's a dance, perform it. This engagement charges the hypersigil with your energy.
- **Integration into Daily Life:** Find ways to incorporate your hypersigil into your everyday life. This could be through regular interaction with your creation or by sharing it with others, depending on your intention.
- **Reflective Practice:** Document your process, feelings, and any changes you observe in your life related to the hypersigil in your journal.

Follow Through:
- After engaging with your hypersigil, it's essential to return to normalcy. Engage in grounding activities like walking, cooking, or other hobbies to balance your energy.

Optional:
- **Digital Expression:** Consider using digital platforms like blogs or social media to create hypersigils. Your online persona and updates can become a living, evolving hypersigil.
- **Collaborative Creation:** If you feel comfortable, collaborate with others to enhance the richness and complexity of your hypersigil.
- **Ongoing Development:** Hypersigils can evolve over time. Feel free to revisit and adapt your creation as your intentions and circumstances change.

PRELIMINARY PREPARATION FOR MAGICKAL RITUAL

Now that we've learned how to do sigil magick, let us set out to enact our first magickal working. A "working" is a system of rituals and spells designed to bring about a certain aim. However, before we can begin, we must undertake some meaningful preparatory measures. These measures should be carried out in advance of any working or ritual.

Now is the time to refer to the Desire List you have been developing in your journal. You should now possess the strongest expressions of your own distinct truth. Also, you may have gone through some journaling to unravel the path of your True Will, your essential role, and your mission in life.

Peruse your desires list and identify which aspirations harmonize together. Which are part of a bigger scheme for manifestation? Next, choose the ambition on the list that feels the most powerful, the most pressing, and that would most completely align with your True Will.

Let us continue by doing some writing on the subject of your "grand aim." To ensure success in achieving our desired outcome, it is of great importance to establish very exact goals and final results. To do this, we must make use of all of our senses and be as certain as possible. This idea is based on neurolinguistic programming. We must create our goals

Jake Kobrin

and outcomes as something uplifting and achievable, uncomplicated by others, and in the context of your designed environment. You can assist yourself in establishing exact outcomes by exploring these tips:

- Generate a positive, specific desire (i.e., expressing "I am wealthy" rather than "I am not poor").
- Make sure your goal is achievable by an action you can take on your own and not contingent on another individual.
- Imagine and write about the environment where the goal will be accomplished, and reflect on any necessary funding, timeline, or other specifics.
- Allow yourself to be as descriptive as you can when formulating the goal, using all of your senses. Ask yourself what you will hear, see, feel, smell, and taste when reaching the goal.
- Recite the many tiny steps that need to be undertaken to achieve the desired result. Consider all elements of it, from the materials needed to the abilities and characteristics required to develop.
- Accumulate a list of all of the necessary resources needed to obtain the desired goal. This could concern people, personal aptitudes, funds, and other material resources, as well as all relevant information.
- Undertake an ecology scan to identify any problems that could prevent the goal. For example, search for values, laws, and personal issues that could be impediments to success. Review Tarot cards or the I Ching for further knowledge related to the aim.
- With the list of mile markers that you have put together, decide on five essential steps that will demonstrate progress toward the desired goal.
- Jot down the endpoint and each of the stages, and then show them in a location that can be seen conveniently.
- Observe the written statement of intent and required steps, referring back to the planned list for guidance when needed.

The Path Within

DESIGNING AND ENACTING YOUR FIRST WORKING

By now, you should have cultivated a daily practice of meditation, as well as the foundational banishing and invoking rituals within a specially prepared ritual space. You should also have taken some time to reflect and determine your True Will and have been diligently reviewing your Desires List to gain clarity on what it is you truly want in life. You should also have kept up your daily routine of recording your dream journal and magickal diary. You have learned the importance of having clearly defined goals and the power of sigil magick. All these practices can be helpful for you to live your life to its fullest potential.

When it comes to manifesting your big desire, you should begin by creating five milestones as stepping stones to your goal. Using these milestones, create a sigil to represent each one. Next, dedicate a part of your daily practice to a special ritual designed to charge your sigils with intent, beginning with the furthest milestone in your future. For example, if your ambition is to become a famous musician, you should start with the sigil for "I am a famous musician," and end with the symbol for "I own a guitar" or whatever milestone is closest to becoming your reality. Although you can do this ritual at any time, it is generally suggested that you perform it in the morning. Nighttime is also a good time for this ritual, though it should be consistent throughout your working. Through regular practice, you'll become adept at meditating on and charging your sigils with the intent to reach your greatest goals.

Begin your daily ritual by preparing your space, maybe drinking some tea or coffee, taking a ritual bath or shower, and donning your robes. Most importantly, relax.

Next, perform the Qabalistic Cross facing your altar (which should be facing east), and place your sigil on the center of the altar.

Jake Kobrin

You can banish the space through a ritual such as the Lesser Banishing Ritual of the Pentagram, and then connect to the magickal force in whatever manner you please, such as through a general invocation.

Meditate for approximately thirty minutes in whatever asana you choose, using your sigil as the object of concentration. Then visualize the sigil vividly in your mind's eye as you focus on it, and if at any point you lose concentration, allow yourself to be drawn back to it. You can create a mantra from the sigil as described previously and repeat it internally as you focus.

Once the thirty-minute period of meditation is complete, close the ritual with the Qabalistic Cross and a banishing ritual, or, in the chaos magicians' style, laughter via a short and light-hearted comedy video that will make you chuckle.

Right after, take a few moments to record your experiences and procedures in your magickal diary. To ground yourself, you might want to eat a meal or a snack.

Once the ritual is officially finished, you can decide whether to burn the sigil during or immediately after the ritual is finished, keep them all together for the week and burn them at the end, or tape it onto your refrigerator or another place that is out of your conscious awareness. I personally prefer to burn my sigils after I charge them in ritual, but you may wish to experiment with these different approaches and see which one works best for you.

If you are to make strides toward your final goal, it is imperative to practice a ritual of this nature for several consecutive days. There is not a specific number of days you have to perform this ritual, but I find five days to be manageable and effective. Do not skip a day and wait to perform your working until you can be sure that you will not miss even one day of the process. If you do miss a day, make sure to perform the ritual on the next day instead.

Begin the process by empowering the sigils in the prescribed order, then make a note of your findings in a dedicated journal or diary. Above all, however, it is important to not forget that you must release any and all expectations after you finish the rituals. It is vital that you relinquish your longing for the result as much as you can, and to keep faith that the ritual

The Path Within

has already manifested. Letting go of your burden of craving achievement while in the middle of a ritual will help the process work in your favor.

EXERCISE: CRAFTING AND EXECUTING YOUR INITIAL MAGICKAL WORKING

This exercise is designed for those who have established a foundational practice in meditation, banishing, invoking rituals, and have a clear understanding of their True Will and desires. The focus is on creating and enacting a magickal working to manifest a significant personal desire, utilizing the power of sigil magick and ritual.

Needs:
- A list of five milestones related to your major desire
- Sigils representing each milestone
- A dedicated ritual space
- Ritual attire (such as robes)
- Items for space preparation
- A journal for recording experiences
- Tools for banishing and invoking rituals (as per your tradition)

Setup:
- **Milestone Identification:** Define five progressive milestones towards your primary goal.
- **Sigil Creation:** Develop a sigil for each milestone, starting from the most distant to the most immediate.
- **Ritual Space Preparation:** Ready your space for the ritual, including cleansing and setting up an altar facing east.
- **Consistent Timing:** Choose a consistent time for your ritual, either morning or evening.

Jake Kobrin

Instructions:
- **Ritual Initiation:** Begin by relaxing and preparing yourself. Drink tea or coffee, take a ritual bath, and dress in your ritual attire.
- **Space Cleansing:** Perform the Qabalistic Cross (or an equivalent) facing your altar. Place the first milestone sigil at the center of the altar.
- **Banishing Ritual:** Use a method like the Lesser Banishing Ritual of the Pentagram to cleanse your space.
- **Invocation:** Connect with the magickal force using a method of your choice (general invocation, specific deity, etc.).
- **Meditation:** Spend thirty minutes in meditation, focusing on the sigil. Use a mantra derived from the sigil if helpful. If distracted, gently return your focus to the sigil.
- **Closing Ritual:** End with the Qabalistic Cross and a banishing ritual. Alternatively, use laughter to close, such as watching a light-hearted comedy video.
- **Recording:** Immediately jot down your experiences and actions in your magickal diary.
- **Grounding:** Eat a snack or a meal to ground yourself.
- **Sigil Disposal:** Choose to either burn the sigil post-ritual, store it out of sight for a week, or place it somewhere unnoticed. Experiment to see which method resonates with you.

Follow Through:
- Perform this ritual daily for a set number of days (five is suggested). Ensure consistency without missing a day. After completing the ritual for each milestone, record your observations and let go of any attachment to the outcome, maintaining faith in the ritual's effectiveness.

Optional:
- **Variable Duration:** While five days is suggested, feel free to adjust the length of the working based on your personal rhythm and the complexity of your goal.

The Path Within

- **Alternative Sigil Disposal:** Besides burning, consider burying or releasing sigils in water as alternative methods of disposal.
- **Reflective Practice:** Regularly reflect on changes in your life related to the working and adapt your approach as needed.

TALISMANS AND AMULETS

Talismans and Amulets can be incredibly powerful and effective tools for manifesting our desires! They are physical objects that have been charged with magickal energy through a ritual and can come in the form of jewelry, stones, rocks, parchment scrolls, and silver cases. When creating a talisman, one can use any ritual they have learned and use it to imbue the talisman with the desired energy of their intention. The ritual of Invoking Archangel Raphael that we will explore later in this book, for example, can be used to create a powerful talisman that can be used in the manifestation of our desires for healing. Talismans and Amulets are powerful tools that can greatly aid us in achieving our goals.

There are many ways—some very complex—to create a talisman. The easiest and simplest way to create a talisman is this:

1. Hold the object you want to turn into a talisman in your hand.
2. Get centered and relaxed.
3. Begin to visualize your desired outcome.
4. Breathe deeply and with each inhale, imagine divine light streaming into your body and filling every cell.
5. With each long exhale, imagine this light, channeled from the visualization of your desired outcome, streaming through your hands and into and imbuing your object with magickal power. Stay with this process as long as you need.

One way to think of charging talismans is to see it as an act of Invocation, an opportunity to connect to and lock in a particular force, be it a planetary energy, a god or goddess, a sphere on the Tree of Life, or an Archangel. We will explore this more in the future. Talismans can be a way of keeping those properties with you at all times.

EXERCISE: CREATING AND CHARGING A TALISMAN

This exercise is about crafting a talisman, a physical object imbued with magickal energy to aid in manifesting desires. Talismans, often in the form of jewelry, stones, or inscribed items, serve as powerful tools for carrying the energy of your intentions.

Needs:
- An object to be transformed into a talisman (e.g., jewelry, stone, parchment)
- A quiet, comfortable space for the ritual
- Focus on a specific intention or desire

Setup:
- **Selection of Object:** Choose an item that resonates with your purpose.
- **Intention Setting:** Clearly define the intention or goal for your talisman.
- **Ritual Space Preparation:** Find a calm space where you can perform the ritual undisturbed.

Instructions:
- **Object Holding:** Begin by holding the talisman object in your hand.

The Path Within

- **Centering and Relaxation:** Take a moment to center yourself. Breathe deeply and relax your body and mind.
- **Visualization:** Clearly visualize the desired outcome you wish the talisman to assist with.
- **Charging the Talisman:** Inhale deeply, envisioning divine light entering your body and filling every cell. With each exhale, visualize this light, representing your intention, flowing from your hands into the talisman, charging it with magickal energy.
- **Duration:** Continue this process until you feel the object is fully charged. This could be a few minutes or longer, depending on your connection with the ritual.

Follow Through:
- After charging the talisman, take a few moments to ground yourself. You might want to eat something light or take a short walk. Carry or keep the talisman with you to maintain a connection with the intention it holds.

Optional:
- **Invocation Integration:** For those familiar with specific rituals, such as invoking Archangel Raphael, these can be integrated into the talisman charging process to align with specific energies (like healing in Raphael's case). We will explore this later.
- **Personalization:** Feel free to embellish or personalize your talisman to strengthen your connection with it. This could involve inscribing symbols, adding colors, or attaching meaningful items to it.
- **Regular Recharging:** Depending on your practice, you may choose to regularly recharge the talisman, especially during significant astrological events or personal milestones, to renew its energy.

CHAPTER NINE

DIVINATION

Divination, which is the art and practice of obtaining rarified information about the future and the gaining of insight and guidance through supernatural means, can be a valuable tool to help make more informed choices in life. Tarot cards, for example, can hold power as a guide to self-understanding. People began to use Tarot cards for divination after they were first introduced in Italy and France, which possibly connects back to the practices of the Romani people, likely brought to Europe from India. Regardless of its origin, one can use the Tarot to tap into the deeper meanings of the pictures on the cards, and it can also contribute to teaching valuable life lessons. We will look into the depths of using Tarot for divination, but only after first relinquishing ourselves to meditation and contemplation of the cards. Ultimately, we can find power in divination as a way to understand the present and prepare for the future.

As one looks to the mysterious, ever-changing nature of life and all its possibilities, divination may give us greater insight into understanding the events that occur in our lives. Tarot and oracle cards, the ancient *Chinese Book of Changes*, the I Ching, geomancy, runes, and many other methods have been used through the centuries as tools to provide us with further information and knowledge in interpreting the cycles and patterns of life. Though the practice of utilizing the cards for fortune-telling may not be as ancient as the cards themselves, this method of reaching beyond the physical world has nevertheless been adopted due to the persistent belief that all things are interconnected, and nothing occurs randomly. Although the I Ching is also quite profound, one particular tool that stands out above the rest is the Tarot; these cards possess symbolism that can provide a person with unique insight and unlock clue's to uncovering the greater patterns of our lives. Horary astrology, which is a recent fascination of mine, is also a remarkably effective form of divination, in which you cast a chart at the time a question is asked and interpret the chart in a specific way so as to divine an answer to your question.

THE TAROT

The Tarot is a deck of cards that has been used for centuries by occultists, mystics, and magicians for the purposes of divination and meditation. It has captivated the imaginations of many, from mere curiosity seekers and dabblers to famous artists, poets, magicians, occultists, and psychologists. Although many people who are unfamiliar with the Western Magickal Tradition think of Tarot cards as charming but strange devices for telling fortunes, the Tarot is in fact a complete and elaborate system for describing the hidden forces which underlie the universe. It is the key to all occult science as well as a blueprint for unlocking the various parts of the human psyche. A comprehensive study of the Tarot is a task which is very nearly

The Path Within

equal to acquiring a college degree in both psychology and theology. Each Tarot card is an astral mirror of the human mind, and each is also an astral mirror of the human soul.

True Tarot cards are not to be confused with *oracle cards* that can be found in many different forms in the marketplace. The Tarot is a deck of seventy-eight cards with twenty-two of them called the Major Arcana, while the other fifty-six are the Minor Arcana. The four suits of the Minor Arcana (Wands, Cups, Swords, and Pentacles) relate to the four Elements: Fire, Water, Air, and Earth. Each suit has four Court Cards: King, Queen, Knight, and Page, which relate to the Tetragrammaton, the unpronounceable name of God: YHVH. The Ace through Ten of each Minor suit relate to the ten Sephiroth on the Tree of Life. The four suits of the Minor Arcana also relate to the four Elements, the four magickal weapons of the magician, and other concepts.

The Major Arcana or "big secrets" are also rich in symbolism. They relate to the twenty-two letters of the Hebrew alphabet, the twenty-two paths on the Tree of Life, the twenty-two archetypes of the subconscious mind, and the twenty-two trumps of the Tarocchi, an Italian Renaissance card game which was the forerunner of the Tarot. The Tarot is a powerful tool for meditation, and it can also be used for divination, either by reading the cards yourself or by having someone else read them for you. In this book we will explore both methods.

The Tarot is an extremely deep subject and could occupy a lifetime of study all of its own. When you begin to draw the cards, before you reach for a book or a website, or the tiny booklet that came with your cards, ask yourself, "what do I see here?", "what do I feel here?", and "what story is this card telling me?", and write down your impressions for at least a paragraph or two in your diary.

Filmmaker and Tarot expert Alejandro Jodorowsky, in his influential book on Tarot,[61] emphasizes forging this personal connection with the cards prior to consulting pre-established meanings of them. Some creativity and free association are required here, as well as careful obser-

---

61   Jodorowsky, Alejandro, and Marianne Costa, *The Way of Tarot: The Spiritual Teacher in the Cards* (Destiny Books, 2009)

☾ 267 ☽

vation. At the end of the day, your definition and intuitive impressions of the cards is what matters, not any high-brow official definitions of the cards. All of the definitions of the Tarot that exist are interpretations, and your interpretations are as valid as any. For this book, I recommend establishing a personal connection with the cards for a given period of time before memorizing more established meanings and interpretations.

THE ORIGINS OF THE TAROT

The roots of the Tarot are shrouded in mystery and intrigue. Various theories abound about its origins, ranging from Atlantis to ancient Egypt, and even as a vessel for preserving Jewish wisdom (namely the Torah). These tales, predominantly found in occult literature and legends, lack concrete historical proof. The earliest known Tarot deck, dating back to the fifteenth century, was crafted by the artist Bonifacio Bembo. Often referred to as the "Visconti Tarot," this deck is displayed in the Metropolitan Museum of Art in New York City.[62]

This deck is composed of four suits with fourteen cards each, making up the Minor Arcana, and an additional set of twenty-two symbolic cards known as the Major Arcana. The Major Arcana's images encompass a range of themes including virtues, religious or mythological stories, societal archetypes, and ethical teachings.

Historically, the Tarot was primarily used for gaming and fortune-telling. However, in the eighteenth century, occultist Antoine Court de Gebelin proclaimed it as a remnant of the Book of Thoth, an ancient Egyptian compendium of knowledge.[63] In the nineteenth century, French

---

62 Pollack, Rachel, *Seventy-Eight Degrees of Wisdom: A Book of Tarot* (Weiser Books, 2007)

63 Crowley, Aleister, *The Book of Thoth: A Short Essay on the Tarot of the Egyptians* (Weiser Books, 1974)

The Path Within

occultist Alphonse Louis Constant, better known as Eliphas Levi, associated the Tarot with the Qabalah.[64] In contemporary times, the Tarot is often viewed as a tool for personal development, aiding in self-understanding and life insights.

This book delves into the Tarot perspectives established by the Golden Dawn and its associates, including Arthur Edward Waite and Aleister Crowley. These figures built upon the foundational ideas of Levi and Court de Gebelin, creating their interpretations of the Qabalistic Tarot.

DIFFERENCES IN TAROT DECKS

The Tarot, with its rich history spanning centuries, is divided into two main sections: the Minor Arcana, consisting of the suits (Wands, Cups, Swords, and Pentacles), and the Major Arcana, often referred to as the "Major Keys" or trumps. While modern Tarot decks closely resemble their fifteenth-century predecessors, the imagery on the cards has evolved, maintaining the foundational concepts with varying artistic interpretations.

In this book, our focus will be on the 1909 Tarot deck created by Arthur Edward Waite, commonly known as the Rider-Waite or Waite-Smith deck. Waite's deck is notable for its unique depictions of several trumps. For example, the traditional Sun card often features two children in a garden, but Waite's version depicts a single child riding a horse out of the garden. Critics argued that Waite was imprinting his personal vision onto the cards, a claim that seems plausible given Waite's strong belief in his interpretations.

The artistic vision of Pamela Colman Smith, the illustrator for Waite's deck, significantly contributed to its distinctiveness. She introduced detailed scenes to all the cards, including the numbered cards of the Minor Arcana.

---

64   Wang, Robert, *The Qabalistic Tarot: A Textbook of Mystical Philosophy* (Weiser Books, 1983)

Jake Kobrin

This was a departure from earlier decks, which typically displayed simple geometric designs for these "pip" cards, with the Major Arcana referred to as Trumps.

An example of Smith's unique approach is seen in the Ten of Swords, which portrays a man under a dark cloud with ten swords in his back and legs. The exact origins of these designs remain unclear. Whether Waite himself conceptualized these designs, particularly the Major Arcana, or if he guided Smith with ideas and qualities, leaving her to create the scenes, is still a topic of debate. Waite described his deck as the "rectified Tarot," suggesting that his designs restored the true meanings of the cards. He often criticized the versions of his predecessors and believed that his deck, possibly influenced by his involvement in secret societies, revealed deeper meanings of the Tarot.

The Waite-Smith deck was chosen for this book primarily for its innovative and meaningful depictions. Additionally, the transformation in the Minor Arcana allows for more interpretative freedom, moving away from rigid traditional meanings. Smith's illustrations invite engagement with the subconscious and personal experience, providing a dynamic and evolving understanding of the cards.

While numerous Tarot decks exist, each with unique attributes and interpretations, this book will focus on decks within the traditional seventy-eight card Tarot system. Some of the other significant Tarot decks available include the Thoth deck and the Marseilles Tarot. Each of these decks presents a distinct perspective of the universe, encapsulated within the symbolic language of the Tarot. While oracle decks, which can vary in the number of cards, offer their own value, they fall outside the scope of this book.

EXERCISE: INTUITIVE TAROT EXPLORATION BEFORE LEARNING THE TRADITIONAL MEANINGS OF THE CARDS

Before consulting any guidebooks, approach the Tarot with fresh eyes. Draw a card and ponder questions like "what do I see here?", "what feelings does this evoke?", and "what story is this card telling me?". Without consulting any guidebooks, write down your observations and feelings about the card in a journal, fostering a personal bond with the Tarot. Keep your journal entries for future reference. Over time, you'll be able to see patterns in your interpretations and how they align with or differ from traditional meanings. This exercise encourages a personal and intuitive connection with the Tarot, inspired by the methods of Alejandro Jodorowsky. It's designed to help you engage with the cards on a deeper level, prioritizing your own insights over established meanings.

Tarot Fundamentals

All Tarot decks are formulated in the same way. Each have seventy-eight cards, consisting of twenty-two Major Arcana cards and fifty-six Minor Arcana cards (ten cards in each of the four suits, plus four court cards in each of the four suits). In this section, I will briefly explain some of the fundamental ideas and concepts of the Tarot and how it is structured.

Major Arcana (The Trumps)

The Tarot archetypes represented in the Major Arcana are pictures that represent life and the stages and experiences we all go through. It's meant to be the story of one's journey through life starting as The Fool (young, pure energy in spirit form), moving through events and cycles and finding completion in The World (the end of our life cycle). This is often referred to as The Fool's Journey. While there are twenty-two Major Arcana cards, they are technically numbered I–XXI in Roman numerals, with The Fool

Jake Kobrin

always being either numbered 0 or, in some cases, without a number at all. The Death card, usually number XIII, is also without a number in some decks. It's also worth noting that in Crowley's Thoth Deck, some of the numbers and names of the cards were changed.[65]

The Hebrew Alphabet and The Tree of Life
You do not need to memorize the Hebrew Alphabet in order to become a good Tarot reader. However, understanding the correlation between the Hebrew Alphabet and the Major Arcana of the Tarot will help to deepen your understanding of The Tarot and its relationship to the Qabalah. It isn't likely that you already know the deeper symbolism of the Hebrew Alphabet as it pertains to the Qabalah, but as you learn about and strengthen your understanding of the Hebrew Alphabet, you can cross-reference the symbols of both the Hebrew Alphabet and the Major Arcana of the Tarot (and the paths they both represent on the Tree of Life) to broaden your symbolic associations.

The Four Suits
The minor arcana of the Tarot is broken up into four suits, similar to those of a regular playing card deck. These four suits of the Tarot are the Wands, the Swords, the Pentacles (or Coins), and the Cups. They correspond to the four Elements, the formula of YHVH, and the Four Qabalistic Worlds in the following way:

- Atziluth, Yod (י), the Element of Fire, the Wands
- Briah, Heh (ה), the Element of Water, the Cups
- Yetzirah, Vav (ו), the Element of Air, the Swords
- Assiah, Heh (final) (ה), the Element of Earth, the Pentacles

Minor Arcana
Minor cards describe the people, events, feelings, and circumstances we encounter on our personal Fool's Journey. It represents events that are

---

65   DuQuette, Lon Milo, *Understanding Aleister Crowley's Thoth Tarot* (Weiser Books, 2003)

The Path Within

within the control of the individual and indicate how you do something. The Minor Arcana closely resembles a traditional deck of playing cards, made up of four suits, including the Queen, King and Knight of each suit, plus the addition of Pages or Princesses. In Crowley's Thoth Deck, there are no Kings, but rather Page, Princess, Queen, and Knight.

The Court Cards

There are Elemental attributions to each of the court cards. They are as follows:

- **Kings:** Element of Air
- **Queens:** Element of Water
- **Knights:** Element of Fire
- **Pages:** Element of Earth

As they go through the different suits, they will be attributed as the Air of Fire (King of Wands), the Water of Fire (Queen of Wands), and so on. We will explore more deeply the attributions and meanings and uses of the court cards in readings later on.

THE TAROT CONTEMPLATION RITUAL

There is no quick or easy way to learn Tarot. Tarot, like language, only comes with time and experience. As you work with the Tarot more and more, you will notice more and more about the cards and relate the archetypes to your personal experiences. This marriage of the Tarot with your actual life and noticing when you see themes represented playing out in your life is the best way to learn the cards, in my opinion.

After you have had time to meditate with each of the cards and contemplate their meaning, you can begin to look into formalized interpretations of the cards. What is most important is your relationship to the cards.

Jake Kobrin

What is important is what they mean to you, not what they mean officially. You'll see in this exercise that I permit you to look at official references for the meanings of the cards, but not until after you have thoroughly contemplated those cards and written your interpretations down first.

1. The first step is to cast space. If you would like to do a banishing ritual, you can perform one, or you can light incense, do a short meditation, or whatever may clear your mind. You might also want to perform a ritual bath and to put on your robes, if you have them.

2. Next, begin to shuffle the cards in your hands. There is no right or wrong way to do this. Personally, I like to shuffle the deck the same as you would a deck of playing cards. Some people prefer to shuffle the cards in a more organic way. Whatever feels right to you is okay.

3. Next spread out all of the cards in a line, facing down so that you cannot see them. Hold your left hand over your heart, and with your right hand, pick two cards that you feel intuitively drawn toward. There is no wrong way to choose your cards. For me, I feel a bit of a buzz, like an electrical current over the card, and that is how I know which to choose. Use your intuition for this.

4. After you pick the two cards, turn them face up so you can see them.

5. Now begin to interpret them. Before you reach towards external sources of information, such as books or using sources online, ask yourself what you notice about the cards. What do they feel like to you? What associations do you personally have to the symbols in the cards—the characters, the colors, the shapes? Contemplate how these symbols and impressions relate to your life experience. Most importantly, what narrative can you construct from the interaction of the two cards together? This is an exercise in creative thinking.

6. I would like you to dedicate a journal specifically to the Tarot, and each day you pull your cards, I'd like you to write down the two cards you pulled, what you think the cards mean separately, and what kind of a story the cards tell together.

The Path Within

7. After you have contemplated the cards on your own, you can look at other sources for interpretation, including the little book that came with your Tarot cards. If you are using the Waite-Smith deck or one of the many decks based on it, I recommend the website Biddy Tarot, as I think they have a very good sense of the cards, and I personally benefit from their interpretations. How has your interpretation shifted after reading other people's interpretations of the cards? What narrative can you now create from the interaction of the two cards together?

8. If you have arrived at a new understanding, you can then write this below your interpretations that you made intuitively through your observations.

Sometimes the meanings of the cards are very clear, and others less so. As with all things, your ability to interpret the cards will grow stronger with time (you will begin to be able to "speak Tarot"). It's important to trust your own interpretations over those of other sources. Your intuition is the authority when it comes to Tarot.

I'll give an example: I drew a couple of cards from one of my decks. I pulled The Lovers and the Seven of Swords.

I associate The Lovers, especially in the context of this deck, with union and romantic love, and I associate the Seven of Swords with deception, thievery, and sneakiness. If I pulled these two cards as my daily contemplation, I would think about how I or my lover might be being deceitful to each other. Is there any cheating occurring, or a lack of honesty or faithfulness? What am I withholding from my lover, what is not being said, or how am I even deceiving myself about the relationship? As you can see, it is the interaction of the two cards and the narrative they form that matter.

I might take some time to write about that, how it might relate to what is happening in my life, and what clarity or questions arise in me from contemplating these cards within my diary.

Do this daily. Over time you will develop a more and more thorough understanding of the cards and their meanings.

It is inevitable that you will eventually draw some unfavorable or harsh cards, like the Ten of Swords or The Tower, so prepare yourself for that! You don't have to let the cards affect you too strongly. These are universal situations to contemplate.

THE MAJOR ARCANA IN A READING

The Major Arcana cards of the Tarot, numbered from 0 to XXI, each embody distinct meanings and stages of life.

- **The Fool (0):** Represents innocence and beginnings, symbolizing the blank slate of new experiences.
- **The Magician (I):** Symbolizes willpower and magick, the power to manifest and transform.
- **The High Priestess (II):** Embodies intuition and the subconscious, delving into hidden knowledge.
- **The Empress (III):** Stands for motherly love and nurture, the embodiment of fertility and abundance.
- **The Emperor (IV):** Represents authority and control, symbolizing structure and stability.
- **The Hierophant (V):** Reflects tradition and learning, the bridge between the divine and the mundane.
- **The Lovers (VI):** Signifies union and harmony, the merging of opposites and choices.
- **The Chariot (VII):** Embodies self-control and determination, driving towards victory.

The Path Within

- **Strength (VIII):** Symbolizes courage and mastery over oneself, the taming of the beast within.
- **The Hermit (IX):** Stands for solitude and contemplation, the quest for inner wisdom.
- **The Wheel of Fortune (X):** Reflects the inevitability of change and the cycles of fate.
- **Justice (XI):** Represents cause and effect, the balancing of scales and fairness.
- **The Hanged Man (XII):** Symbolizes letting go and sacrificing control for greater insight.
- **Death (XIII):** Embodies endings and transformation, the necessary conclusion for new beginnings.
- **Temperance (XIV):** Reflects balance and moderation, blending opposites for harmony.
- **The Devil (XV):** Stands for materialism and addiction, the chains of physical desire.
- **The Tower (XVI):** Represents sudden upheaval and the destruction of ego, a dramatic shift.
- **The Star (XVII):** Symbolizes hope, faith, and inspiration, seen as a guiding "star."
- **The Moon (XVIII):** Reflects the unconscious, illusions, and the spiritual "dark night of the soul."
- **The Sun (XIX):** Embodies clarity, success, and confidence, the light after darkness.
- **Judgement (XX):** Signifies honest self-evaluation and the call to a new paradigm or awakening.
- **The World (XXI):** Represents wholeness, completion, and fulfillment, the culmination of the journey and spiritual ascension.

THE FOOL'S JOURNEY

The Major Arcana of the Tarot unfolds a narrative akin to our quest through life, often called "The Fool's Journey." These cards serve as a visual narrative of life's events and existential cycles, starting with the untapped potential of The Fool (0) and culminating in the cycle's completion with The World (XXI).

The journey commences with The Fool, akin to a newborn, eager to explore and learn. They first meet The Magician (I) and The High Priestess (II), representing the duality of the conscious and subconscious, the masculine and feminine energies within. The nurturing Empress (III) follows, symbolizing motherly care and nature's bounty. The Emperor (IV) then introduces structure and authority, guiding The Fool in understanding life's frameworks.

The Fool, now emerging from childhood, encounters societal norms and traditions through The Hierophant (V). Love and inner harmony are explored with The Lovers (VI), confronting the Fool with the concepts of Jung's Anima and Animus, the internal feminine and masculine. Here, The Fool confronts personal beliefs and values, stepping beyond societal norms to forge an individual path.

As an adult, The Fool embodies the traits of The Chariot (VII), exuding confidence and control. Life's challenges call for inner fortitude, represented by Strength (VIII), teaching The Fool about passion management and self-discipline.

Deep reflection ushers in with The Hermit (IX), prompting The Fool to seek life's greater truths. The Wheel of Fortune (X) symbolizes life's inevitable changes and cycles. Justice (XI) demands The Fool to confront past actions and decide on future paths.

Confronting life's hardships, The Fool learns humility and acceptance, symbolized by The Hanged Man (XII) and Death (XIII). Temperance

(XIV) brings balance, harmonizing The Fool's being. The Devil (XV) then challenges with material temptations, highlighting the dangers of ignorance and addiction.

The Tower (XVI) shatters illusions with a lightning bolt of knowledge, leading to The Star (XVII), which offers hope and inspiration. However, The Moon (XVIII) presents illusions and emotional ambiguity, challenging The Fool's discernment.

The Sun (XIX) brings clarity and joy, illuminating The Fool's path with understanding and confidence. Judgment (XX) signifies self-realization and decision-making, urging The Fool to embrace their true self and values.

Finally, The World (XXI) marks the journey's end, where The Fool emerges integrated, whole, and fulfilled, ready to share their gifts with the world. The Fool's Journey illustrates the evolution of The Fool, a never-ending process of self-discovery and potential, embodying the essence of life itself.

TAROT ATTRIBUTIONS

The concept of attribution is a major part of Tarot, it's clear to see that each Tarot card has its own sovereign power, yet also has pathways to connect to further symbols and associations. With this understanding, you can unlock the information you need to gain a richer understanding of each symbol, as well as purposeful meditations and readings with the cards.

The Major Arcana are primarily linked to one of the paths of the Qabalistic Tree of Life, each path numbered and attributed to a certain Hebrew letter as part of the Hebrew alphabet. For example, path eleven is attributed to The Fool and the letter Aleph. Although The Fool is the first Tarot card, numbered 0, it is the eleventh path because the first ten paths are concerned with the ten sephiroth. It's not just the Tree of Life that has attributions of the Tarot cards, but also the astrological signs and planets. This is important to remember, as it helps us to understand the cards and how they relate to the zodiacal signs and the planets above us. Furthermore, four of the cards—The Fool, The Hanged Man, Justice, and The World—share the attributes of the four Elements.

Cards share the same attributes as the other symbols that they correspond to. The Strength card of the Tarot, for example, which corresponds to Leo, reflects the same underlying qualities of Leo, the Sun, and fixed Fire. They are connected through the ancient and sacred energies of astrology, all of which share the same fundamental attributes, emanating a brilliant and all-encompassing light. Just as the Sun sends out its warmth to the world and Leo is symbolized by its strength, so too does the Strength card encapsulate both the powerful dynamism of fixed Fire and the luminous, creative spirit of the Sun.

Paths of the Tree of Life and the Tarot's Attributions to Astrology

Tarot transcends its common perception as a tool for divination or a collection of beautiful cards. It represents a key to unlocking secret mysteries. In this section, we delve into the deeper secrets of Tarot, exploring its connections to the spiritual journey of the soul and its relationship with other symbolic systems like the Qabalistic Tree of Life, astrology, and the Hebrew alphabet.

Consider the Tarot in relation to the Qabalistic Tree of Life. You don't need to memorize the Tarot attributions to the Tree; it's more for reference. However, understanding the meanings of the Sephiroth or Spheres, is crucial. These Spheres represent dimensions of consciousness, with Paths acting as conduits to these dimensions, much like a railway system.

The Tree of Life is analogous to an extensive train network. We start our path up the Tree at Malkuth, the Kingdom, symbolizing our current 3D earthly plane. As we ascend the tree, we traverse various Tarot paths, akin to train lines, guiding us toward Kether, the Crown. This Sphere represents the pinnacle of consciousness and unity with the source.

There's a notable correspondence between the twenty-two Major Arcana cards and the twenty-two pathways of the Tree of Life, each linked to one of the twenty-two letters of the Hebrew alphabet. This connection enriches the Tarot with a multitude of symbols and attributes.

The Path Within

The Tarot, the Qabalistic Tree of Life, and astrology, though distinct, all map the same celestial territory. Understanding zodiacal signs and planets allows for a deeper exploration of the Major Arcana archetypes, each associated with a specific planet or sign. Beyond this, there are numerous other attributions, including colors, gemstones, incense, and plants, each serving a purpose in ceremony and ritual. By grasping the connections between the paths, Hebrew letters, and astrological symbols of the Major Arcana, you gain a profound insight into the Tarot.

Here is a table listing the Major Arcana cards, their corresponding zodiac signs, planets, and Elements:

Major Arcana Card	Zodiac Sign	Zodiac Symbol	Planet	Element
The Fool			Uranus (♅)	Air
The Magician			Mercury (☿)	
The High Priestess			Moon (☽)	
The Empress			Venus (♀)	
The Emperor	Aries	♈		
The Hierophant	Taurus	♉		
The Lovers	Gemini	♊		
The Chariot	Cancer	♋		
Strength	Leo	♌		
The Hermit	Virgo	♍		
The Wheel of Fortune			Jupiter (♃)	
Justice	Libra	♎		
The Hanged Man			Neptune (♆)	Water

Jake Kobrin

Major Arcana Card	Zodiac Sign	Zodiac Symbol	Planet	Element
Death	Scorpio	♏		
Temperance	Sagittarius	♐		
The Devil	Capricorn	♑		
The Tower			Mars (♂)	
The Star	Aquarius	♒		
The Moon	Pisces	♓		
The Sun			Sun (☉)	
Judgement			Pluto (♇)	Fire
The World			Saturn (♄)	Earth

While understanding the Tarot's deeper meanings and attributions can be extensive, with even more insights available in esoteric texts like *Liber 777*, remember to take your time. Integrating these attributions into rituals and ceremonies can add significant depth to your Tarot practice.

The Minor Arcana

The Minor Arcana cards of the Tarot deck represent the daily challenges and experiences of life. Despite their designation as "minor," these cards hold significant power in shaping our day-to-day affairs, offering insights into current events and guiding us toward achieving our goals.

The Minor Arcana is comprised of four suits, each connected to an Element and a corresponding Archetypal World in the Qabalistic tradition:

- **Pentacles:** Associated with Assiah (action/doing) and represented by the Hebrew letter Heh-Final (ה). Pentacles focus on work, finances, and material aspects of life.
- **Swords:** Linked to Yetzirah (formation/thinking) and symbolized by the letter Vav (ו). Swords pertain to the domains of the mind and intellect.

The Path Within

- **Cups:** Connected to Briah (creation/feeling) and denoted by the letter Heh (ה). Cups deal with emotions and relationships.
- **Wands:** Corresponding to Atziluth (emanation/spirit) and represented by the letter Yod (י). Wands are related to willpower, energy, and creativity.

Each suit progresses through cards numbered from Ace to ten, correlating to the spheres on the Tree of Life, with the Ace representing Kether, the Divine Crown. Additionally, each suit contains four court cards, embodying various personality traits that might be expressed in different situations.

All of these cards have many complex meanings, but here is a brief summation of the cards.

Wands

- **Ace of Wands:** This card symbolizes the birth of creativity and enthusiasm, akin to a spark igniting a flame. It's about seizing new opportunities with zeal, much like an artist finding sudden inspiration. (Thoth Title: The Root of the Powers of Fire)
- **Two of Wands:** Represents a moment of decision-making and future planning, much like a strategist mapping out their next move. It embodies the power of choice and direction. (Thoth Title: Dominion)
- **Three of Wands:** Symbolizes the establishment and expansion of plans and ideas, similar to a business owner seeing their company grow. It reflects foresight and preparedness. (Thoth Title: Virtue)
- **Four of Wands:** This card is about celebration and harmony, akin to a family enjoying a festive gathering. It signifies the joy and satisfaction of achieved goals. (Thoth Title: Completion)
- **Five of Wands:** Indicates competition and conflict, like rivals in a sporting event. It suggests challenges but also the growth that comes from overcoming them. (Thoth Title: Strife)
- **Six of Wands:** Represents victory and acclaim, as when an inventor receives accolades for their innovation. It speaks to success and public recognition. (Thoth Title: Victory)

Jake Kobrin

- **Seven of Wands:** Symbolizes resilience and courage in adversity, akin to a defender standing their ground against odds. It's about protecting one's stance or beliefs. (Thoth Title: Valour)
- **Eight of Wands:** Indicates swift action and rapid progress, like a runner sprinting towards the finish line. It represents momentum and quick developments. (Thoth Title: Swiftness)
- **Nine of Wands:** Represents resilience and endurance, akin to a marathon runner persisting through fatigue. It's about preparedness and fortitude. (Thoth Title: Strength)
- **Ten of Wands:** Symbolizes the burden of responsibilities, like an overloaded worker. It suggests the need to reassess one's commitments. (Thoth Title: Oppression)
- **Page of Wands:** Embodies exploration and discovery, similar to a young student exploring a new field of study. It suggests the beginning of an adventure or creative project. (Thoth Title: Princess of the Shining Flame)
- **Knight of Wands:** Represents a daring and adventurous spirit, like a young entrepreneur embarking on a new venture. It suggests energy and passion but warns against recklessness. (Thoth Title: Prince of the Chariot of Fire)
- **Queen of Wands:** Symbolizes confidence and vibrancy, akin to a successful leader inspiring their team. It represents boldness and determination. (Thoth Title: Queen of the Thrones of Flame)
- **King of Wands:** Embodies leadership and vision, like a CEO steering their company to success. It suggests charisma and the ability to motivate others. (Thoth Title: Lord of the Flame and the Lightning)

Cups

- **Ace of Cups:** Represents the beginning of emotional experiences, like the first stirrings of love. It symbolizes new relationships or emotional awakenings. (Thoth Title: The Root of the Powers of Water)

The Path Within

- **Two of Cups:** Symbolizes a union or partnership, akin to a deep and meaningful relationship forming. It's about connection and mutual understanding. (Thoth Title: Love)
- **Three of Cups:** This card is about community and friendship, like old friends reuniting to share joy. It represents celebrations and emotional bonds. (Thoth Title: Abundance)
- **Four of Cups:** Indicates contemplation and reassessment, similar to an individual pausing to reflect on their life's path. It suggests reevaluation of one's emotional state. (Thoth Title: Luxury)
- **Five of Cups:** Represents loss and disappointment, akin to mourning a missed opportunity. It's about learning from emotional setbacks and looking towards what remains. (Thoth Title: Disappointment)
- **Six of Cups:** Symbolizes nostalgia and looking back, like revisiting childhood memories. It suggests innocence and the comfort of the familiar. (Thoth Title: Pleasure)
- **Seven of Cups:** Represents choices and illusions, like a dreamer envisioning various paths. It suggests the need to ground dreams in reality. (Thoth Title: Debauch)
- **Eight of Cups:** Indicates a departure or moving on, similar to leaving a job or relationship that no longer serves. It's about seeking deeper meaning and letting go. (Thoth Title: Indolence)
- **Nine of Cups:** Symbolizes contentment and fulfillment, akin to enjoying the rewards of one's efforts. It represents satisfaction and gratitude. (Thoth Title: Happiness)
- **Ten of Cups:** Represents emotional abundance and family bliss, like a harmonious family celebration. It suggests joy, peace, and familial contentment. (Thoth Title: Satiety)
- **Page of Cups:** Embodies curiosity and emotional exploration, like a young artist experimenting with new mediums. It suggests the beginning of an emotional or creative pursuit. (Thoth Title: Princess of the Waters)
- **Knight of Cups:** Represents a romantic and idealistic pursuit, akin to a suitor wooing their beloved. It suggests charm and allure but

Jake Kobrin

warns against being overly fanciful. (Thoth Title: Prince of the Chariot of the Waters)

- **Queen of Cups:** Symbolizes emotional depth and intuition, like a therapist providing compassionate counsel. It represents empathy and understanding. (Thoth Title: Queen of the Thrones of the Waters)
- **King of Cups:** Embodies emotional maturity and control, like a counselor guiding others through challenges. It suggests wisdom and emotional leadership. (Thoth Title: Lord of the Waves and the Waters)

Swords

- **Ace of Swords:** Represents mental clarity and breakthroughs, akin to an epiphany or sudden realization. It's about sharp intellect and clear thinking. (Thoth Title: The Root of the Powers of Air)
- **Two of Swords:** Symbolizes difficult decisions and stalemates, like a diplomat facing a challenging negotiation. It suggests balance and the need for impartiality. (Thoth Title: Peace)
- **Three of Swords:** Indicates heartache and sorrow, akin to experiencing a painful separation or betrayal. It's about dealing with emotional pain and grief. (Thoth Title: Sorrow)
- **Four of Swords:** Represents rest and recovery, like taking a sabbatical to rejuvenate one's spirit. It suggests a pause for reflection and recuperation. (Thoth Title: Truce)
- **Five of Swords:** Symbolizes conflict and tension, akin to a disagreement escalating into an argument. It suggests caution in conflicts and the potential for hollow victories. (Thoth Title: Defeat)
- **Six of Swords:** Represents a movement towards healing, like moving to a new place for a fresh start. It suggests moving away from turmoil towards peace. (Thoth Title: Science)
- **Seven of Swords:** Indicates deception and strategy, akin to a strategist planning a covert move. It suggests the need for caution and vigilance. (Thoth Title: Futility)

The Path Within

- **Eight of Swords:** Symbolizes restriction and entrapment, like feeling stuck in a limiting situation. It suggests the need to find a way out of self-imposed constraints. (Thoth Title: Interference)
- **Nine of Swords:** Represents anxiety and worry, akin to lying awake at night troubled by fears. It suggests the need for confronting one's inner fears and seeking support. (Thoth Title: Cruelty)
- **Ten of Swords:** Symbolizes defeat and endings, like the final scene of a tragedy. It suggests the end of a cycle and the necessity of moving on. (Thoth Title: Ruin)
- **Page of Swords:** Embodies curiosity and mental agility, like a student eagerly learning a new subject. It suggests vigilance and a thirst for knowledge. (Thoth Title: Princess of the Rushing Winds)
- **Knight of Swords:** Represents ambition and assertiveness, akin to a young professional climbing the career ladder. It suggests determination but warns against aggression. (Thoth Title: Prince of the Chariot of the Winds)
- **Queen of Swords:** Symbolizes clear communication and objectivity, like a judge presiding over a court. It represents honesty and intellectual clarity. (Thoth Title: Queen of the Thrones of Air)
- **King of Swords:** Embodies leadership and intellectual authority, akin to a respected academic or lawyer. It suggests rationality and ethical judgment. (Thoth Title: Lord of the Winds and Breezes)

Pentacles/Coins

- **Ace of Pentacles:** Represents new financial opportunities and material gain, like receiving a lucrative job offer. It's about the manifestation of wealth and security. (Thoth Title: The Root of the Powers of Earth)
- **Two of Pentacles:** Symbolizes adaptability and balance, akin to a business owner managing multiple projects. It suggests juggling responsibilities with skill. (Thoth Title: Change)
- **Three of Pentacles:** Represents collaboration and skill development, like an artist working on a commissioned piece. It suggests craftsmanship and the value of teamwork. (Thoth Title: Work)

Jake Kobrin

- **Four of Pentacles:** Indicates security and control, like a saver guarding their nest egg. It suggests stability but warns against being overly possessive or miserly. (Thoth Title: Power)
- **Five of Pentacles:** Symbolizes hardship and need, akin to facing financial challenges. It suggests seeking support and recognizing the value of perseverance. (Thoth Title: Worry)
- **Six of Pentacles:** Represents generosity and sharing of wealth, like a benefactor donating to a cause. It suggests fairness in financial dealings and the joy of giving. (Thoth Title: Success)
- **Seven of Pentacles:** Indicates patience and long-term planning, like a farmer waiting for the harvest. It suggests perseverance and the foresight to reap future rewards. (Thoth Title: Failure)
- **Eight of Pentacles:** Symbolizes dedication and mastery, akin to an apprentice perfecting a craft. It suggests hard work and attention to detail in pursuit of excellence. (Thoth Title: Prudence)
- **Nine of Pentacles:** This card reflects the satisfaction of achieving prosperity through hard work. Imagine an artist stepping back to admire a masterpiece that has taken years to complete, a testament to their dedication and skill. (Thoth Title: Gain)
- **Ten of Pentacles:** Symbolizes the culmination of material success and the joys of family legacy. It's like the heartwarming scenes at a family reunion where generations come together, celebrating their shared heritage and prosperity. (Thoth Title: Wealth)
- **Page of Pentacles:** Represents the eagerness to learn and the pursuit of tangible achievements. Picture a young, ambitious graduate, diploma in hand, ready to conquer the world with their newfound knowledge and aspirations. (Thoth Title: Princess of the Echoing Hills)
- **Knight of Pentacles:** This card embodies the virtues of patience, reliability, and thoroughness in work. Envision a skilled artisan meticulously crafting a piece of fine jewelry, where every detail is carefully considered and executed. (Thoth Title: Lord of the Wild and Fertile Land)

- **Queen of Pentacles:** Reflects the embodiment of nurturing and practical care. She is like a loving parent who not only provides for her family's physical needs but also creates a warm, stable environment where every member thrives. (Thoth Title: Queen of the Thrones of Earth)
- **King of Pentacles:** Illustrates the archetype of a benevolent and prosperous leader. He is the successful entrepreneur who uses his wealth and resources not just for personal gain but to uplift his community, fostering growth and stability around him. (Thoth Title: Lord of the Gates of Matter)

Ultimately, what is most important is your own contemplation of the cards, and the meanings and interpretations that you arrive at from your own participation with the symbols.

THE THREE CARD TAROT SPREAD

With a three-card draw, one can tap into the power of simplicity and focus on the present moment to divine answers to simple questions. By positioning the cards in advance and reading into the story they tell, you can get a better understanding of the current situation or relationships. For a reading designed to understand a situation, you can assign the positions of past, present, future; current situation, obstacle, advice; where you stand now, what you aspire to, how to get there; and what will help you, what will hinder you, what is your unrealized potential. When it comes to understanding relationships, you can assign the positions of you, the other person, the relationship; opportunities, challenges, outcomes; what brings you together, what pulls you apart, what needs your attention; and what you want from the relationship, what your partner wants from the relationship, where the relationship is heading. To understand the physical, emotional, and spiritual state of your being, you can use the positions of mind, body, spirit; material state, emotional state, spiritual state; or you, your current path, your potential. To gain experience in facilitating Tarot readings for other people, I suggest you make it a weekly practice to do at least one three-card reading for someone else. Even if your experience level is low, you can still offer your services to those who are willing to receive them. The more you practice, the better you will get at it, so I suggest you do as many readings as possible, even daily.

This is also a great practice to have as a daily Tarot-reading practice. Allow your intuition to guide you through your daily Tarot reading. Shuffle your cards and hold your question in your mind, spreading them out face down in front of you. Then, pick up and study the card you've chosen. Consider the images, symbols, and colors on the card. After you have personally contemplated the card, you can read any explanations that you have of the cards in books or online. Think about how the card's message relates to your intention and what it might mean for your life. Write down any reflections or thoughts in your magickal diary and treat yourself as though you were doing a reading for someone else.

ASTROLOGY

Although we won't be delving deeply into astrology in this book—a vast and complex subject that can be studied for lifetimes—it is nevertheless a profound and powerful form of divination. Astrology is more than just a system of prediction: it is a science that examines the influences of celestial bodies on all living and non-living things, and the reactions these effects have. It is one of the oldest known sciences, stretching back to ancient Sumer and beyond, and it was well-known to the Egyptians, Indians, Chinese, Persians, and the civilizations of the ancient Americas.

The Path Within

Astrology is the precursor of astronomy, and for a long time, the two were one. Nowadays, astronomy is seen as an "objective" science of distances, masses, and speeds, while astrology is considered a "subjective" and intuitive science which not only deals with the mathematical elements of charting horoscopes and predicting the future, but also as a philosophy which helps to explain the spiritual nature of life.

Astrology is divided into two branches: *exoteric astrology*, which concerns itself with the mathematics and predictive arts of the subject, and *esoteric astrology*, which deals with the mysteries of the universe, the spiritual, moral and intellectual dynamics of the cosmos. Esoteric astrology reveals the universal pattern of living and how human beings can align themselves with the spiritual fabric and pattern of the universe. It is a system for understanding celestial energies, and a method for viewing the world as a whole.

Have you ever heard someone say, "I'm a Scorpio" or "I'm a Taurus"? For some of us, it might seem like a basic and reductive concept, while for others it could be a fresh and new understanding of the zodiac. In any case, the symbolism of the zodiac is fundamental to modern and ancient magick. While it may not have been essential for your practice until now, it can be very valuable for creating talismans and for certain kinds of invocation work.

The zodiac is simply a stretch of sky with twelve constellations that the planets, including Earth, rotate through, which is why astrologers will say things like "the moon is in Virgo," or "Venus is in Capricorn," meaning that the Moon and Venus are literally passing through these constellations.

There are two main kinds of astrology: Western and Vedic. Western astrology is based on a calendar that was established during the Hellenistic era and is "fixed." Vedic astrology, which is practiced mostly in India, is based on the sidereal zodiac, meaning positions of planets are calculated based on where they are actually observed in the sky in relation to constellations. Currently, Vedic astrology is more accurate, but Western astrology is more common in the Western world.

The symbols of the zodiac represent aspects of the mind of God, or different aspects of the human soul, and everyone is born with an archetype that they embody more fully than others. However, it's not as simple

Jake Kobrin

as "if your sun sign is in Aries, you are selfish and aggressive." There are many different planetary aspects to consider when looking at one's personality, such as the placement of the Moon, Mars, Venus, and the Ascendant. Furthermore, each zodiac sign passes through three decans, which adds even more subtle differences in characteristics.

The zodiac signs are associated with the four Elements, Air, Earth, Fire, and Water. Each Element has three signs, one of which is a cardinal sign, one fixed, and one mutable. Cardinal signs are the initiators; they start a season. Fixed signs are the embodiments of each season, and mutable signs conclude each season and transition us into the next. Fire signs (Aries, Leo, and Sagittarius) are full of passion and enthusiasm but can be too forceful and domineering. Water signs (Cancer, Scorpio, and Pisces) are intuitive and sensitive, but can be moody and self-pitying. Air signs (Libra, Aquarius, and Gemini) are great communicators but can be cold and insensitive. Finally, Earth signs (Capricorn, Taurus, and Virgo) are dependable and practical, but can be dull and possessive. The order of the signs is Aries, Taurus, Gemini, Cancer, Leo, Virgo, Libra, Scorpio, Sagittarius, Capricorn, Aquarius, and Pisces. Each sign is unique and offers its own gifts and challenges. The four Elements and twelve signs work together to create a beautiful, balanced cycle of life.

The planets, like the zodiacal signs, are symbols of astrology that can help us to gain an understanding of the universe and our place within it. These planets, in Classical systems, are Saturn, Jupiter, Mars, the Sun, Venus, Mercury, and the Moon—the Earth is omitted as the perspective from which we look. Each planet is said to rule one or more of the zodiac signs, and the energy of a planet is strong in the sign(s) that it rules. Furthermore, every planet also has one sign, aside from the one it rules, where it expresses itself in a compatible fashion. When a planet is in the sign directly opposite to the one it rules, it is in the sign of its detriment, and when a planet is in the sign opposite of its exaltation, it is in the sign of its fall.

The Path Within

A few other planets have been discovered in modern times, such as Neptune, Uranus, and Pluto, which are therefore not part of Classical astrology. However, many modern astrologers use these planets, referred to as "transcendental planets," to gain a deeper understanding of our place in the universe.

Astrology is a tool for peering into the cosmic weather of any event, but it is primarily used to examine the planets' positions in relation to one's birth. This is what is known as your natal chart, and it is believed that the positions of the planets when a soul is born—from the perspective of the place of its birth—will determine its personality, abilities, tastes, and challenges. It is essentially a map of one's karma. Houses represent the areas of life in which you will be affected, and the signs denote the characters of those areas. Meanwhile, planets are the aspects of the personality: the Sun in Aries in the second house, for example, could mean that one's sense of self is fiery and impulsive (Aries), and dependent upon their finances, money, and possessions (second house). Additionally, decans are the divisions of each zodiac sign, and each decan is ruled by a different planet. In order to fully examine one's natal chart, an astrologer must look at the interactions between each planet, sign, decan, and house. This includes conjunctions (when two or more planets are close together in the zodiac wheel), sextiles (when two planets are 60° apart), squares (90° apart), trines (120° apart), and oppositions (when two planets are 180° apart). The use of astrology has been popular for centuries, with famous occultists such as Dr. John Dee and Aleister Crowley having once earned a living from it. Fortunately, there are now many good free online natal chart reading programs which can do the complex calculations for you. Still, it useful to pay a professional astrologer to read and analyze your natal chart.

Jake Kobrin

BEYOND THE BASICS: THE I CHING

The I Ching, or Book of Changes, dates to around 1000 BCE in ancient China and is a revered divination system known as *cleromancy*. It provides ethical and moral guidance, drawing from the philosophical depths of Confucianism, Taoism, and Buddhism. Its unique feature is offering specific, balanced insights into various aspects of life.

This ancient text has guided significant decisions for centuries, captivating scholars and thinkers worldwide. For a genuine divination experience, it is recommended to use the Richard Wilhelm translation and set aside three identical coins specifically for your I Ching readings.

To consult the I Ching, begin with a clear, open-ended question. It's best to avoid simple yes or no inquiries and overly complicated questions. Instead, frame your question in a straightforward manner, like asking about the outlook of your finances for the year instead of combining multiple topics such as travel and investments.

The divination process involves shaking and tossing the three coins six times, each toss building a line of a hexagram. The formation of these lines depends on the coin toss results: three heads yield an "- o -" line (yang changing to yin), two heads and a tail produce a "- -" line (yin), one head and two tails create a "- - -" line (yang), and three tails result in a "- X -" line (yin changing to yang). The appearance of all heads or tails indicates a changing hexagram, leading to the creation of two hexagrams reflecting present circumstances and potential future changes.

The Path Within

Coin Toss Result	Line Formed	Description
3 heads	- o -	Yang changing to Yin
2 heads, 1 tail	- -	Yin (Unchanging)
1 head, 2 tails	- - -	Yang (Unchanging)
3 tails	- X -	Yin changing to Yang

The I Ching communicates through specific phrases or sentences in its text that resonate with your query. These messages are to be interpreted as intuitive guidance, offering insight into your current situation and suggesting possible future developments. Each reading is a blend of ancient wisdom tailored to your personal question, providing a unique perspective on your life's path.

Example I Ching Reading: "Engaging with Jake's Magick Book"
Situation (First Hexagram: Hsiao Ch'u/The Taming Power of the Small)
- **Returning to Spiritual Fundamentals:** "Return to the way. How could there be blame in this? Good fortune." This line suggests a return to basic spiritual practices, similar to an artist revisiting the fundamentals of their craft to enhance their work.
- **Importance of Discipline and Learning:** "If you are sincere and loyally attached, you are rich in your neighbor." This emphasizes the value of sincerity in spiritual practice, akin to a student diligently learning from their mentors.
- **Consistency and Ego Regulation:** "The wind drives across heaven: The image of *The Taming Power of the Small*. Thus, the superior man refines the outward aspect of his nature." The imagery of the wind symbolizes the gentle, yet consistent effort required in spiritual growth, much like a sculptor patiently shaping a masterpiece.

Jake Kobrin

- **Gratitude for the Present:** "The rain comes, there is rest. This is due to the lasting effect of character." Acknowledging the transient nature of experiences, this line encourages appreciating the present moment, as one would cherish a fleeting yet beautiful sunset.

Future Outlook (The Changing/Second Hexagram: Ting/The Cauldron)

- **Nourishment of the Soul:** "Fire over wood: The image of *The Cauldron*." This imagery suggests the nurturing and transformation of the soul through spiritual practice, similar to the way fire transforms ingredients in a cauldron into a nourishing meal.
- **Kindling of Spiritual Energy:** "There is food in the ting. My comrades are envious, but they cannot harm me. Good fortune." Here, the ting represents the vessel for spiritual energy, like a garden that flourishes under the care of a devoted gardener.
- **Overcoming Obstacles:** "The handle of the ting is altered. One is impeded in his way of life…. Good fortune comes in the end." Despite potential challenges in the spiritual path, perseverance leads to success, akin to a traveler overcoming obstacles to reach a cherished destination.

This reading from the I Ching provides nuanced guidance for spiritual endeavors. The first hexagram, The Taming Power of the Small, advises focusing on foundational aspects of spiritual practice and maintaining sincerity and humility. It highlights the importance of consistent effort and gratitude for current experiences. The second hexagram, The Cauldron, symbolizes the nourishment and transformation of the soul. It suggests that spiritual practices serve as a vessel for inner growth, and despite any challenges, continued dedication will lead to fruitful outcomes. This reading, with its specific lines and imagery, offers a roadmap for personal and spiritual development, encouraging introspection, persistence, and adaptability.

CHAPTER TEN

UNLOCKING THE POWER OF DREAMS

Dreaming, a universal experience, is one of the vital first steps towards practicing magick. To effectively incorporate it into magickal practices, one must develop the skill of dream recall, which often necessitates lifestyle adjustments. For instance, sleeping separately from a snoring partner, minimizing exposure to blue light from screens before bedtime, avoiding late-night caffeine, and possibly using sleep supplements or herbs that can all aid in dream recall.

Mastering dreamwork allows us to recognize the precognitive nature of our dreams, serving as tangible proof of magick and challenging the materialistic worldview imposed by our culture. Embracing this perspective transforms our understanding of the world. The fascinating book *Dreaming Ahead of Time: Experiences with Precognitive Dreams, Synchronicity and Coincidence* by Gary Lachman gives detailed accounts of this phenomena.

The skill of dreaming can unveil new realms of possibility. Documenting your dreams immediately upon waking, either by writing them down or recording them, is crucial for magicians. Dreams reveal a universe far more magickal than commonly perceived. For instance, my early experiences with lucid dreaming were transformative for my entire outlook and perception of reality. Developing a system to record dreams, such as using a voice memo app upon waking and later transcribing these recordings into a dream journal, can be effective.

Maintaining a dream journal, similar to a magickal journal, is highly beneficial for dreamwork. Choosing a special notebook for this purpose can enhance your commitment to the practice. Remind yourself to remember your dreams upon awakening and promptly record them. Audio recordings can be particularly useful, capturing the emotional nuances of dreams, which aids in analysis. As you delve deeper into dreamwork, you may notice increased dream recall, thematic continuity, and variations in dream intensity.

DREAM ANALYSIS

Dream analysis stands as a crucial tool for magicians seeking deeper self-understanding. Comparable to the benefits of psychotherapy, it facilitates self-discovery and personal growth. Freud regarded dreams as pathways to the unconscious, revealing insights that balance our conscious and subconscious selves. He saw dreams as messages from deep within, guiding us toward equilibrium and completeness.

Dreams function as informants of self-awareness, unearthing the unknown within us, integrating shadow aspects, and deciphering symbolic content. They often grant access to our deeper self, an exploration typically veiled in our daily lives. Despite debates about their nature and purpose, engaging with dream symbols, mythological motifs, and diverse cultural symbolism can bring a conscious understanding of our dreams. Exploring

The Path Within

these irrational symbols, even if the idea of subconscious wisdom is debated, offers a unique form of self-discovery.

This exploration resembles a form of divination or scrying, especially from a psychological standpoint. It allows for introspective questioning and receiving responses from unexplored parts of oneself. These insights can transcend prior self-perceptions. For effective dream interpretation, personal symbol associations are crucial. Relying on generic dream dictionaries can lead to misinterpretations. Carl Jung, the astounding archetypal wizard and renowned depth psychiatrist of the twentieth century, was adamant about this. Do not use dream interpretation dictionaries.

In understanding dreams, it's often beneficial to research mythological themes for unfamiliar archetypes. Typically, personal associations with symbols yield the most meaningful interpretations. According to Jungian theory, every dream element symbolizes a facet of the dreamer. For example, dreaming about conversing with a sibling isn't about the actual relationship but represents the interplay between different parts of your psyche.

To analyze dreams, first document the narrative and symbols. Imagine dreaming about walking through a bustling city you've never visited and having a conversation with an unknown person. The first step involves associating the city with feelings of exploration, unknown territories, or perhaps aspirations. The unknown person might represent unexplored traits or desires within you. Avoid drifting into unrelated associations; stay focused on the dream's elements. Visual aids, like drawing the symbol with associations radiating from it, can assist in this process.

Next, connect these images to your inner dynamics and amplify them using traditional symbols, seeking what Jung referred to as "luminous" elements—those with a special significance beyond their personal interpretation.

For instance, the bustling city in the dream might symbolize your ambition or longing for new experiences, while the unknown person could represent undiscovered aspects of your personality. The third step is weaving these dynamics into an interpretation that resonates with your current life. Perhaps the dream suggests embracing new opportunities or exploring hidden facets of your personality.

In this process, listen to your unconscious, the dream's narrative, and act on insights that bring comfort and self-care. This approach, although simplified, offers a starting point for delving into the rich and enlightening world of dream analysis.

PRACTICAL STEPS FOR DREAM RECALL AND ANALYSIS

1. Recording Dreams: Upon waking, immediately record your dreams. A voice memo app can be invaluable here, allowing you to capture the dream while it's fresh, as you're still lying in bed with closed eyes. Later, transcribe these recordings, either digitally or in a dream journal. This step is fundamental in capturing the ephemeral nature of dreams.

2. Dream Analysis: View dreams as a tool for self-exploration akin to psychotherapy. Analyzing dreams involves not just interpreting their symbols but also integrating their insights into our conscious awareness. This process helps balance our inner selves, promoting psychological and spiritual growth.

3. Personal Symbolism in Dreams: Steer clear of generic dream dictionaries. Instead, focus on your personal symbolism and associations. This approach yields more meaningful and accurate interpretations, as dreams are highly personal experiences. Remember, in Jungian terms, every dream element represents an aspect of yourself.

4. Dreamwork Process: Begin by jotting down all dream elements, then analyze each symbol by exploring your personal associations with it. Avoid getting sidetracked by irrelevant associations; keep the focus on the dream elements. This method allows for a deeper understanding of the inner dynamics represented in the dream.

The Path Within

5. Amplifying Dream Symbols: Enhance your understanding by connecting dream symbols with traditional sources or mythological themes. This step adds depth to your interpretation, offering broader perspectives and insights.

6. Interpreting and Integrating the Dream: Weave the identified inner dynamics into a cohesive narrative. Look for an interpretation that resonates, even if it's slightly uncomfortable. This process often illuminates aspects of self-care and personal growth that need attention.

RITUALIZING DREAMS

After analyzing your dream, the subsequent step is to engage in a ritual that honors its message. The idea here is that by making the dream's insights tangible, you acknowledge and integrate its lessons more deeply into your life.

Taking the dream about wandering through an unfamiliar, bustling city and conversing with an unknown person as an example, an imaginative way to honor this dream would be to create a symbolic representation of the city and the person. You could, for instance, craft a small model of a cityscape or create an abstract painting that captures the essence of a bustling urban environment. For the unknown person, you might write a letter to this aspect of yourself, expressing a willingness to explore and understand these uncharted parts of your personality.

Once your symbolic creations are ready, conduct a small ritual where you dedicate these items as physical embodiments of your dream. You might place them in a special area of your home, such as on a shelf or a personal altar, as a daily reminder of your commitment to exploring new experiences and unexplored traits within yourself. Let this ritual be a creative process, a physical manifestation of your connection to the dream, reinforcing its message in your waking life.

EXERCISE: HONORING THE DREAM THROUGH RITUAL

Recognizing and honoring the messages of dreams through ritual reinforces their significance and integrates their lessons into our lives.

Needs:
- A journal
- Space for ritual
- Any specific items related to the dream (e.g., a jar of earth if dreaming of a specific location)

Setup:
- Prepare your space for the ritual, making it conducive to reflection and respect for the dream's message.

Instructions:
- Conduct a ritual that symbolizes the dream's message. For example, if dreaming of a childhood home, you might collect earth from that location and place it in a jar, setting it in a special place as a reminder of the dream's insights.

Clean Up/Follow Through:
- After the ritual, take time to reflect on the dream's impact and how it might influence your actions or mindset moving forward. Maintain the ritual space as a physical reminder of the dream's message.

ACTIVE IMAGINATION

Expanding on our exploration of dreams, I'd like to introduce you to a complementary technique known as *active imagination,* a concept developed by Carl Jung. This technique involves entering a semi-meditative state and consciously re-engaging with characters or elements from your dreams. The process is akin to stepping back into the dream's unique universe to delve deeper into its meanings and messages.

Active imagination can be a profoundly insightful practice. It's about more than just recalling a dream; it's an interactive experience where you can dialogue with dream figures or explore dream environments more thoroughly. To begin, you might create a quiet, ritualistic space where you feel relaxed and undisturbed. Some may find it helpful to perform a simple banishing ritual to clear the space of any distracting energies.

Once in this space, mentally call forth a particularly striking character or element from a vivid dream. Imagine yourself re-entering the dream's landscape and encountering this character or element. Engage in a conversation with it, asking for clarity or further insight. Questions like "what message do you have for me?" or "is there something more I need to understand?" can prompt revealing responses.

To document this inner dialogue, you might adopt a unique method of recording, such as typing your questions in lowercase and the dream character's responses in all caps. This distinction helps in later analysis, making it easier to differentiate between your conscious inquiries and the responses from your subconscious.

For those interested in deepening their practice of active imagination, Robert Johnson's book *Inner Work* is an excellent resource. It provides detailed guidance on using active imagination techniques along with other methods of personal exploration and understanding of the unconscious mind.

Active imagination can be a transformative tool, offering a bridge between your conscious mind and the deeper wisdom held within your subconscious. Through this practice, you not only gain a richer understanding of your dreams but also foster a deeper connection with your inner self.

EXERCISE: THE ACTIVE IMAGINATION TECHNIQUE

Setup:
- Create a quiet, meditative space. Perform a simple banishing ritual if desired.

Instructions:
- Visualize a character from your dream, engaging in a dialogue to seek further information and insights. Record this dialogue for later analysis.

Clean Up/Follow Through:
- Reflect on the insights gained from this interaction, considering how they apply to your personal growth and magickal practice.

The Path Within

LUCID DREAMING

Lucid dreaming represents a unique state of consciousness that straddles the boundaries between sleep and wakefulness, characterized by the dreamer's awareness of being in a dream. This phenomenon allows individuals to potentially influence the narrative, characters, and environment of the dream, though such control is not a defining feature of lucid dreaming. My own fascination with lucid dreaming led me to join a community of "oneironauts" or dream explorers. This group, spanning different countries, achieved remarkable feats within the dream world, including collective gatherings in shared dream spaces. The potential of lucid dreaming is vast, offering boundless opportunities for exploration and experience, akin to the limitless possibilities portrayed by Neo in "The Matrix."

Lucid dreaming serves as a gateway to extraordinary and archetypal dominions, providing a conduit to profound states of being. Creatively, it offers unparalleled inspiration; one might dream of visiting an art gallery and later materializing the observed artworks, or, like Toby Driver of *Maudlin of the Well*, dream music and then transcribe it upon waking. Dr. Stephen LaBerge's research on lucid dreaming underscores its practical applications, demonstrating how athletes and musicians improve their waking skills through dream practice, underscoring the brain's inability to distinguish between dreamt actions and real ones.[66]

In the context of ritual magicians, mastering both magickal rituals and lucid dreaming can potentiate one's magickal practices, making it one of the most powerful techniques in the magician's toolkit.

---

66 LaBerge, Stephen, and Howard Rheingold, *Exploring the World of Lucid Dreaming* (Ballantine Books, 1991)

Jake Kobrin

Lucid dreaming exists on a continuum of consciousness. At one end is full waking consciousness, followed by active imagination where we have significant control, then lucid dreaming with moderate control, and finally regular dreaming with minimal conscious involvement. The degree of control and involvement varies depending on the specific instance and the individual's proficiency.

In the waking state, the idea of defying gravity seems far-fetched, yet in the dream world, such feats are not only possible but commonplace. The practice of lucid dreaming enables this liberation from physical constraints, allowing for dream manipulation. The challenge lies in recognizing the dream state and achieving lucidity, which can be facilitated by regular reality checks, such as attempting to breathe with a pinched nose or reading text, looking away, and then reading it again.

Lucid dreaming also serves as a path to transcendent consciousness, comparable to meditation, brainwave entrainment, and psychedelic experiences. For example, in my exploration of lucid dreaming, a particularly vivid experience in 2009 stands out. In this dream, I found myself in an ancient, surreal library, filled with books bearing unknown symbols. The scent of old parchment was pervasive. A majestic tree in the library, with roots deep in the ground and branches reaching into a canopy of stars, symbolized growth and connection between the earthly and divine.

Aware of my dreaming state, I touched the tree's bark and was instantly transported above an endless ocean, the tree transforming into a guiding path through the stars. The flight was exhilarating, symbolizing liberation from physical constraints. I encountered a wise old man among the stars, who communicated wordlessly, imparting insights about the unity of all things and the illusion of time.

The ocean below me turned into a web of memories and emotions, each wave a memory, every ripple an emotion. This figure, possibly my higher self, guided me to embrace these aspects of my being. The dream culminated in the ocean and sky merging, a powerful realization of the unity of my conscious and unconscious mind.

This lucid dream was a profound manifestation of my inner world, offering insights into my existence and consciousness. It reinforced the

The Path Within

transformative power of lucid dreaming in personal and spiritual growth, underscoring the boundless potential within our minds for exploration and understanding. This was only one of many such transcendent experiences encountered in my lucid dream explorations.

Despite growing interest and research in lucid dreaming since the late 1980s, skepticism remains. Stephen LaBerge's *Exploring the World of Lucid Dreaming* delves into the scientific study of the phenomenon, including experiments that validate the experience of lucidity. Yet, the personal nature of dreaming means that universal interpretations and applications may not always be pertinent.

Lucid dreaming, while misconceived by some as harmful or exhausting, poses no threat to mental or physical well-being. In this simulated dream environment, negative experiences can be reframed as valuable parts of our psyche. Given that we dream extensively each night, with lucid dreams being only a fraction of these dreams, there is ample opportunity for physical and mental rejuvenation during REM sleep. The movie *Waking Life* poignantly illustrates the fluidity of dream reality, but it also warns of the potential dissociative effects where the line between dreaming and waking life becomes blurred. If such confusion arises, it is advisable to pause dream work to reestablish a clear distinction between these states.

Utilizing the third of our lives spent in sleep, lucid dreaming offers a means to enhance personal development. Whether for fulfillment of desires or deeper exploration, this practice invariably yields positive outcomes.

HOW TO LUCID DREAM

We all have the potential to lucid dream, but we must learn to recognize the signs and signals of our dream state first. We must cultivate strong dream recall and good quality sleep in order to prepare ourselves for what lies ahead. To start, we must be intentional in our practices, such as turning

Jake Kobrin

off our phones; sleeping in a dark, silent room; and abstaining from blue light and caffeine before bed. Additionally, we must focus on our overall health and well-being, such as eating nutritious food, limiting alcohol, and managing our stress.

Once we have done this groundwork, we can begin our lucid dreaming practice. Lucid dreaming, a phenomenon where the dreamer becomes aware they are dreaming, is within the potential of every individual. However, achieving lucidity in dreams requires preparation and practice. This preparation involves cultivating strong dream recall and ensuring quality sleep. Integral to this process are intentional practices like disconnecting from digital devices, ensuring a dark and silent sleeping environment, and avoiding blue light and caffeine before bedtime. Additionally, overall health and wellbeing, including nutritious diet, limited alcohol consumption, and effective stress management, lay the foundation for successful lucid dreaming.

Techniques for Lucid Dreaming

- **Dream-Induced Lucid Dreaming (DILD):** The crux of DILD lies in recognizing anomalies within the dream that trigger awareness of the dream state. Practitioners should incorporate regular reality checks into their waking life, such as examining hands, attempting to manipulate light switches, pushing hands through walls, and observing clocks. These checks, when habitualized, transcend into the dream state, leading to lucidity.
- **Wake-Induced Lucid Dreaming (WILD):** This technique involves transitioning from wakefulness directly into a dream state. It requires recognizing hypnagogic hallucinations that occur as one drifts off to sleep. Although conceptually straightforward, WILD can be challenging to master, with individual variations in the ease of falling asleep affecting its success rate.
- **Wake Back to Bed (WBTB):** An alternative to WILD, WBTB involves waking after five hours of sleep, remaining awake for approximately thirty minutes, and then returning to sleep. The heightened alertness during this interim period increases the likelihood of enter-

The Path Within

ing a lucid dream.

- **Mnemonic Induction of Lucid Dreams (MILD):** Developed by Dr. Stephen LaBerge, MILD utilizes intentional thought to induce lucidity. By visualizing a recent dream, identifying an anomaly or "dreamsign," and repeating a mantra like "the next time I dream, I want to remember that I am dreaming." This technique harnesses intentionality to achieve lucid dreaming. Combining MILD with reality testing and WBTB is considered particularly effective.
- **Utilization of Sigils in Lucid Dreaming:** Sigils can also be employed to facilitate lucid dreaming. A sigil bearing an intention such as "I always dream lucidly" can be visualized or ritually charged before sleep to promote lucidity. Additionally, sigils can be creatively integrated into the lucid dream itself to manifest specific experiences or encounters.

It's worth noting that novices in lucid dreaming often encounter initial challenges such as waking up immediately upon achieving lucidity. To counteract this, spinning around in the dream, akin to the practices of Sufi mystics, can stabilize and shift the dream environment. It is also not unusual for lucidity to fluctuate within the dream, so perseverance is key. Maintaining a dream journal and promptly recording experiences upon waking enhances the ability to recall and benefit from lucid dreams.

DREAM INCUBATION

Dream incubation is an artful technique of using the power of the mind to direct our dreams in order to gain insight or solve a problem. You can invite the dream world to help you by going to bed with intention and focus and setting the stage for dream work. Before going to bed, write down the problem as a brief phrase or sentence and place this near your bed. Spend a few minutes reviewing it, then as you drift off to sleep, visualize the problem as an image if it lends itself to this. Tell yourself you want to dream about the problem. Place a pen and paper, and possibly a lamp or flashlight, if necessary, on the night table. When you awaken, lie quietly and recall any traces of the dream, then invite more of the dream to come back to you. Then write down as much of it as you can recall. You might also arrange objects related to the problem on your night table or wall, create a sigil, or even make an altar specifically for the purpose of dream incubation. By doing this, you utilize the dream world to gain knowledge and insight.

EXERCISE: DREAM INCUBATION

Needs:
- Journal and pen for recording thoughts and dreams
- Any objects or symbols related to the problem or question at hand
- Materials for creating a sigil or an altar, if desired

Setup:
- Create a calm and focused atmosphere in your sleeping area conducive to introspective thought.
- Place any objects or symbols that relate to your question or problem near your bed as visual cues.

Instructions:
- **Problem Articulation:** Write down the issue or question you wish to explore in your dream as a concise statement or phrase. Keep this note near your bed.

The Path Within

- **Pre-Sleep Ritual:** Before bed, spend a few minutes focusing on this problem. If possible, visualize it as an image or scene.
- **Intention Setting:** As you prepare to sleep, affirm to yourself the desire to dream about this specific issue. This verbal or mental assertion guides your subconscious towards the problem during sleep.
- **Bedside Preparation:** Ensure you have a pen and paper, and a light source if needed, on your nightstand for immediate dream recording upon waking.
- **Sigil or Altar Creation (Optional):** If it resonates with you, create a sigil or set up a small altar related to your query to reinforce your intention and focus.

Follow Through:
- Upon waking, stay still and gently recall any fragments of your dream. Invite more of the dream to return to your memory.
- Write down as much as you can remember. Even small details can be significant.
- Reflect on the dream and its possible meanings or solutions to your problem throughout the day.

Additional Tips:
- Consistency is key. It may take several nights of practice before you successfully incubate a dream related to your problem.
- Combining this practice with lucid dreaming techniques can enhance your control and recall within the dream space.
- Consider meditating on your intention before sleep to deepen your mental focus and clarity.

Jake Kobrin

DREAM HERBS AND DREAM TECHNOLOGIES

Dreams often offer us a portal to a world of endless possibilities. To enhance and deepen this exploration, various natural and technological methods can be employed.

Herbal Enhancements for Vivid Dreams
- **Mugwort *(Artemisia vulgaris)*:** Commonly available in health-food stores and often found growing wild, mugwort can be utilized as a potent dream enhancer. Consumed as a tea or smoked before bedtime, it has been known to intensify dream vividness and clarity. Mugwort's properties can stimulate the subconscious, potentially leading to more lucid and memorable dreams.
- **Blue Lotus *(Nymphaea caerulea)*:** Revered in ancient Egyptian culture, blue lotus is celebrated for its ability to heighten dream awareness and psychic sensitivity. It is believed to amplify the "lunar qualities" of perception, enhancing the depth and intensity of the dream experience. Blue lotus can be consumed as a tea or in other preparations to facilitate more subtle, insightful, and profound dream states.

Scientifically Researched Agents
These agents can be dangerous when used improperly; be mindful and smart about your use.

- **Galantamine:** A compound derived from certain flowers and used clinically for dementia treatment, galantamine has been the subject of scientific studies for its ability to induce lucid dreaming. It is thought to influence the brain's chemistry in a way that increases the likelihood of achieving lucidity during the dream state.

The Path Within

- **Choline (alpha-GPC):** Another agent that has shown promising results in the induction of lucid dreams is choline, specifically in its alpha-GPC form. This compound is believed to enhance cognitive function and, when used in conjunction with dreaming, may assist in achieving a greater level of control within the dream.

Technological Tools for Lucid Dream Induction
- **Lucid Dreaming Devices:** Products like the Lucid Dreamer and Remee represent the cutting edge in dream technology. These devices employ techniques such as transcranial alternating current stimulation and light and audio stimulation. The goal is to enhance gamma activity within the brain, a state associated with heightened awareness and consciousness, thereby facilitating the onset of lucid dreams.

Each of these methods, whether natural or technological, offers a unique pathway to explore the rich and diverse landscape of dreams. By integrating these techniques into a regular practice, individuals can unlock the potential of their subconscious, journeying into a world where the boundaries of reality are expanded and the depths of the psyche are explored. Of course, your personal research and discretion are required when taking the responsibility to experiment with any drugs or herbs. Each person will have a different reaction, so some caution is necessary.

Jake Kobrin

ASTRAL PROJECTION

Embarking on the practice of astral projection necessitates a foundational understanding of its theoretical underpinnings, particularly the astral body's nature. The Tree of Life, as outlined in the nineteenth-century Golden Dawn tradition, serves as a valuable conceptual framework. It symbolizes the manifestation of the material world and the intricate facets of human spiritual anatomy. At its base, the physical body is conceived, reaching above connected by an astral framework—a more subtle and diverse energetic structure not confined to physicality. The astral plane, rather than an extraordinary otherworld, aligns more closely with the realms of our imagination, encompassing our daydreams, dreams, imaginations, and visualizations.

In this text, the focus is on astral projection, distinct from etheric projection. Etheric projection involves the etheric body's separation from the physical, exploring nearby locales, potentially useful for remote information gathering. This is often also called "remote viewing." However, it is not the subject of this book and is purported by some to be potentially detrimental to the energetic body. Astral projection, in contrast, transports you to a domain not anchored in the physical world but existing in the vastness of the mind. This plane of existence is infinitely malleable, capable of creating forms nonexistent in the physical sphere.

The Path Within

EXERCISE: ASTRAL PROJECTION

Preparatory practices for astral projection are key. Ensure a state of physical ease—avoid being too full of food, particularly with meat, and ensure restfulness. For men, it is advisable to abstain from orgasmic release for a minimum of twelve hours beforehand. Should significant fatigue arise while astral traveling, it is wise to conclude the session. In moments of uncertainty or fear, imagine commanding a chariot led by formidable steeds to return you safely to your body.

To embark on astral projection, dedicate an hour in a sacred, undisturbed space. Create an ambiance conducive to spiritual work—dim the lights, use candles, or cover windows during daylight. A sleep mask or your robe's hood can aid in blocking out residual light. Ritual bathing signifies the transition into this sacred practice. Clothe yourself in your magickal robes and settle into your designated space, initiating the ritual with rounds of fourfold breathing or the relaxation ritual to achieve a relaxed state.

Commence with foundational banishing rituals, such as the Lesser Banishing Ritual of the Pentagram, and potentially the Lesser Banishing Ritual of the Hexagram if invoking specific planetary energies aligns with your intent. Bless the forthcoming endeavor with a general invocation like Psalm 23 or the Bornless One Invocation. You can also use your own invocations or the one that I included earlier in this book. If your aim is to connect with a specific astral location or entity, this is the moment for tailored invoking rituals or invocations, complemented by incense corresponding to the sphere, planet, or deity of focus.

Once relaxed, visualize energy emanating from your physical form, shaping into an astral double mirroring your physical presence, connected by a light cord. Transfer your consciousness into this ethereal duplicate, perceiving your surroundings from this new perspective. Then, visualize yourself ascending upwards, transitioning beyond the confines of your physical environment into an astral landscape ripe for exploration. Energize your astral form with mental enactments of rituals like the Lesser Invoking Ritual of the Pentagram or the Middle Pillar Ritual, requiring internalization and mental rehearsal.

Call upon a guide within this space, remaining receptive to the forthcoming experience. Authenticate the guide by securing a name, verifying correspondences (if need be), and engaging with signs and words. Journey with the guide through the astral landscape, immersing in the exploration. Upon concluding your astral experience, respectfully dismiss your guide or any encountered entities.

To return to your physical form, enact the Sign of Silence, deeply inhaling to reconnect with your corporeal self. Engage in muscle movements to reinforce your physical presence. Perform another round of the Lesser Banishing Ritual of the Pentagram for safety and conclude the ritual in a manner befitting your practice.

Astral projection can be a profound traversal of unseen dimensions, guided by intention, ritualistic discipline, and a profound connection to the mystical dimensions interwoven in our existence.

THE ENOCHIAN CALLS

One of the most commonly practiced forms of Astral Projection in magick is Scrying the Enochian Aethyrs, using the Enochian Calls, which were discovered by Dr. John Dee and his assistant Edward Kelley in the Renaissance era. Enochian is an angelic language, and the idea is that you recite the Enochian Calls as incantations and travel to these subtle dimensions and have psychic experiences of these dimensions. There are thirty Enochian Aehtyrs. According to Aleister Crowley, the magician starts with the thirtieth aethyr and works up to the first, exploring only so far as their level of initiation will permit. The ritual, in its most simplistic version,

The Path Within

is the same as the previously described. You should get into the state of mind to do ritual and prepare yourself by banishing. Then, out loud, recite the Enochian Call. Immediately afterward, lay down, close your eyes, and induce an astral experience. Let your mind go and have whatever experience comes to you. Directly after the experience finishes, banish again, and then record your results in your diary.

The thirtieth Enochian Aethyr, TEX (pronounced *tah-eh-atz*), phonetically is:[67]

Madariatza das perifa Tah-Eh-Atz cahisa micaolazoda saanire caosago od fifisa balzodizodarasa Iaida. Nonuca gohulime: Micama odoianu MADA faoda beliorebe, soba ooaona cahisa luciftias peripesol, das aberaasasa nonucafe netaaibe caosaji od tilabe adapehaheta damepelozoda, tooata nonucafe jimicalazodoma larasada tofejilo marebe yareryo IDOIGO; od torezodulape yaodafe gohola, Caosaga, tabaoreda saanire, od caharisateosa yorepoila tiobela busadire, tilabe noalanu paida oresaba, od dodaremeni zodayolana. Elazodape tilaba paremeji peripesatza, od ta qurelesata booapisa. Lanibame oucaho sayomepe, od caharisateosa ajitoltorenu, mireca qo tiobela Iela. Tonu paomebeda dizodalamo asa pianu, od caharisateosa aji- latore-torenu paracahe a sayomepe. Coredazodizoda dodapala od fifalazoda, lasa manada, od faregita bamesa omaoasa. Conisabera od auauotza tonuji oresa; catabela noasami _ tabejesa leuitahemonuji. Vanucahi omepetilabe oresa! Bagile? Moooabe OL coredazodizoda. El capimao itzomatzipe, od cacocasabe gosaa. Bajilenu pii tianuta a babalanuda, od faoregita teloca uo uime. Madariiatza, torezodu!!! Oadariatza orocaha aboaperi! Tabaori periazoda aretabasa! Adarepanu coresata dobitza! Yolacame periazodi arecoazodiore, od quasabe qotinuji! Ripire paaotzata sagacore! Umela od perdazodare cacareji Aoiveae coremepeta! Torezodu! Zodacare od Zodameranu, asapeta sibesi butamona das surezodasa Tia balatanu. Odo cicale Qaa, od Ozodazodame pelapeli IADANAMADA!

---

67   Turner, Robert, *Enochian Magic for Beginners: The Original System of Angel Magic* (Llewellyn Publications, 2002)

Jake Kobrin

In English, this translates to:

O you heavens which dwell in the [Number of Aether, e.g. First Ayre], the mighty in the parts of the Earth, and execute the Judgment of the Highest! To you it is said, Behold the face of your God, the beginning of comfort, whose eyes are the brightness of the heavens: which provided you for the government of the Earth and her unspeakable variety, furnishing you with a powerful understanding to dispose all things according to the providence of Him that sits on the Holy Throne, and rose up in the beginning, saying: the Earth let her be governed by her parts and let there be division in her, that the glory of her may be always drunken and vexed in itself. Her course, let it run with the heavens, and as a handmaid let her serve them. One season let it confound another, and let there be no creature upon or within her the same: all her members let them differ in their qualities, and let there be no one creature equal with another: the reasonable Creatures of the Earth let them vex and weed out one another, and the dwelling places let them forget their names: the work of man, and his pomp, let them be defaced: his buildings let them become caves for the beasts of the field. Confound her understanding with darkness. For why? It repents me I made Man. One while let her be known and another while a stranger: because she is the bed of a Harlot, and the dwelling place of Him that is Fallen. O you heavens arise: the lower heavens underneath you, let them serve you! Govern those that govern: cast down such as fall! Bring forth with those that increase, and destroy the rotten! No place let it remain in one number: add and diminish until the stars be numbered!

Arise, Move, and Appear before the Covenant of his mouth, which he has sworn unto us in his Justice. Open the Mysteries of your Creation: and make us partakers of Undefiled Knowledge.

When reading the calls, only read them in Enochian.

The Path Within

EXERCISE: SCRYING THE ENOCHIAN AETHYRS

Needs:
- A quiet, undisturbed space for ritual work
- A copy of the Enochian Calls, particularly the call of the Aethyr you intend to explore
- Ritual items for banishing and grounding
- A journal or diary for recording experiences

Setup:
- Begin by creating a sacred space, ensuring it is free from external interruptions.
- Familiarize yourself with the Enochian Call of the Aethyr you wish to explore. The thirtieth Aethyr, TEX, is often the starting point.

Instructions:
- **Preparation:** Engage in a state of ritual readiness through relaxation and mental focus. Perform a banishing ritual to clear the space and align yourself with the task ahead.
- **Recitation of the Enochian Call:** Recite the Enochian Call of the chosen Aethyr aloud with clear intention and focus. Refer to the transcription above for TEX, the thirtieth Enochian Call.
- **Astral Journeying:** Immediately after reciting the Call, lie down, close your eyes, and allow your mind to enter the astral realm. Be receptive to the experiences and visions that arise, letting them unfold naturally.
- **Recording and Reflection:** After your astral journey, perform another banishing ritual to ground yourself. Then, promptly record your experiences in detail in your journal.

Jake Kobrin

Additional Tips:
- Ensure you only read the Calls in Enochian during the ritual to maintain authenticity and effectiveness.
- Approach this practice with respect and a clear mind.
- Gradually progress through the Aethyrs, starting from the thirtieth, and only advance as your experience and understanding grow.
- Regularly reflect on your experiences and insights gained from each Aethyr to deepen your understanding and connection with the Enochian system.

EXPLORING THE ASTRAL PLANE: TECHNIQUES FOR ASTRAL PROJECTION, LUCID DREAMING AND INTEGRATING THE QABALAH BY GUEST TEACHER MARK STAVISH

Our topic for discussion is going to be lucid dreaming, astral projection, and the body of light. Wonderful. Well, I think we need to look at a few things whenever we look at any esoteric practice. We have to look at what is its foundation, what is its philosophical view.

It is important to remember that when working with any of these practices, it is not a race. It takes at least two years to begin to understand, whether you like it or not, and five to six years to gain a sense of competency. After ten to fifteen years, you will begin to understand what you are good at and what you don't know. The most talented people I have known have practiced for decades before achieving tangible results.

It is important to have a phenomena buddy to help keep you grounded and to understand the difference between subjective and objective experiences. Subjective experiences are personal and internal, while objective experiences are verified by others. When doing meditations, particularly on the Elements, it is important to understand the nature of stability so that when entering into meditative states, your mind is stable. This is criti-

The Path Within

cal for those involved in lucid dreaming, which is the gateway to astral projection.

The Golden Dawn has many wonderful techniques and methodologies, but it has no core philosophical view. Without a philosophical view, it is difficult to understand where you are going. Therefore, it is important to understand how it all began.

Within some esoteric practices, there is a notion of the path of spirituality being the path of return. This path is said to return to a primordial awareness or beginning. This beginning is thought to be God, who is omnipresent, omnipotent, and all-knowing. However, this means that God is big, dumb, and stupid, as there is nothing else to know.

To solve this problem, creation must take place. Jean Duwe, the founder of The Fosters of Nature, described this as the breaking of the speed of light. This is the end of instantaneousness and is what we are talking about when we discuss the holy opportunity on the Tree of Life.

The model of the tree is effective for the descent, but not as effective on the ascent. This is due to the role of Saturn and Binah as gatekeepers. Creation is the first phase, which is the end of spaceless and timelessness. We now have time, space, and duality.

At the sphere of Jupiter, knowledge and power are vast, but awareness of what? If we have just come out of unity, it must have been terrifying. As we go down the Tree, we end up with seven faces of limitation. This is due to the slowing down of the speed of light.

At the sphere of Malkuth, or Earth, we have almost no memory of what we once were. The journey up, or the path of return, begins. As long as we are dealing with duality, we are dealing with cause and effect, or karma. The most important thing to learn is discrimination, so we can know what is good for us and what is not. We must also consider opportunity cost, as we must choose to do one thing, which means we are not doing something else.

Everything has obvious and not so obvious effects. In this world, we are under what is called *determinism* or fate. We can look at it this way: in the physical world, everything is karma. It is all cause and effect. We have some freedom in the sense of choices we make, but once we make a

Jake Kobrin

choice, that is all there is. For example, we are free to smoke all we want, but don't be surprised if we end up with cancer. We are free to drink all we want, but don't be surprised if our liver craps out.

Sometimes we get a glimpse of something other, perhaps in a dream, under a hypnotic state, or even under a hallucinogen. We get a sense of otherness, though it may not be terribly clear. We are moving from the physical domain of Malkuth to the lunar dimension, the realm of dreams, and the realm of imagination. We seek to understand this, to make sense of it, to see if there is a pattern at work.

We move up to the realm of Mercury or Hod, and then to the Sun, Tiphareth. Here, something wonderful happens: our inner Sun is awakened. We have graduated and are now an adult in the universe. We have reached the gate of Saturn, and with each step, more freedom has occurred.

Using the traditional initiatory systems, we have the potential to experience profound unity or eternity, sometimes called "touching the face of eternity." This is possible because Kether is in Malkuth and Malkuth is in Kether. We can experience this unity or Nirvana of one taste, duality, unity, or enlightenment. To do this, we use maps such as the Tree of Life and other hermetic and neoplatonic maps. However, the map is not the territory we seek to experience. We develop methods such as meditative and ritual means to study the effect of symbolism on energy and consciousness.

We are also concerned with energy and how symbols move energy and how energy affects and moves consciousness. We need more juice, and that is why breathing practices are so important. The first element of life is prana, and we focus our energy on this. We also see this in traditional magickal practices, which involve blowing the airs and psychic energies.

When we move into the practices of alchemy, we are dealing with matter, consciousness, and energy. Alchemy requires a tremendous amount of energy and releases a tremendous amount of energy, which is why it is so dangerous. We also have plant work such as *spagyrics*, which involves extracting a concentrated essence according to astrology.

Alchemy, astrology, and Kabbalistic ritual magick are the three fundamental approaches we use on the path of return to unity. We can

The Path Within

never return as we were, but rather with all the knowledge and freedom we have acquired and built for ourselves. Our psychic structures are the ones we have built for ourselves, and no two are identical.

No two cars are identical, yet they serve the same purpose. We can easily enter into the dream world by going to sleep. Many of us have experienced lucid dreams, which can be more intense or clear at different times of the month. This is related to the lunar cycles and the planetary energies of the day and night. We can use planetary hours and rituals to influence our dreams. Generally, from sunrise to midday, the Element of Fire is strongest, and from evening to the middle of the night, the Element of Water is strongest. As we go to sleep and deepen our sleep until sunrise, the energies of Earth are strongest. Lucid dreaming is a ritual that can be used to enter into the lunar world. It is the gateway to other things, and when we have a lucid dream, we can feel a shift in our awareness as we try to stabilize it. This is why the Earth Elements are so important.

What you're doing is awakening the stability of your own mind. This is critical. Then, you get to have sub-lucid dreams. You say, "Hey, okay, this is a lucid dream, right? I want to do stuff." And you kind of get to do stuff.

It takes work because now you must overcome the inertia or the force of gravity of resistance in that psychic dimension. Each of these dimensions has its own qualities, which is why we talk about becoming light or lighter. Not only are we quite literally filled with more light, but we become lighter like air. That's why the Element of Air is so important in this, because it also rules our neurological structures and communication structures. So, it's the senses and our neurology, but also our psychic neurology.

You want to keep those clean—that's why we have different practices. The easiest is good breathing practices and some of the good visualizations. Don't go too overboard on a lot of this stuff. Give yourself patience and time, otherwise you'll burn out. But the nice thing about lucid dreaming is every night you're going to go to sleep. So, every night, you can remind yourself to just make the simplest affirmation: "Tonight, I will sleep, I will dream. I will know that I am dreaming. I'll become aware of my dreams. I will take control of my dreams, and I will remember them upon awakening."

Jake Kobrin

Of course, there are more. One of the things you can do is use the psychic centers as you understand them. And there are several different locations which are beneficial for that. One is the heart. Certain centers are better for night, and some are better for day. The other is the throat, which is very important, but that may cause you to be awake. Now, when you're awake like that, as long as your mind is alert but your body is rested, that's all that matters.

If you feel your body is heavy but your mind is alert, that's not a problem. The problem is all in your head, which is what you wanted anyhow. You wanted to be awake and outside of your body. (Well, we're working on that.) So then, as you do the meditations on the throat, the tendency is to visualize a brilliant red sphere. But these spheres are small, about the size of a marble. Most of the stuff you read about the Middle Pillar exercise is interesting, but not terribly effective for a variety of reasons.

One issue is the energy centers need to be smaller with a greater radiance, like an LED light like you might see on your Christmas tree. You'll want this luminosity to light up your room, preferably an area of about forty or fifty feet around you, but nine to ten feet around you is sufficient. It's as if when you were going to sleep, you had this luminous red light (or if you had white like the sun) just lighting up your whole room.

The other place you'll want to visualize something special aside from the throat is the back of the head. Now, some of it is in the medulla oblongata. Some of the French schools have moved that around a little bit. But the medulla oblongata is a good point because when you start meditating back there, you're affecting the flow of blood to the parts of the brain that have to do with auditory and visual reception. What you do is visualize different symbols back there, and those symbols can direct you in the direction you want to go. If we want to awaken ourselves in the lunar realm, we visualize a lunar symbol with the intention of the direction we're going to go. And it's not terribly complex.

Dreaming is very important because it allows us to enter into the unconscious and make what is in the unconscious conscious. We are trying to make the objective subjective and the subjective objective. Astral projection is an effort to leave the body and roam this dimension, usually the physical

The Path Within

world, but not always. When many people begin to experience the first phases of it, there is a profound sense of spinning or dizziness, which can be very terrifying. To prepare for this, we can practice by sitting anywhere and imagining ourselves walking out of our body and then back in.

We don't need to worry too much about the notion of a silver cord. We just need to get the idea in our head that we are capable of walking. When we do this, we will notice that it is easy to visualize, but difficult to feel. We have to make a conscious effort to feel gravity and density in the experience. We also have to imagine any odors, tastes, or anything else that we would experience in the physical world.

By doing this, we create an avatar that we inhabit to varying degrees. If we do it really well, we can create a body of light that is capable of doing all the things that our physical body can do in one or more of the psychic dimensions. Ultimately, the reason we do this is so that we can create a locus of consciousness within ourselves that is stable enough to withstand the pressures of the nothingness from which we have come.

Understanding the purpose of our practices is essential for our capacity to survive death. Without the continuity of awareness, we spend a great deal of time starting from the beginning again. It is natural to feel scared when we think of this, but it is important to understand the importance of each step and to celebrate our victories.

Classical magick and traditional systems emphasize the importance of this. We should take our practices joyfully, but with understanding. It may take a long time for the fruit to drop, but we must be patient and allow the cycles of time to grow and bear fruit.

We must think of our body in terms of energy, with clarity, brilliance, purity, and blissfulness. Fire is the element of awareness, awakening, and transformation. Love is an intense state of blissfulness, not a neurotic or adolescent state. It is also erotic, as it is the energy of Netzach, which allows us to bring energies under our control.

To understand this, we must read and annotate books on occult philosophy, such as Agrippa's *Three Books of Occult Philosophy*, published by Inner Traditions. A good paperback edition is recommended, as it will be easier to annotate.

Jake Kobrin

The notion of eros as the foundation of all magick is known as meaning an intimate union and a deep emotional affection. This is how any magick occurs. Your inner energies don't respond just because you call; they require something external to you. We are dealing with two dimensions: the psychospiritual dimension of awakening what's within us, and something external to us. This is why the concept of "as above, so below; as within, so without" exists.

When dealing with planetary forces, you can create a resonance between two poles by imagining gods or angels, or something with an intense desire to enter that dimension. It's important to remember that the map is not the territory, and experiences may be different from day to day. Saturday is Saturn, Sunday is the Sun, Monday is the Moon, Tuesday is Mars, Wednesday is Mercury, Thursday is Jupiter, and Friday is Venus.

When lucid dreaming, pick an image such as a planetary symbol for the night. With this, you can also use the images of the gods of those realms or the Archangels. Your goal is to overcome the period of unconsciousness through the intention and stability of your awareness.

When you do this, please do not show off your experiences on social media. If you have been doing this, stop it immediately. Stop talking to everyone about your experiences. This shows that you don't really understand what you're doing and don't trust yourself to understand yourself.

Part of you may be arrogantly prideful and want to show everyone how special you are. I know that hurts, but you must get over it. As you go through each of these realms, you must deal with virtues and vices. The first virtue is discrimination, the second is inertia. It is easy to get stuck in the dream world, where it is easier to avoid life than to deal with it. This dream realm exists in our own minds and in much of our experience, which is why the silver screen is so attractive. The virtue of honesty is important, as we must be honest with ourselves and with others. Love is the virtue of Netzach, which is about right relationships and taking the right action in a relationship. In Tiphareth, the virtue is selflessness, meaning we must learn how to get out of our own way. The divine name of Kether is "I am

The Path Within

that I am," which is about identifying with something other than what we think of ourselves normally. When we make "I am" statements, we must be careful not to fill in the blank with an identifier. In Kether, the virtue is courage, and in Geburah or Mars, it is energy. We must be careful of its tendency to cause profound destruction. In Saturn, the virtue is silence, and we must learn to be quiet. This will give our words meaning and potential. When we take ourselves seriously, we can experience something that is completely subjective and move it into an objective action. This will not be easy, as it is called the Great Work for a reason.

You have to be prepared for the disruptions that will occur in your life when you practice magick. Magick is inherently disruptive because it requires you to get rid of something in order to change. You want this disruption to be as harmonious as possible, just like going to the dentist. Generally speaking, it is best to invoke in the morning and banish in the evening. Do not feel the need to do it more than twice a day. If you tire of doing it, stop for about a month. Doing too much can lead to burnout, like a sponge that has absorbed too much water.

Pace yourself accordingly for the long haul. Take advantage of short practices during the day. Recognize that everything is a spectrum of energy, like a piano keyboard. Think of everything that is solid as relating to Earth, but also consider the planetary references. For example, a computer screen is Mercurial. Or, look at the colors someone wears and the way they walk. This is known as the doctrine of correspondences.

Now you may have been told that stereotypes don't exist, but that's wrong. We just call them target audiences, preferred consumers, or archetypes. What are the commonalities of expressions in those energetic preferences? Begin to notice and identify them, but also notice the subtle differences, particularly when dealing with human beings, as they are far more complex.

You are trying to ascend not only through four Elements but through seven planes and twelve possible cyclic expressions. There are some people who are not that complex, but you can see within yourself that there are

Jake Kobrin

probably three or four qualities that dominate within you, and three or four qualities that dominate in most of the people you're with, and that they have planetary as well as Elemental expressions.

Look at a room. What are the qualities of that room? Is it lunar or solar in nature? (Why do we call it a solarium where all the sunlight is? Right?) I'd be very concerned for you if your bedroom was very haunted in nature or extremely Martial.

How do these symbolic realities exist in the terra firma that we experience? One way to get a sense of them is noticing every time you cross a threshold, because what is astral projection, what is death, and what is meditation if not crossing the threshold. And what do we do when we cross the threshold? We encounter the guardian of the threshold: the totality of our own awareness.

Some have asked about the tangible, felt distinctions in passing through the different spheres of the Tree of Life, and what makes it distinct from the experience at only the Malkuth level. Are those shifts into the different spheres only shifts in consciousness, or is it something that is primarily noticed in the sort of psychic realms, or is it also tangibly noticeable within one's physical form?

To answer that question, it's going to be depending on each person, the intensity, because of course there's different realms, but we'll just say for the most part, there's going to be a shift in who you are. It can be very subtle or very strong. Very few people touch Saturn and get away unscathed. The same thing with Mars. You may just get terribly angry and terribly aggressive. It doesn't mean that energy isn't used worthwhile. I always tell people, if you're going to do a lot of Mars work, make sure you have a good schedule of activity so that you can channel that energy and just not let it fly off.

The best measure of magickal practice is the sort of tangible objective results that you can get from the practice itself, rather than being lost too much in the subjectivity of what experiencing. We must also remember to do purification practices and different acts of offerings or sacrifices early on in the game. If we are too concerned with objective phenomena, nature will clean that plate for us, and that can be very unpleasant.

The Path Within

When you're going to work with symbol sets, it's important to recognize that most of the stuff you work with is pretty straightforward. Don't be overly confused by its simplicity. At the same time, you'll find that some of the understandings of these planetary energies can be very sophisticated. It's important to be consistent in what you do, and remember that you're forming mental, emotional, and physical patterns for specific results.

When you are looking at complex symbol sets, it is important to recognize that the modern Tarot is just that: modern. The use of it in terms of occult symbolism doesn't date back much before the French Revolution, and most of the symbols and ideas that you are familiar with really only go back to the French court revival. This is okay because it works quite well, but you'll notice that the French approach to the Tarot—like if you use the Oswald Worth Tarot of the magicians or Papus—is going to be very different from the British or the Golden Dawn.

That's okay because they are a means to an end. They are not an end in and of themselves, and that's important to know. Whenever you get a practice, it's okay for you to ask the questions, "where did it come from? How do I do it? And what can I expect?" You need to know if you're doing it correctly and if you're benefitting from it.

So, when you're looking at Tarot cards, you're looking at someone's particular view of the cosmos of the universe, and that's important to know. You don't want to be too overly influenced by their particular vision. When you use something like Crowley's deck, the art is spectacular, but it can be overwhelming because of that spectacular nature. That is, it doesn't allow you a realm to realize in because it both directly and indirectly is already guiding you there, limiting you to some degree.

The Tarot of Marseilles is a very simple and somewhat crude deck, and there are some Italian variations which are a little nicer in the art, but it's fundamentally the same symbols. You don't get that same direction. You just get the impulse, the push in a direction, but then you have to allow it to unfold where it's going to go for you.

There are decks out there that are not Tarot, although they carry the name Tarot. An example would be something like the Tarot of Martin. These are truly from the Renaissance and are really teaching tools that

Jake Kobrin

represent the entire philosophical view of the Renaissance, which is essentially occultism. So, these are a very useful type of deck. If you can get one for a reasonable price, that's very useful in understanding those views. The same thing applies to using texts like the secret symbols of the Rosicrucians or the alchemical plates: they represent a particular view. When you're looking at the decks, remember, you have to look at them and say, "what does this say about the creator?" (It's their worldview.) "Where is it taking me? Where is it taking my mind?"

To continue with the discussion about lucid dreaming, yes, you can use patterns in lucid dreaming to manifest something in the physical world. To combat the inertia of the dream realm, it is important to remember to bring something back into the physical dimension and into your brain. This is the overlap between the forces of the dream and the physical world. When you enter into a state, the idea is to bring something back. To do this more effectively, it is important to be able to navigate the interior realms and maintain clarity of awareness. If you are really good at it, you don't even need to do this, as you can manifest the energy right away. However, this is only possible for a few people. To make this possible, it is important to break down the barrier between consciousness, energy, and matter so that they are in continuity. Otherwise, creative visualizations will be of no use.

The Tree of Life and the Tarot cards, in regard to astral traveling, are a great topic for discussion because there are several versions of the Tree of Life and adding the cards to them is a relatively new phenomenon. The French schools apply different cards to the Tree than the British schools, so it's a different lineup. The paths represent relationships of forces, so to truly understand them, you have to work them. When I worked with the Tree of Life, I worked with it twice for three and a half years, which is a month for each path and a month for each sphere, and then a month for each Element. You can do it in about two weeks and get a decent idea, but if you really want to understand it, it's best to work with it every day for a year or a year and a half.

The rituals have to be done in a very simple manner so that an awakening takes place and the cards can be useful for that. Pathworking is a

The Path Within

relatively new phenomenon, and it's often approached with fantastic stories and a kind of fairytale, which is a kind of guided visualization or guided imagination. However, if the images in the story have no meaning to you, it won't be of any value. It's better to have a very simple opening and closing with a clear intention. You can find this in my book of all for health and wellness.

There are specific practices related to cultivating the virtues of each of the spheres. It is important to:

- Be aware of your actions and the consequences of them.
- Not be lazy and do something.
- Not lie to yourself or to others.
- Work on your emotional relationships.
- Be selfless in a healthy way and to be willing to help others in an intelligent way.
- Not be so attached to yourself and your notions and to expand outward.

These practices all work together to help you expand your potentialities and cultivate the virtues of each sphere. Don't be stupid or lazy. Think about the consequences of your actions and be honest with yourself and others. Work on your emotional relationships and be selfless in a healthy way. Be willing to help others in an intelligent way and don't be too attached to your own ideas and philosophies. Expand your potentialities and look outward.

In the *Corpus Hermeticum*, there is a short section which outlines a path of practice. It encourages us to be courageous and not be cowards, as this is the path of heroes. We should also have compassion for others and obey the laws of the universe, the biggest one being karma. We should also remember to "do what thou wilt is the whole of the law" and that "love is the law." We should be responsible for our actions and learn to be silent, as there are beings who have trodden this path long before us.

Jake Kobrin

We should also remember that these beings have their own agendas and to be mindful before asking the universe for more. Finally, we should remember that even glimpses of these qualities are very impersonal, and they do not care about us as individuals.

It is not often discussed, but it is there if you know the right people. People often ask when the Rishis, the thirteen beings that rule the universe in Indian philosophy, and the unknown superiors, the brotherhoods, will step in to solve the world's problems. The answer is almost always the same: they will only step in when necessary.

This means that you are on your own. You have your own lifeguard, your inner self, your guardian angel, but it cannot force you to make the right decisions. It cannot stop you from drinking, smoking, or eating high fructose corn syrup.

The same is true for the holy saints. They will not stop the world from doing whatever it does. There is a point where they cannot be crossed, but it is best to not reach that point. The virtues are gatekeepers in the classical sense. They are virility or power, and they are actual psychic qualities and awakenings.

Notice how your life changes when you are honest and shut up. Observe yourself and others. Meditation is not a system that will solve all your problems. It is important to get space and distance between the things you do and the things you believe. This will help you to identify with the other and understand them better.

You may be afraid of what will happen to you if you change inside, as you have an unstable sense of self. To stabilize your sense of self, you can do rituals for love. However, you may realize that it is not love, but lust that you are feeling. Lust can be a good motivator, but it is not a good way to get through life. When you lust for something, you are using people in relationships without any real care or concern for the other.

In order to become a better person, you must face the demons you seek to overcome. If you are asking for help to become more courageous, you must face your cowardice. If you are asking for help to become more silent

The Path Within

and inward, you must face the weight of that. You must also face why you like to keep your mind active so much and what you are running from.

When this happens, there is nowhere to run in the dream world except back into your body. In some cases, it may even be someone else's body, which is why you hear stories of possession or hauntings.

The relationship between astral projection, lucid dreaming, and practical magick is an interesting one. There is an application within these practices for manifesting things by your will. The stronger your mind, the greater your clarity, and the better your ability to do lucid dreaming, the easier it will be to manifest stuff. This is because your mind is stabilized. As you are falling asleep, you can use the same process to imagine or visualize yourself carrying out the activity that you wish to be successful at.

When you have internalized something through habit, you may find yourself dreaming about it. This is why it is important to form good habits and to internalize thought, word, and deed. Ritual brings all of these together and can help to solidify them in your inner visualizations. It is important to be as concrete and realistic as possible when doing this.

It is quite well-known that making the strongest circle for your temple depends on the operation you are doing. It is best to do it on the ground and it should be nine feet in diameter. You can use painter's canvas, chalk, or red thread. But, it is important to have confidence in the efficacy of the circle. Virtual reality circles are the ultimate expression of your inner energies and aura.

The circle is your aura. In fact, when you say, "around me flames the pentagrams and in the middle of the pillar shines the six-ray star," that middle pillar is an expansion of a primordial dot of awareness—your inner awareness which allows you to have consciousness. The more you focus on being in the middle pillar across the day, the stronger your fundamental psychic anatomy becomes. This pillar is not rigid, but quite dynamic and static in potential, extending from Malkuth, which is our physical domain. The feet, spine, and knees are the same psychic center, functionally speaking.

Jake Kobrin

When your aura is purified, it is your protective barrier. Until then, you can use tools to help you, such as visualization of the spheres and drawing it. Visualization creates a small force field, and when working with alchemy, the force field is about nine feet. When working with minerals, the force field is about fifty yards, but you don't feel it when you are in it. You only feel it when you cross the barrier.

You can play a game with this by imagining your energy moving in and out and visualizing the sphere around you. Notice people's actions when they walk towards you: they will usually stop about four or five feet away, as this is the edge of the sphere. This is known as personal space, and it is an unconscious thing. The more you strengthen the tangibility and permeability of your aura, the more real and tangible it becomes. Ultimately, this comes from a little point within you.

The most effective your ritual circle will be is when you visualize it, as well as when you draw it. Do you understand? I just saved you about five years, and this whole thing saved you about ten, maybe more.

Also, be careful when using crystal dust. You don't want to wear a lot of crystals or gems. Be selective in what you wear, particularly quartz crystals. Don't wear it at all, just leave it somewhere. When changing crystals for their planetary Sefirotic alignment, go with the geometric structure of the crystal rather than attributes given to it. This works a little better and you're a little cleaner that way. There is some good evidence that these geometric structures also line up with salt structures when doing plant work, although more research needs to be done on that.

Forms, structures, and patterns affect the psychic structures. This is the same thing you're trying to do when you do geometric forms on a talisman, when you're working with geometric structures in your room, or when you're creating a pattern on the floor with rituals.

CHAPTER ELEVEN

INVOKING THE DIVINE

Invoking is the art of drawing a being into oneself and becoming one with it. It is not unlike Channeling, and Channelers are, in truth, invoking, though usually with more intent and purpose. This practice can be used for a variety of reasons: firstly, to learn from entities with higher wisdom; secondly, to amplify a quality that one wishes to cultivate (for example, the invocation of the Egyptian deity Thoth can be used to become more articulate and refined in communication); and thirdly, it can be used in combination with astral projection to explore a certain astral dimension or to contact and interact with an entity there. We can also use invocation to direct a being's energy towards a specific purpose, as we will demonstrate with an example ritual to invoke the Archangel Raphael for purposes of healing.

Jake Kobrin

While a general invocation is used to access the universal source of energy, specific invocations such as those we will discuss in this chapter are intended to connect one to a particular force, which can then be directed with purpose and precision in rituals. The ends to which such invocations can be put are limitless.

The confusion between invocation and evocation can be likened to the difference between bringing something within yourself, as in invocation, and summoning something from without, as in evocation. Evocation is often done with the magician in the circle and the spirit called forth into a triangle just outside the circle. Invocation is when one brings a deity into oneself and merges their consciousness with it, while evocation is when a spirit is pulled towards the magician and made subservient to their will but still kept apart from them. Many spirits can be worked with using Evocation, but not all of them are safe to have one's consciousness merged with!

When it comes to evocation, I'm not qualified to teach it—and some feel it can be dangerous—so I'm going to omit teaching it here. Evocation, as mentioned in the first chapter is the intentional conservation of spirits or entities and the aid of employing them to do your will. It is the summoning of spirits, angels, or demons; binding them or bribing them; and asking them for favors. This is the type of magick that you will encounter most often in mediaeval grimoires and in the tradition of Solomonic magick. It is certainly very powerful, but we will not be exploring this practice in this book. However, I would suggest that invocation is usually the better way to go in terms of achieving your goals and desires, as it involves merging your consciousness with a Divine aspect to enhance your own abilities rather than relying on external forces. Yet, when I do perform invocation, I always refer to the entity I'm invoking in the third person when I make my appeals and state my Will. Dr. Stephen Skinner is one of many who does a great job of teaching this skill.

The Path Within

WRITING YOUR OWN INVOCATIONS

Writing an invocation can be deeply personal, a tribute to the divine and a connection to the ancient. Invocations often start with the magician making an appeal to the deity, and end with the perspective of the deity itself.[68] If you don't feel like you have the poetic prowess to write your own invocation, don't fret; there are many traditional invocations out there that you can find with a simple Google search or in books about magick. But the power of an invocation is magnified when it is created from your own devotion.

The process of creating magickal invocations is typically structured around seven perspectives:

- **Imprecation:** This aspect is akin to a servant addressing their lord, demonstrating humility and subservience.
- **Oath:** Similar to a vassal pledging loyalty to their liege, this part involves a commitment or promise.
- **Memorial:** Resembling a child speaking to a parent, this perspective reflects a familial, nurturing relationship.
- **Orison:** Like a priest praying to their god, it signifies a formal and reverent appeal to the divine.
- **Colloquy:** This is a conversation between equals, like a brother speaking to another brother, denoting a sense of camaraderie.
- **Conjuration:** Comparable to a friend addressing another friend, it's more informal and personal than colloquy but still between equals.
- **Madrigal:** This final perspective is romantic or passionate, like a lover speaking to their mistress.

---

68   Shoemaker, David, *Living Thelema: A Practical Guide to Attainment in Aleister Crowley's System of Magick* (Anima Solis Books, 2013)

An invocation typically begins with the magician appealing to the deity and concludes by adopting the perspective of the deity itself. While it's possible to use traditional invocations found through research, the effectiveness of an invocation is greatly enhanced when it is crafted from one's own feelings of devotion and creativity.

EXERCISE: CRAFTING YOUR PERSONAL INVOCATION

Invocations are powerful tools in magick and spirituality, serving as bridges between the practitioner and the divine. This exercise is designed to guide you through the process of creating your own invocation, using seven distinct perspectives. By engaging with each perspective, you'll craft an invocation that is not only deeply personal but also resonates with the various aspects of your relationship with the divine. This practice not only enhances your creative and spiritual expression but also deepens your connection to the ancient traditions of magick.

Needs:
- A quiet, comfortable space for reflection and writing
- Writing materials (pen and paper, computer, or tablet)
- Any relevant magickal tools or symbols that inspire you
- Optional: Reference materials for traditional invocations or poetic inspiration

Setup:
- Begin by creating a sacred space where you can work undisturbed. This could involve lighting candles, burning incense, or setting up an altar.
- Have your writing materials ready.

The Path Within

- If you wish, start with a brief meditation or ritual to center yourself and connect with your intent.

Instructions:

- **Imprecation:** Start by writing a passage where you humbly appeal to your deity or divine force, acknowledging your subservience and need for guidance.
- **Oath:** Write a pledge of loyalty or a promise to your deity, expressing your commitment and devotion.
- **Memorial:** Reflect on your relationship with the divine as a nurturing force. Write a passage that honors this familial bond.
- **Orison:** Craft a formal prayer or appeal to your deity, showing reverence and respect.
- **Colloquy:** Write a conversational piece, as if speaking with a brother or an equal, sharing your thoughts and feelings in a familiar tone.
- **Conjuration:** Create a passage where you speak to the divine as a friend, focusing on a more personal and intimate connection.
- **Madrigal:** Conclude with a passionate or romantic expression of your love and adoration for the deity.
- Throughout this process, let your words flow naturally. Don't worry about perfection; focus on the sincerity of your feelings.

Follow Through:

- After completing your invocation, take some time to reflect on what you have written. You may wish to read it aloud in your sacred space. If any part of the invocation feels inauthentic or forced, consider revising it until it truly resonates with your inner voice. Store your invocation in a safe and sacred place or consider using it in a future ritual or meditative practice.

Optional:

- If writing from all seven perspectives feels overwhelming, start with just one or two that resonate most with you and gradually build up to including more. You can also integrate traditional elements from invocations you admire, blending them with your personal touch. If you are artistically inclined, consider accompanying your invocation with drawings, symbols, or other visual elements that enhance its meaning.

AN INVOCATION TO LOVE

This is an invocation that I wrote, though some of the lines of the poem are from Crowley's *Book of the Law*, specifically the chapter attributed to Nuit.[69] I have used this invocation in rituals dedicated to the planet Venus and its associations, to bring about love and beauty:

Magnet of my heart, Electric pulse of breath and blood, living lord of light and goodness, self-shining flame of the dawn, shimmering glory of all that is boundless and immutable.

Love, Eros, Agape, and numerous titles hence, I call thou forth to me.

My Beloved, who art of the stars and of the heavens, mover of spirit who doth cradle my soul before birth and shall again in the abodes of death hereafter, the warmth of the bosom that doth sound the rhythm of my beating chest, thee I invoke, it is thee I invoke.

Eternal mother,
From thine abode beyond the Silences
Thee who hath the power to come forth to me,
Mere mortal man, enshrined in shackles, prisoner of mind and concept,
And set free mine heart,
To initiate my whirling soul,

---

69 Crowley, Aleister, *The Book of the Law* (Dover Publications, 1976)

The Path Within

to free me from my endless discursions,
And thrust me forth into the realms beyond the separation and
the illusion.

To thou secret pillar, who indwells as an undying spark, even in
the most wicked and terrible of men,
I bid thee come forth and unto me.
Strengthen and purify these holy aspirations of my soul,
To know thee. To be drunk of thee. Veiless, unending, enraptured
in your fire and ecstasy, I say unto thee to let me know thy sweetness,
and in the darkness of this world to hold you in thine heart as a lamp
amongst the storm.

Love, love, come forth unto me. Enshrine of my heart a temple of
your dwelling.
Purge me and consecrate my heart,
Burn through all of my walls and limits,
Render aside all of my barriers and bounds.
Cast aside these chains that torture my spirit,
Let me dance with thee in the scarlet flame,
The waters of my heart rush forth to merge with thee,
In the oceantide of your voluptuous embrace.
Lightbringer bring forth your light,
Whereupon the everlasting lamps rejoice,
Their pedestals upon the Universe,
Are set in rolling clouds, in thunder gusts,
In vivid flames and tempest; burn unto me and burn me unto thee,
So I may be a vehicle worthy of your divine spark to carry a
million such sons into the dim light of this darkened world.

Come unto me so that I may be a spark that may ignite the tender
flames of yearning in the fertile hearts of women and in the cold chests
of men.

Burn unto me now, oh lord of Love and Beauty, I desire thee so.
Take of me a worthy servant.
Like a slave to my lord, oh lord of the hearth and sweetness, She who

Jake Kobrin

maketh the God's adore thine beauty and fall lovestruck in your company,
    To thee do I swear my fealty and allegiance.
    Great goddess of Unity,
    She who created separation solely for the ecstasy of reunion,
    Thou that wieldest the flower and dove,
    The rose and the lily,
    To thee do I cower in servitude and devotion.
    Great Mistress of mystery,
    The lover of All and refuser of none,
    To thee do I swear my fealty and devotion.

    Aphrodite! Venus! Isis! Nuit! My Scarlet Flame!
    And to Love, like a Beloved friend do I call,
    My name to you is grace, to you I call thee friend and trickster,
    Great goddess of fertility and abundance,
    Lover of wine, and candles, and warm cuddles in the night,
    I bid to you as a companion in your midst,
    That my mind may be open to the influence of the highest,
    That my heart be flooded with love,
    That my soul be purged of Selfishness,
    And that my whole Being be attuned to the hum of your graces.

    And may I coo to you like a lover in the night,
    Mistress! Wife! Lover!
    I call thee hence,
    Thou adored and adoring!
    Bend close to me Thou Lover, that I may be intoxicated by the
ardor of thy breath!
    Thy dear, delicious perfumes in my nostrils!
    At the touch of Thy body I am caught up in a Rapture of Delight!
    The Heavens and the Earth and the silver stars of night!
    All are dissolved in Thy Blissful Embrace!
    And Thy Being merged in mine carries me through Aeons of Time,
    Love is the Law!

The Path Within

I stand towering now with the gods!
My heart is enflamed with thee!
Mistress! Wife! Beloved!
I adore thee!
Love unto me!

And in the starry abode of night
Do I feel thou calling me forth.
To take refuge in thine heart.
I shall make of thee a fertile ground to grow upon,
So my stocks may grow tall and my fruits shall feed the hungry
hearts of Legions.

Under sapphire skies of night,
The sacred beauty of Nuit is revealed,
In blissful rapture, she bends in love,
To embrace the hidden ardor of Hadit.

What is the sign, you ask?
My answer is a flame of blue,
Dancing, penetrating, my hands upon the earth,
My body arching in love, my feet gentle upon the flowers,

You know, I say!
The sign shall be my ecstasy!

For I am divided for the sake of love,
So the pain of parting can be forgotten,
And the joy of union be all.

To love me is better than all things,
If you burn incense in the desert beneath the stars,
Invoking me with a pure heart and the Serpent flame,
You shall come and lie a little in my bosom.

Jake Kobrin

For one kiss, you can have all things,
But he who gives a single grain will lose all in that hour.

You can gather goods and take your fill of pleasure and spices,
You can be adorned in rich jewels,
You can surpass the nations of the earth in splendor,
But always from the love of me, and so shall you come to my joy,

I charge you earnestly to come before me in a single robe,
Crowned with a rich headdress, I beg of you.

Pale or purple, veiled or voluptuous, I'm all pleasure and purple,
and the drunkenness of the innermost sense, I desire you.
Put on the wings and arouse the coiled splendor within you: come
unto me!

Come to me! Come to me!

I'm the azure-lidded daughter of Sunset,
I'm the naked brilliance of the voluptuous night sky!

Sing the love-songs, burn the perfumes,
Wear the jewels, and drink to me, because I love you! I love you!
Come, for the gates of Heaven are open wide.
Come, for the joy of love is waiting inside.
Come, for the beauty of my love is eternal light.
Come, for the rapture of my embrace is pure delight.

The Path Within

ARCHANGELS

Delve into magick and you will find that one of its most powerful and effective practices is to work with Archangels. These entities, however, are not quite the same as the "Hallmark card" version we were raised to believe in Catholic school; they are unimaginably larger and older than we could ever be, and working with them is an intense and humbling process, not always as sweet as we might think. Yet, with the right tools and skills, we can access them safely and begin a relationship that can be both powerful and enlightening.

Archangels are the highest entities in the spiritual hierarchy, beneath the Unicity of Undifferentiated Divinity and the gods and goddesses, and they exist in the world of Briyah, the archetypal realm which coexists with our own. They are powerful, not limited by space and time, and they can be called upon for a vast array of purposes, both spiritual and mundane. If you wish to explore the many roles of the various Archangels, I recommend Damien Echols' book *Angels and Archangels: A Magician's Guide*, which contains a comprehensive list of these entities and their divine purposes.[70] No matter what you choose to work on, remember that with the right knowledge and mindset, you can tap into the power of the Archangels and open yourself up to a whole new world of possibilities.

The Archangels associated with each sphere of the Tree of Life are:

1. **Kether: Archangel Metatron**
    - **Appearance:** Clothed in robes of crystal-clear light, seated on a throne of brilliant light.
    - **Benefits of Invocation:** Helps break free from the wheel of samsara, complete the Great Work, and align will with the Universal Will.
    - **Sphere:** Kether.

---

70 Echols, Damien, *Angels and Archangels: A Magician's Guide* (Sounds True, 2020)

Jake Kobrin

2. **Chokmah: Archangel Raziel**
   - **Appearance:** Wears gray robes and holds a large book.
   - **Benefits of Invocation:** Assists in setting plans in motion, gaining energy, breaking free from ruts, and gaining wisdom and insight.
   - **Sphere:** Chokmah.

3. **Binah: Archangel Tzaphkiel**
   - **Appearance:** Wears black robes and holds an hourglass.
   - **Benefits of Invocation:** Helps bind enemies, repel curses and negative energy, and destroy plans and schemes of enemies.
   - **Sphere:** Binah, associated with Saturn.

4. **Chesed: Archangel Tzadkiel**
   - **Appearance:** Wears blue robes and holds a scepter.
   - **Benefits of Invocation:** Brings prosperity, inner harmony and joy, and luck in gambling.
   - **Sphere:** Chesed, associated with Jupiter.

5. **Geburah: Archangel Kamael**
   - **Appearance:** Wears red robes, crimson armor, and a helmet, and holds a spear and shield.
   - **Benefits of Invocation:** Helps repel negative energy, defeat enemies, and gain bravery in adversity.
   - **Sphere:** Geburah, associated with Mars.

6. **Tiphareth: Archangel Raphael**
   - **Appearance:** Wears golden robes and brilliant armor with the sun on the breastplate, holds a scepter.
   - **Benefits of Invocation:** Assists in all manners of healing, repairing rifts, and attaining fame and popularity.
   - **Sphere:** Tiphareth, associated with the Sun.

The Path Within

7. **Netzach: Archangel Haniel**
   - **Appearance:** Wears seafoam green robes and is accompanied by the scent of rose.
   - **Benefits of Invocation:** Helps bring peace to lovers, encourage fidelity, and turn enemies into friends.
   - **Sphere:** Netzach, associated with Venus.

8. **Hod: Archangel Michael**
   - **Appearance:** Wears orange robes and holds a caduceus.
   - **Benefits of Invocation:** Aids in making intelligent decisions, protection during magick, and eloquent expression.
   - **Sphere:** Hod, associated with Mercury (note: Raphael can also be invoked for Mercury).

9. **Yesod: Archangel Gabriel**
   - **Appearance:** Wears purple robes and a silver headband with a crescent moon.
   - **Benefits of Invocation:** Helps bring more love, peace, subdue aggression, and enhance artistic inspiration.
   - **Sphere:** Yesod, associated with the Moon.

10. **Malkuth: Archangel Sandalphon**
    - **Appearance:** Wears pale brown robes and holds a cornucopia.
    - **Benefits of Invocation:** Aids in manifesting material desires and blessing magick harmlessly.
    - **Sphere:** Malkuth, associated with the Earth.

Each Archangel is associated with a specific sphere on the Tree of Life and can be invoked for different purposes, helping to access the creative forces of the Sephiroth and tap into powerful divine energy. These are a few among many angels and Archangels available for work.

A RITUAL TO INVOKE ARCHANGEL RAPHAEL

If you are feeling ill and seek healing, then you may wish to perform a ritual to invoke the Archangel Raphael, who is the Archangel of Healing. This ritual requires the use of the Lesser Banishing Ritual of the Pentagram, and it can be improved if you also know how to perform the Lesser Banishing Ritual of the Hexagram, the Supreme Invoking Ritual of the Pentagram, and the Greater Invoking Ritual of the Hexagram. Additionally, you will need your usual ritual tools, altar and circle, robes, candles, and a glass or cup of water, or an object to charge as a talisman if you are performing this for another person. Lastly, you will need to print out or draw the traditional Seal of Raphael and place it on your altar.

If you have studied and practiced all of the techniques we have covered thus far, then you will be able to perform this ritual successfully. However, even if you don't feel confident in your abilities, if you are ill, it is still worth making an attempt. The caduceus, the double-entwined serpent which Raphael carries, is symbolic of medicine and healing—so this ritual can be used for physical healing, whether it is a cold, COVID, or a broken leg. If you perform this ritual for yourself, you will be charging

The Path Within

the glass of water before drinking it, a variation of the Eucharist practice common to Catholicism and other traditions. If you are performing this ritual for another person, you can charge an object as a talisman and give it to them, or simply make your appeals to Raphael at the altar.

After the temple is fully set, take a ritual bath and dawn your robes.

Enter the temple and perform a brief centering and relaxing ritual by doing a few rounds of Fourfold breathing.

When you are ready to begin, ring the bell or knock however many times feels intuitively correct for you in the moment.

Banishing
- Perform the preliminary banishing by commanding:

   "Hekas, Hekas, Este Bebeloi!"

   This is a traditional way of banishing, and means, "Begone, begone, all profane influences!"
- Perform the Lesser Banishing Ritual of the Pentagram.

   (If you know how, you can also perform the Lesser Banishing Ritual of the Hexagram)

Preliminary Invocation
Here you can use any preliminary invocation you would like, such as my own personal preliminary invocation. There is also a "Conjuratio" given in *The Grimoire of Armadel* that you can use as a preliminary invocation for this purpose.[71] It is recited as follows:

O Eternal Omnipotent God, who hast formed every creature unto Thy praise and honour, and for the Ministry of Man: I beseech Thee to send unto me the Spirit Raphael of the Archangels, who may inform and teach me concerning those things which I shall demand of him, nevertheless not my Will, but Thine, be done, through Thine Only-begotten Son Jesus Christ. Amen.

---

71   Translated by S. L. MacGregor Mathers, *The Grimoire of Armadel* (Samuel Weiser, 2001)

Jake Kobrin

Or you can recite it in Latin, if you are feeling adventurous:

Omnipotens Aeterne Deus, Qui totam Creaturam condidisti in laudem et honorem tuum, ac ministerium hominis, OTO ut Spiritum Raphael de Archangels, qui me informat et doceat quo ilium interrogavero, non mea voluntas fiat, sed Tua, per Jesum Christum Filium Unigenitum. Amen.

The Oath/Proclamation

At this point, it is appropriate for us to proclaim our intent for this ritual. Stand behind the altar and say:

"It is my Will to Invoke Archangel Raphael for the intention of healing [my or insert the name of the person you intend to heal here] [state your or the other person's illness]."

Specific Invoking Rituals

To invoke Archangel Raphael, we will use a specific invoking ritual that is based off a ritual known as the Supreme Invoking Ritual of the Pentagram. In my own practice, I also use a ritual that is a form of the Greater Invoking Ritual of the Hexagram, but we will not explore this ritual in this book. The Supreme Invoking Ritual of the Pentagram allows you to invoke specific planetary energies associated with a specific sphere. I would typically invoke the energies of the Sun when approaching Archangel Raphael.

The Supreme Invoking Ritual of the Pentagram for Archangel Raphael

First, perform the Kabbalistic Cross.

Drawing the Pentagrams:

1. Stand facing east. Trace the Equilibrated Active Pentagram of Spirit. While doing so, vibrate *ex-ahr-pey* so that the last syllable occurs after you finish drawing and while you are thrusting your hands forward as the Enterer. This pentagram should be white.
2. Make the sign of Spirit—a wheel—in the center of the penta-

gram, and vibrate *eh-heh-yeh*, saving last syllable for the sign of the Enterer once again. The wheel symbol should be made by first making a clockwise circle, starting and ending at the top. Then, draw the vertical, then horizontal, spokes. Follow this with the two diagonal spokes. See this wheel as white.
3. Still facing east, make the Invoking Pentagram of Air directly on top of the figures you just made. Vibrate *oh-row ee-bah-hah ah-oh-zohd-pee*, once again vibrating the last syllable with the sign of the Enterer (this should always be done). See this pentagram as yellow.
4. While forming the sign of Aquarius in the center of the pentagram, vibrate *yud-heh-vahv-heh*. See this sigil as yellow.

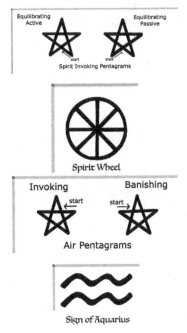

5. Draw the Sigil of Raphael while vibrating *Ra-fay-el*. Visualize this sigil glowing bright yellow.
6. Now turn and face south, and repeat this same exact process, drawing these pentagrams and sigils.
7. Now do the same for west and north, and then return to your altar.

Jake Kobrin

Evoking Archangel Raphael

1. Extend arms straight to the sides, forming a cross. Visualize yourself as a white cross in the center of the Universe. Visualize before you a looming Archangel, dressed in yellow robes with some purplish highlights. The figure carries a caduceus wand and its robes wave in the wind. Feel a breeze coming from behind the Archangel. Vibrate: "Before me, Rah-fay-el."
2. Now repeat the evocation of Raphael behind you, to your right side, and to your left side in the same manner.
3. Stand with feet shoulder-width apart and visualize another electric blue pentagram outlining your body. Vibrate: "For about me flames the pentagram..." Visualize a brilliant golden hexagram at your heart area. Vibrate: "...and in the column shines the six-rayed star."
4. Perform the Kabbalistic Cross again.

The Invocation

Now recite this invocation to Archangel Raphael, which is not of my original design, or you could find another invocation you resonate with more or write your own.[72]

> *Raphael of the glorious seven who stand before*
> *the throne of Him who lives and reigns;*
> *Angel of health, the Lord has filled thy hand with*
> *balm from heaven to soothe and cure our pain.*
> *Heal and console the victims of disease and guide our*
> *steps when doubtful of our ways.*
>
> *Holy Raphael, I entreat thee to help me in all my needs*
> *and in all the trials of this life. And since thou art the*
> *physician of God, I pray thee to heal my soul of its many*
> *infirmities, and my body of the ills that afflict it, if this*

---

72 Original writer unknown. See the St. George's and St. Matthew's website for more information: www.stgandstm.org/st-raphael

The Path Within

favor be for my greater good.
I plead for angelic purity that I may be fit to be the
living temple of the Holy Spirit.
Amen.

Vouchsafe, O Lord God, to direct thy Holy Archangel
Raphael to our help, and may he whom we believe to be
ever in attendance on thy majesty, present our poor prayers
to thee for thy blessing, through Jesus Christ our Lord, who liveth
and reigneth world without end.
Amen.

Then say the following:

"I [your name or magickal motto] do Conjure thee Archangel Raphael by the
virtue of the Great and Holy Names of God, that immediately and without
delay thou art to appear unto me under an agreeable form, and without noise,
nor injury unto my person, to make answer unto all that I shall command
thee; and I do conjure thee herein by EL ELOHIM ELOHO ELOHIM
SEBAOTH ELION EIECH ADIER EIECH ADONAY JAH SADAY
TETRAGRAMMATON SADAY AGIOS OTHEOS ISCHIROS
ATHANATOS AGLA. Amen."

Bringing Down the Magickal Force

There are many ways that you could theoretically bring down the magickal force. You could, for example, perform the Middle Pillar Ritual and imagine that you are channeling the energy of Archangel Raphael, intensifying it for each round. For the purpose of this ritual, I will suggest that you circumambulate (pace around) your circle while chanting the divine names associated with Raphael. This will sound like:

"Shaddai El Chai, Raphael, Chassan, Ariel, Hiddikel, Mizrach, Ruach."

Jake Kobrin

Circumambulate the circle six times (six is a number that corresponds to Tiphareth) while chanting this.

Each time when you reach the East, make the Sign of the Enterer and imagine that the circle is building more and more strongly with energy. Perform the Sign of the Enterer in the direction of the circle (towards the curve going South), not facing towards East.

Locking in the Force

Now return to your altar and take your cup of drinking water in your hands. Go first to the direction of the East and say "Archangel Raphael, great Angel of Healing and whose hands filled with balm from heaven to soothe and cure our pain, bless this water with your light and radiance so that it may become a healing elixir, and cure whatever sickness ails me."

Now imagine the great looming angelic presence of Archangel Raphael and imagine him filling the cup with his light and his energy. Breathe deeply and with each long inhale imagine he is filling your entire body up with his light and energy, and with each long exhale imagine this energy is moving through your heart, out through your arms, out through your hands and into the cup. Stay with this experience for as long as you need until it feels complete.

Now proceed to the South, the West, and the North and repeat the same process, with the same appeals.

If you are doing this for another person, do the same only modify the statement to suit them and bring whatever object you are charging to the four quarters.

If you have any other appeals, wishes, desires, and prayers for Archangel Raphael, return to your altar and say them. Say them with a commanding voice, not as one who is asking, but rather commanding, though not in a cruel way.

Now standing at your altar, take the cup of water in your hands and drink it with full and complete presence, imagining the healing light of Archangel Raphael to pass through every cell of your body. This is no longer just water that you are drinking, but a powerful energetic and magically healing elixir.

The Path Within

If you are charging a talisman for another person, you should now cover it by wrapping it with a black silk cloth.

Now make a definitive statement of completion, such as, "I am healed now by the powers of Archangel Raphael and all of the hosts of heavens that he commands. I am now free of my illness. As it is, as it was, and so shall it be."

Stand in the Sign of Silence behind your altar and take as much time as you need to feel this to be true, to observe and interact with Archangel Raphael, and to soak up and experience all of the potent energy that was cultivated during the ritual.

The Lesser Banishing Ritual of the Pentagram

If you want to be extra thorough, you can perform the Lesser Banishing Ritual of the Hexagram as well as the banishing form of the Supreme Ritual of the Pentagram, and the Greater Ritual of the Hexagram, with the Air pentagrams, and Mercury hexagrams, but in their banishing forms.

You can also, if you would like to "leave the tap on" and maintain a connection with Archangel Raphael, choose not to banish after the climax of the ritual.

Ring the bell and declare the ritual finished.

License to Depart and Closing

For this you can use any License to Depart that you know and like, but there is also a special License to Depart given in *The Grimoire of Armadel* that you can use as a preliminary invocation for this purpose. It is as follows:

Seems that peaceably and in quiet thou has come, and hast made answer unto me in this (my) petition, I return thanks unto God, in Whose Name thou hast come. Depart hence in peace unto thine habitations and be thou ready to return whensoever I shall have called thee. Through Christ our Lord Amen.

Jake Kobrin

Or in Latin:

Quia Placide et quiete ven isti, et hac petitione mihi res pondisti, ago Deo gratias in Cujus Nomen venisti, ite in pace ad loca tua et rediturus ad me cum te vocavero per Christum Dominum nostrum. Amen.

Then, recite the following:

Go in peace unto the place which hath been destined unto you from all Eternity; let there be peace between us and you.

Ring your bell three times to close the ritual. Immediately record the results in your magickal diary upon completion.

Perhaps afterward take a shower, have a bit of food, and maybe laugh with a friend (on your phone, perhaps, if you are sick). Whatever you can do to fully arrive back in your body and put the ritual behind you is important. What is done is done, and now you must trust that it has worked and that the healing you are seeking has arrived.

Additionally, at the point after the Bringing Down of Magickal Force, you could charge a sigil in whatever fashion you like (my preference is through meditation) that you may have drawn prior to the ritual for a purpose related to healing your illness. This is optional, but would give even more juice to an already very powerful ritual.

CHAPTER TWELVE

CREATING PERSONAL RITUALS

As we approach the final chapter of this book, we find ourselves at a pivotal juncture. The preceding chapters have given you some of the fundamental theories and practices of esoteric knowledge, threading together the practices of magick with the transformative art and self-inquiry of methods for your personal evolution. It is here, in this final chapter, that we delve into the practice of personal creative rituals for anything you may desire.

Rituals, the lifeblood of magickal practice, transcend mere ceremonies or rites; they are vibrant manifestations of our innermost yearnings and intentions. In this chapter, we will summarize and explore the process of transmuting the mundane into the sublime through the artistry of ritual.

The craft of personal ritual-making is an intimate, creative process—a symbiotic relationship to powerful forces that weave the fabric of our universe and a profound dialogue with our souls. We will aim to uncover the art of designing rituals that echo the unique timbre of who you are, empowering you to infuse your daily existence and ritual practice with your own creative intent.

This chapter serves as your creative milieu: a space where the theories, practices, and wisdom gathered becomes the tools for your magickal and artistic expression. Regardless of your experience in magick prior to reading this book, this chapter contains a fundamental resource to guide you in forging rituals that mirror the singularity of your essence, the authenticity of your aspirations, and the potency of your vision.

Our exploration will guide you in discerning what you desire to achieve, in selecting symbols and elements that resonate with your specific intentions, and in orchestrating these facets into a ritual that aligns with your personal expression.

Magick is an art that demands practice. Now is the time to take everything you've learned up to this point and to put it towards practical and tangible use. Each ritual you conceive is a small part of an infinite path of discovery, a path that beckons you towards a deeper communion with your inner self, your Holy Guardian Angel, and the cosmos.

MAGICKAL RITUAL FORM

What we are discussing here is the form of magickal ritual—a way to create a talisman, activate a sigil, call upon an Archangel or a particular spirit, or tap into a planetary energy. Although the form of the ritual remains more or less the same, some of the details may be more complex than we are ready for at this stage of your practice. I wanted to give you this information so that you can refer to it and so that we can define the terms.

Reflecting on why you are doing a magickal ritual is a crucial part of the process: it's important to understand why you're doing something, and what you hope to gain from it. Before you begin, you should take the time to ask yourself what your goals and intentions are and why you truly

The Path Within

want to do this ritual. You should also do divination to make sure that no harm is done to yourself or any other person by performing it.

At this stage, you should take any practical steps needed to achieve your aim. "Pray to catch the bus, and then run as fast as you can."[73] If you have done the exercise about Mastering Creative Visualization on page 116, you have already done the work necessary in preparing for your magickal ritual. You can use that worksheet any time you would want to do a ritual, prior to enacting the ritual itself.

Additionally, this is the time when you should plan the ritual itself; write or find any invocations necessary; draw sigils; consider the symbols, Qabalistic correspondences, and timings for use in the ritual; and so on.

Cleansing

The first step in the ritual is to purify and consecrate the temple and yourself by cleaning the temple and altar, using incense, and taking a ritual bath. It is also customary to light candles, decorate the space according to your ritual's intention, and turn on some complimentary music. It is important to perform a relaxation ritual or four-fold breathing to help center and purify your mind. Ringing a bell marks the start of the ritual, and banishing declarations such as "Hekas, Hekas, Este Bebeloi" or "Apo Pantos Kakodaimonos!" are made to purify and sterilize the temple and create a circle of protection. This I learned from the Star Ruby ritual and means "away, every evil daimon!" in Greek.[74]

Banishing

The next step is banishing. It can be seen as a way to create a space of safety and stillness, where one can carry out their magickal work without the interference of any foreign influences or energies. It is a way of purifying and stabilizing the energies, creating a protective circle and calming and centering the mind. It can take many forms, such as the Lesser Banishing Ritual of the Pentagram, the Lesser Hexagram Ritual, and the Star Ruby,

---

73   Cameron, Julia, *The Artist's Way: A Spiritual Path to Higher Creativity* (Tarcher-Perigee, 1992)

74   Duquette, Lon Milo, *The Magick of Aleister Crowley: A Handbook of the Rituals of Thelema* (Weiser Books, 2003)

Jake Kobrin

all of which have specific uses and effects, but generally serve the same purpose. Banishing is essential for successful magickal practice and can help to create an atmosphere of clarity and power.

General Invocations
Connecting to the magickal force of the universe is like plugging into an infinite source of energy and guiding it to manifest our desires. General invocations are a way to tune in to the Divine Light Energy that is present everywhere, and accessible to us all. Think of it as "the Force" from Star Wars—a powerful energy that is available to us any time we choose to access it. The Middle Pillar ritual is an excellent way to do this.

The Oath/Proclamation
This is when you state your intention for your ritual, and your aims in performing the ritual. This generally looks like standing behind the altar and proclaiming, "it is my Will to...."

Specific Invocations
There are many specific invocations and rituals that are designed to aim your cosmic GPS toward a very specific energy and call it down into the space of your ritual. These are invocations to gods, goddesses, or Archangels, or rituals designed to connect to and bring down the energies of specific planets, Elemental energies, or spheres on the Tree of Life.

Locking in Magickal Force
Calling down the magickal force is a process of connecting to the highest level of Divine Light energy and then working through a hierarchy of planes to channel that energy into the working. This hierarchy can be symbolically enacted through a ritual that includes the following. We'll use the Archangel Raphael and his correspondences as our example:

1. **Invocation of the Divine Light Energy:** Connect to the highest level of Divine Light energy.

The Path Within

2. **Invocation of the God Name:** Invoke the specific God Name associated with the Element. For Air, use "Shaddai El Chai."
3. **Archangel Invocation:** Call upon the Archangel related to the magickal Element. For Air, this is "Raphael."
4. **Angel Invocation:** Invoke the name of the Angel associated with the Element. For Air, the Angel is "Chassan."
5. **Ruler of the Element:** Invoke the name of the ruler of the Element. For Air, this is "Ariel."
6. **River Associated with the Element:** Invoke the name of the river linked to the Element. For Air, it is "Hiddikel."
7. **Direction Associated with the Element:** Mention the direction related to the Element. For Air, the direction is "Mizrach."
8. **Name of the Element in Hebrew:** Conclude with the Hebrew name of the Element. For Air, it is "Ruach."

This structured approach assists in methodically channeling the energy from the highest divine source through various planes, culminating in the specific Element of focus, in this case, Air.

This process can be a creative one, as exemplified by David Shoemaker's group ritual to charge a talisman for the sphere of Hod on The Tree of Life, wherein he created a giant Tree of Life on the ground and had each of the participants run all the way through the Spheres up until Hod, and then give the Sign of the Enterer to direct magickal force into the talisman. In this way, we can see how the ritualistic bringing down of magickal force can be both a spiritual and creative endeavor.

Charging

Charging is where you direct the mysterious power that you have called forth to carry out a certain objective for you. This could appear like charging a sigil, which can be done through sex magick, meditation, or a range of other techniques. It may also look like making your requests to the angels, Archangels, or gods that were invoked. You usually will stand before your altar and command the power of the invoked to bring your Will into being.

Jake Kobrin

This could also be where you direct the magickal energy into a talisman, or some other kind of "locking in the Force." One way to do this is to charge a glass of water or piece of food with this magickal energy, and then consuming it. This is especially successful if what you are creating is a shift in yourself, as a way of metaphorically taking in that energy. This is, especially in the case of the use of sex magick (pun somewhat intended), the climax of the ritual.

Second/Closing Banishing
After completing your ritual, and having charged the sigils or talismans, or having called forth the divine agents to execute your will, it is wise to perform a second banishing. This second banishing serves both as a symbolic closure and a way to ensure that the energy of the ritual does not carry over into your daily life. Tales have been told of natural disasters occurring near where rituals have been performed without the proper banishing. There are, however, some exceptions—such as when invoking Elemental Air energy to be more effective in communication. In such cases, it is perhaps more prudent to either not banish at all, or to wait until the communication is concluded before performing the banishing. Ultimately, it is safer and more traditional to banish again in order to close the ritual.

License to Depart
After finishing a ritual, it is customary to give "License to Depart" which is to command all of the spirits and energies invoked to leave. An example might be:

> *"O thou spirit(s) [either name directly the spirit, or just say spirits—I often say "all spirits and energies who are present here"], because thou have diligently answered unto my demands and hast been very ready and willing to come at my call, I do here license thee to depart unto they proper place. Go now in peace to thy abodes and habitations, causing neither harm nor danger unto humans or beasts. Depart, then,*

The Path Within

I say, and be thou very ready to come at my call, when duly conjured by the sacred rites of magick. I charge thee to withdraw peaceably and quietly and may the peace of God be ever continued between thee and me! So mote it be!"

This is a traditional and quite old version of the License to Depart, but you may prefer to formulate your own.

At this point I like to ring the bell again. Generally, three times feels correct to me.

Finishing

After you finish the ritual, you might want to take a moment to sit or stand behind your altar and soak up all of the energy that has been raised and feel it charging you and your energy body. I tend to prefer to hold the Sign of Silence while I do this and do it standing, but you can do whatever feels right for you, including simply sitting, standing, or even lying down. Performing an intense magickal ritual can be quite energetically taxing, so do not feel ashamed if you feel quite tired after your ritual is finished. Conversely, in certain cases, you might feel extremely energized.

Afterglow

Once you finish your ritual, it is wise to record your experience, procedures, and results in your magickal diary. It is best to do this before leaving the temple space, as the details will still be fresh in your mind. You can also record it as a voice note and transcribe it later, if that feels more comfortable. After ritual, it is customary in some traditions to take a shower. This is a way to symbolically transition back to "normal" life. Laughter is also a great way to banish dark energies and lighten the energy of the space. Cakes and ale are a great way to celebrate the completion of a ritual—eating something can help you transition back to your physical body and establish a boundary between magickal practice and the rest of your life. With this, you have come to the end of the general ritual form.

Jake Kobrin

Timing

Timing is an enigma, and when it comes to magick, it is an ever-unfolding mystery. Elections, astrology, and other time-based factors are often used to influence magickal work—the planets, days, and hours all have their own special properties and meanings. For instance, if you wanted to create a charm to attract love, you could work with the planet Venus, the symbol of love, and do your ritual on Friday during the hour of Venus. Astrology is an intricate and complicated subject, and you could also look to chaos magick, which suggests the number twenty-three. Popularized by William Burrows, this superstition suggests performing rites on the twenty-third day of the month or the twenty-third hour, a tradition of Thee Temple ov Psychick Youth.[75]

PLANETARY HOURS AND THE DAYS OF THE WEEK

Planetary energies and their frequencies can be accessed and embodied through spell and ritual work. For example, certain magickal operations, such as talismans, should only be undertaken during certain times, such as within the time of the Moon's increase in the waxing phase or full phase of the Moon. Furthermore, invocations should be performed during the hour of the planet associated with the ritual.

By developing a relationship with the planets, one can tap into the deeper relationship with oneself that ensues. The path to gnosis can be profound through the lens of planetary magick, stirring up ancient remembrance within and aligning with our multidimensional selves. Life becomes synchronistic, and we're reminded that the gods are here to teach us wisdom and knowledge that contributes to our growth and evolution. Just be careful what you ask for, for you just might get it!

---

75   P-Orridge, Genesis, ed., *Thee Psychick Bible: Thee Apocryphal Scriptures ov Genesis Breyer P-Orridge and Thee Third Mind ov Thee Temple ov Psychick Youth*. Updated and Expanded Edition (Feral House, 2010)

The Path Within

Ordinary life is bursting with magick when you really begin to look for it. While it's one thing to practice magick, it's another to live a truly magickal life. Apart from the designated practice sessions or other magickal works you might be engaged with, there are fun ways to integrate magick into your day-to-day life.

One delightful way to do this is to reflect on the magickal meanings behind the days of the week. Each day is named after an ancient god and each of these deities, which correspond to the seven classical planets, have unique qualities that can inspire us and guide us in how we choose to live. Although these planetary correspondences are not as powerful as the organic movements of the planets through the houses, we can still use them to enjoyably reflect on their unique qualities. The days of the week as we know them have deep roots in mythology, primarily drawing from the Norse pantheon, with fascinating correspondences to Roman and Greek gods. They are as follows:

Sunday
- **Norse:** Sunna or Sol
- **Roman:** Sol Invictus
- **Greek:** Helios
- **Planetary Association and Keywords:** The Sun; protection and prosperity

Monday
- **Norse:** Máni
- **Roman:** Luna
- **Greek:** Selene
- **Planetary Association and Keywords:** The Moon; emotions and intuition

Tuesday
- **Norse:** Tyr
- **Roman:** Mars
- **Greek:** Ares
- **Planetary Association and Keywords:** Mars; war and bravery

Jake Kobrin

Wednesday
- **Norse:** Odin (Woden)
- **Roman:** Mercury
- **Greek:** Hermes
- **Planetary Association and Keywords:** Mercury; wisdom and communication

Thursday
- **Norse:** Thor
- **Roman:** Jupiter
- **Greek:** Zeus
- **Planetary Association and Keywords:** Jupiter; thunder, opportunity, Ruler of Gods

Friday
- **Norse:** Frigg or Freya
- **Roman:** Venus
- **Greek:** Aphrodite
- **Planetary Association and Keywords:** Venus; love and fertility

Saturday
- **Norse:** No direct counterpart
- **Roman:** Saturn
- **Greek:** Cronus
- **Planetary Association and Keywords:** Saturn; wealth and time

These etymological connections highlight the syncretism in the evolution of cultures and their mythologies.

The Path Within

MAGICKAL PROPERTIES OF EACH PLANETARY DAY

Sunday, the Sun
Personally, I associate the Sun with self-expression and joy. It represents the vital and lifegiving power within us. Therefore, Sundays are a brilliant day to celebrate, attend an ecstatic dance or a rock concert, or to do anything that connects you with that sense of vitality, joy, and freedom which the Sun radiates. It's a day of fun and freedom. It would be a great day to try acting or singing or some other mode of self-expression. Parties and festivities are best organized on a Sunday.

Monday, the Moon
The Moon is reflective, and as such it relates to our subconscious and subtle patterns within our perception like our psychic abilities, clairvoyance, and dreams. It also relates to our emotions. Therefore, Mondays are good times for divination, meditation, or astral projection—anything that deals with the subtle levels of the mind (like getting high on cannabis, psilocybin, or the like…if it's legal for you to do so where you live, and you do so safely and responsibly, of course!). The Moon also represents consistency and stability, and routines, so it could be a good time to do any chore-work.

Tuesday, Mars
Mars is the planet of war, aggression, dynamic action, competition, and dominance. Tuesdays are excellent days for a climbing expedition, a hard workout in the gym, learning a martial art, or taking dynamic action and initiative towards your goals and projects.

Jake Kobrin

Wednesday, Mercury

Mercury rules communication, learning, and the intellectual qualities of life. Wednesdays are ideal for study and learning, teaching a class, starting a podcast, or anything that requires intellectual faculties such as reading and writing. Mercury is also the planet most associated with magick, due to the fact that Hermes, the Greek version of the Roman Mercury (who is also the Egyptian God Thoth or Tahuti), is considered to be the god who taught magick to humankind. This is why the Hermetic Tradition is called "Hermetic," relating to the Thrice-Great Hermes, or Hermes Trismegistus, who was mythologized to have written the core texts and developed both the philosophy and techniques of Hermetic magick. In the Tarot, Mercury is associated with the Magician card.

Thursday, Jupiter

Jupiter is the planet of abundance and expansion. It's been associated with good luck, bounty, optimism, and growth. Therefore, Thursdays are a great day for activities that involve luck and growing wealth, like gambling or investing. Jupiter also rules foreign travel and moving, so these activities are best done on this day.

Friday, Venus

Ah, Venus day! It's my favorite. Venus relates to the "icing on the cake of life" which guilds and decorates reality, and all of the sensual pleasures of life including good food, art, poetry, and music. She is also the goddess of love and fertility! Therefore, Fridays are a great night for a romantic date night, making paintings, composing music, or to find yourself in a starlit rose garden overlooking the ocean.

Saturday, Saturn

Saturn is the planet of boundaries, discipline, and constriction. Therefore, Saturdays are a good time to do things that relate to structure, like organizing your home, doing your taxes, and balancing your checkbook. It's a good day to undertake work that relates to very tight and structured systems, like a Ph.D. program or something within a university setting. If you have to visit the DMV or deal with any kind of bureaucracy, a Saturday would be a good day to do it.

Optionally, if you decide to experiment with planetary impacts on days, you can record your observations and results in your magickal diary to see if it had an impact. By consciously observing and reflecting on the magickal meanings of each day of the week, we can add an extra layer of mystery and enchantment to our lives, and perhaps even tap into the divine power of the Ancient Gods!

HOURS

Connecting with the planets each day is something we can do through the planetary hours in addition to the planetary attributions of each day of the week. There are many tools available to help us, such as online calculators and phone apps that tell us what planetary hour it is and how to plan our magickal work around it. We can use these hours to our own advantage and make life feel more aligned and powerful, by using the energies of each planet to our benefit.

Properties of the Planetary Hours (organized in the order the hours occur)
- **Mars Hour:** Ideal for physical activity and exercise, martial arts, leadership duties, sports, and activities requiring energy and willpower.
- **Sun Hour:** Suitable for play, recreational activities, performance, and self-expression.
- **Venus Hour:** Great for making love, art, writing poetry, and visiting gardens and art galleries.
- **Mercury Hour:** Best for study, magickal work such as reading and writing, and making phone calls.
- **Moon Hour:** Perfect for meditating, Tarot reading, astral travel, contemplation, dreaming, and visualization.

- **Saturn Hour:** Best for organization and administrative work.
- **Jupiter Hour:** Optimal for investing and traveling.

Experimenting with these specific activities during their corresponding planetary hours can enhance the effectiveness of your magickal work. Exploring the planetary hours and writing down your experience in a magickal diary can help you to become more in tune with the energies of the universe and make your life even more magical.

Both the planetary hours and planetary days can be helpful to plan your magickal work. For example, you might find it best to perform a sigil magick ritual to gain a romantic relationship on a Friday during a Venus hour.

MOON PHASES

The ever-changing phases of the Moon and their influence upon us and our magick is a fascinating thing to behold. We've all heard our witchy friends talk about doing rituals on the new or full moon, but why? Well, the Moon is the closest heavenly body to us, and its waxing and waning controls the rhythm of the sea and all its creatures, as well as the flow of blood in the human body. Farmers have found that certain crops yield more nutritious vegetables when picked at certain phases of the Moon, and dogs respond to the full moon in their own special way. Menstrual cycles are even related to the Moon phases.

Each night, the Moon gives off different amounts of light depending on its relationship to the Sun and its cycle of eight phases, each lasting around three and a half days, completes in approximately twenty-eight days. Each of these phases has its own unique qualities and influences all life on Earth.

The Path Within

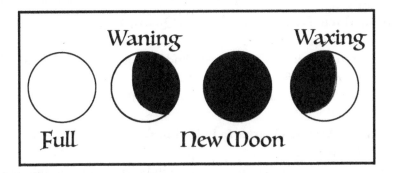

The Moon's phases will affect your magick differently and you can use certain apps to track the phases. Lunar energy is traditionally seen as feminine and receptive, and those with feminine gender may be more naturally affected by the Moon's cycles. Solar energy is seen as masculine and assertive, and there is also a solar cycle of three months that can influence your magick in a subtler way. Finally, there are also specific lunar hours called the "lunar mansions" which are governed by specific lunar deities, but this is beyond the scope of this book.

Let's talk a bit about the Moon phases and how they might relate to your magick: like the ebb and flow of the tides, the Moon's phases can be seen as a reflection of our own inner cycles and rhythms.

New Moon (First Quarter to New Moon)
- **Element:** Water.
- **Significance:** Time of new beginnings, fresh opportunities, and positive changes.
- **Activities:** Setting intentions for the month, dream work, divination.

Dark Moon (Around New Moon)
- **Timing:** One day before and one day after the new moon.
- **Focus:** Discarding unwanted aspects of life, reflecting on accomplishments, planning future goals.

Waxing Moon (New Moon to Second Quarter)
- **Element:** Air.
- **Attributes:** Focus on growth and increase in various aspects like knowledge, finances, relationships.
- **Activities:** Healing, enhancing communications.

Full Moon (Second Quarter to Full Moon)
- **Element:** Fire.
- **Significance:** Moon's most powerful phase, a time of fulfillment and activity.
- **Activities:** Increasing psychic ability, perfecting ideas, celebrations, renewing commitments, performing any kind of magick, harvesting crops and fruits.

Waning Moon (Full Moon to First Quarter)
- **Element:** Earth.
- **Attributes:** Time of decrease, release, letting go, and completion.
- **Activities:** Dieting, breaking bad habits, ending relationships, addressing legal matters.

Thus, by recognizing the power of the Moon's phases, you can use the energy that they embody as a potent ingredient in your rituals.

DESIGN YOUR OWN RITUAL

By now you have all the knowledge to craft your own rituals for your own purposes. It's time to take what you've learned and put it into practice: to create a ritual of your design. Review your intentions from the start of this

The Path Within

book and pick one that resonates with your True Will. Perform divination to ensure that it will bring only benefit and no harm to yourself or others. After that, complete the preliminary ritual exercise to make sure that this ritual is in line with your aspirations and that there are no mundane actions that need to be taken.

Then, consult the Magickal Ritual Form guide and work with *Liber 777* or other correspondences found from other sources. Attend to the colors, smells and incenses, symbols, plants and flowers, as well as the correspondences to the planets, Tarot cards and their associated paths on the Tree of Life, and the spheres of the Tree of Life. If you wish to invoke any gods, goddesses, or Archangels, find invocations or write your own. You may also want to draw a sigil; structure the ritual around planetary days, moon phases, and planetary hours; and choose an object that you would like to make into a talisman that you can carry until your desire is fulfilled. Sometimes talismans can have special physical properties, like being adorned with certain symbols and sigils, and it may make them more effective, but you can also just use any physical object for a talisman.

You are free to use anything you have learned in this book to accomplish your Will. Do what feels right, what is most potent and aligned with your desire, but also what is correct. Record the results of your ritual and the procedure you used in your magickal diary, and if necessary, draft invocations or draw sigils. You can also use scripts to read during your ritual—it's alright to read from books or notes, no need to memorize everything.

Good luck! This ritual is a learning experience, so have fun with it and don't put too much pressure on the result. As Aleister Crowley said, "[f]or pure will, unassuaged of purpose, delivered from the lust of result, is every way perfect."[76] Let go of the expectation that your desire will be fulfilled and focus on the ritual itself. After you're done, write it down in your magickal diary and then forget about it. Have confidence in your magick but move forward without being fixated on the outcome.

---

76   Crowley, Aleister, *Liber II: The Message of the Master Therion* (Ordo Templi Orientis, 1913)

EXERCISE: CRAFTING YOUR PERSONAL RITUAL

This exercise empowers you to create a ritual tailored to your specific intentions and aligned with your True Will. It is a practical application of your accumulated knowledge and skills in ritual magick, allowing you to manifest your aspirations effectively.

Needs:
- Your intentions from the start of the book
- Divination tools (Tarot cards, pendulums, etc.)
- Preliminary ritual worksheet
- Magickal Ritual Form guide
- *Liber 777* or other correspondence resources
- Materials for sigils, talismans, or invocations (paper, pen, etc.)
- Ritual components (colors, incense, symbols, etc.)
- Magickal diary for recording

Setup:
- Reflect on your intentions set at the beginning of this book. Choose one that resonates deeply with your True Will.
- Use divination to confirm the chosen intention will bring benefits without harm to yourself or others.
- Fill out the preliminary ritual worksheet to align the ritual with your goals and to check for any required mundane actions.

The Path Within

Instructions:
- Consult the Magickal Ritual Form guide. Use *Liber 777* or other sources for correspondences related to your ritual.
- Pay attention to the specific colors, scents, symbols, plants, and other correspondences that align with your intention.
- If invoking deities or Archangels, prepare or write your invocations.
- Craft a sigil and consider the timing of the ritual based on planetary days, moon phases, and planetary hours.
- Consider creating a talisman that symbolizes your intention and carry it with you. Choose an object that you feel would work well as your talisman.
- Perform the ritual with focus and intent, using any scripts or readings as needed. Remember, it's acceptable to read from notes.

Follow Through:
- Record every detail of your ritual and its results in your magickal diary.
- If necessary, refine your invocations or sigils for future use.
- Release your attachment to the outcome, as advised by Aleister Crowley, focusing on the process rather than the result.
- Document your experience in your magickal diary and then let go of the ritual mentally, trusting in the efficacy of your magick.

Optional:
- You may incorporate elements from various magickal traditions if they resonate more with your practice.
- Feel free to adapt or modify the ritual structure to better suit your personal style and spiritual path.

CONCLUSION

Though you have come to the end of this book, you have not reached the end of your quest of learning, discovering, and practicing magick. Magick is vast and filled with potential to explore. Everyone has the potential to unlock a hidden power that has been kept secret for centuries. To do this, we must follow our curiosity and be brave. We must read books, find teachers, take courses, and, most importantly, do the work. Magick is a skill that is learned through experience.

Magick is a potent and real force, as I've learned through my own experiences and the teachings of renowned authors like Dion Fortune, Israel Regardie, Austin Osman Spare, and many others. If this book has sparked your curiosity, I encourage you to put its principles into practice. Tonight, focus on a desire that is within reach, write it down clearly, and give it a go. Remember, it's important to be realistic—aiming for something like traveling to Mars might be a stretch if you don't have a rocket! And if you're thinking of performing a ritual to manifest riches, it's practical to take a corresponding action, like investing in a small venture.

Jake Kobrin

Together, let's venture on the experimental quest of changing our reality and our world. Approach magick not as an unshakable truth but as a fascinating aspect of human capability. We are engaging with a system that can be influenced by our words and intentions. So, why not experiment tonight? You never know, we might just tap into a profound power that has been elusive for ages.

Life is a dream, and we are all dreamers in this "dreaming." We are so deeply immersed in this dream of life, often unable to recognize the other possibilities available to us. The dreamer is without shame, operating at a profound subconscious level. It traps us in its trance, commanding us to obey. Whatever we dream ourselves to be, whatever we are conditioned to believe we should be, we will become. This trance of dreaming is as integral to human life as water is to fish. However, we have the capacity to alter the dream. This requires us to wake up out of the dream, to wake up out of the trance, which is a difficult task. Most people never manage to do this, as it requires a level of awareness that is rare. But if we do wake up, then a new reality is revealed: the truth of awareness, which gives us access to an infinite range of alternate possibilities. Just as lucid dreaming can show us how to take control in a dream world, we can also take hold of our lives and choose our own paths rather than submitting to fate. Lucid dreaming is a metaphor for this awakening, offering us true freedom.

In order to make our dreams come true, we must be open to the possibility of the seemingly impossible and explore our depths to understand what it is we truly want. By utilizing symbols such as sigils, ceremonies, and rituals, we can access and condition our unconscious. We must also be aware of any unconscious biases that are holding us back and be willing to consider a new dream, even if it means going beyond the usual boundaries of thought and facing something we may find disagreeable or unusual.

When we take control of our dreams and make them reality, our lives can be dramatically changed for the better. But it is essential to remember that freedom comes with responsibility and the consequences of our choices. To make joy and contentment for ourselves and those around us,

The Path Within

we should be guided by love. We must understand the physical laws that restrict our actions, but also remember that any rules from society, such as religions and governments, may not be applicable to the fundamental nature of things, seeing things from a limited perspective.

Breaking free from the confines of man-made social expectations and conventions grants us the power to be in control of our own destiny. We can learn from our mistakes, construct a life in line with our values and ideals, and establish our own personal truth without interference. Once we realize our power and potential as lucid dreamers and agents of change, we have the ability to give life and existence greater meaning and to choose how our individual lives should be lived.

At the core of our being lies a power—an infinite divine energy that is the source of all life and consciousness. This power is the source of our freedom and autonomy, and it is our right to express it in whatever way resonates most deeply with us. We can choose to think, feel, do, and say whatever we wish, unhindered by anyone else. Every individual is their own guiding star, and no one else can claim superiority. We have the right to eat and drink what nourishes us, to live where our heart desires, to think and express ourselves freely, and to love whoever we choose. In the end, we are responsible for our own actions, and no one else can dictate them.

The path of spiritual ascension is one of returning to our true selves, of remembering who we truly are and freeing ourselves from the illusions of our minds and the deceptions of the world. It is not a path of gaining power, but rather a path of rediscovery and recognition of the divine nature within us all. We are expressions of this divine consciousness, a timeless potentiality that is manifested in a multitude of forms. We can become lost in our own contracted sense of self and in the limited perspectives of our minds, but through practices such as magick, Yoga, and meditation, we can come to understand and access the divine powers that lie within us, and our sense of self will be dissolved into the radiant perfection of wholeness.

Jake Kobrin

It is important to remember to have fun with our practice and not take things too seriously. We should also remember that even if our new path is something that we are rebelling against, we can still find insight and illumination from it, regardless of what our family or culture may think. The phrase "do what thou wilt" is an invitation to discover and activate the prime directive of our existence—our own unique will—and to understand that love is the ultimate law. We can find strength, creativity, and power in love, and it is through love that we can discover our purpose and destiny. Our adventure is one of self-discovery and self-empowerment, and we should always remember to embrace our freedom and autonomy.

Magick is an exploration, a path of discovery that transcends rules and set paths. It invites us into a sphere of endless possibilities, encouraging us to view the world through a lens of wonder and inquisitiveness. Your interest might be drawn to diverse traditions like Wicca, Kabbalah, or exploring ancient mystic practices like those of the Druids. Whatever sparks your interest, pursue it with passion and don't let anyone limit your exploratory spirit.

Finding joy in your magick is essential. Fun can manifest in various forms—for some, it's deep, introspective, and serious, while for others, it's more whimsical and playful. Embrace what fun means to you. It could involve delving into mystical texts, experimenting with obscure rituals, or rediscovering the enchantments and legends that captured your imagination as a child, be it Narnian tales or the lore of Greek mythology. Anything that ignites your sense of curiosity and wonder is worth exploring.

At its core, magick should be enjoyable. If you're not finding joy in your practice, you might want to reevaluate its role in your life. While magick encompasses self-discovery, seeking truth, and exploring exotic mystical dimensions and practices, the experiences should also be fun.

Listen to what resonates with you deeply and follow that path. Your intuition is a powerful guide, leading you to this moment for a reason. If the allure of magick captivates you, then it's time to embrace the path wholeheartedly.

The Path Within

Magick should bring joy and facilitate your authentic expression. When practiced earnestly, it can lead to unexpected, sometimes intense or eerie experiences. But remember, this is all part of the adventure—the mystery and excitement of the magickal path.

Believe in yourself and your chosen path. You're here for a meaningful reason, and this book is no coincidence. If the call of magick resonates with you, trust your inner voice. Magick is more than a practice; it's a lifelong adventure. Your starting point is just the beginning of what will become a transformative and enriching path. If you embrace magick as a lifelong pursuit, your exploration will be filled with profound change and growth. Revel in your unique adventure with magick, trust its progression, and know that you are destined to become a true and great magician.

I sincerely want to thank you from the bottom of my heart for trusting me as your guide on this expedition into ritual magick. I hope that the information you have gained through this book has enhanced your life and empowered you to take control of it. You can now create and envision the life you truly want to live and become the person you want to be. On an even deeper level, you may have experienced realizations about yourself, the true nature of the self and reality, and the pursuit of the great work.

I understand that this has not been easy. It has been a huge amount of work and a lot of information. Therefore, I want to congratulate you on your success in undertaking this big endeavor. You have taken the time out of your busy lives, despite the chaos in the world, to learn, digest, and practice all of this information. You are now a fully-fledged magician.

However, you have the rest of your life to continue to explore, discover, grow, experiment, and discover your own magick. The examples I have given in this book are just some of the systems, practices, and techniques I have used, as well as from our guest teachers and the particular lineages they come from. It is now up to you to discover your own magick through your own experimentation and life. Hopefully, through this book, you have discovered that this is something you want to pursue for the rest of

Jake Kobrin

your life. This was just an introduction in all of these subjects. Now is the time for you to leave the nest and fly.

Thank you for joining me on this adventure. I hope you have been able to explore your own direct experience and experiment with the disciplines and practices you have learned in this book. You may even develop your own rituals and practices. I cannot tell you where to go next, you must listen to your inner compass and the whispers of your Holy Guardian Angel. Pursue your own True Will and your own unique path as a magician, wizard, witch, or sorcerer.

I want to thank you for coming along this ride with me and my fellow guest teachers. I have found sharing this information to be a deeply meaningful experience and I am grateful for your readership and trust.

EXPANDED BIBLIOGRAPHY

Abrahamsson, Carl. *Source Magic: The Origin of Art, Science, and Culture.* Park Street Press, 2023.

——. *Occulture: The Unseen Forces That Drive Culture Forward.* Inner Traditions, 2018.

Adler, Margot. *Drawing Down the Moon: Witches, Druids, Goddess-Worshippers, and Other Pagans in America.* Penguin Books, 2006.

Aristotle. *Nicomachean Ethics.* Translated by W. D. Ross. Batoche Books, 1999.

Asprem, Egil. *The Problem of Disenchantment: Scientific Naturalism and Esoteric Discourse, 1900-1939.* Brill, 2014.

Bardon, Franz. *Initiation Into Hermetics.* Dieter Rüggeberg, 2001.

——. *The Key to the True Kabbalah.* Dieter Rüggeberg, 2002.

——. *The Practice of Magical Evocation.* Dieter Rüggeberg, 2001.

Batchelor, Stephen. *Buddhism without Beliefs.* Riverhead Books, 1997.

Besant, Annie. *Esoteric Christianity: or The Lesser Mysteries.* Quest Books, 2006.

Blackburn, Simon. *Being Good: A Short Introduction to Ethics.* Oxford University Press, 2001.

Blavatsky, Helena Petrovna. *The Secret Doctrine: The Synthesis of Science, Religion, and Philosophy.* Theosophical University Press, 1977.

Bogdan, Henrik. *Western Esotericism and Rituals of Initiation.* State University of New York Press, 2007.

Buckland, Raymond. *Buckland's Complete Book of Witchcraft.* Llewellyn Publications, 2002.

Butler, W. E. *Magic, Its Ritual, Power and Purpose.* Samuel Weiser, 1971.

Cameron, Julia. *The Artist's Way: A Spiritual Path to Higher Creativity.* TarcherPerigee, 1992.

Campbell, Joseph. *The Hero with a Thousand Faces.* New World Library, 2008.

——. *The Power of Myth.* Anchor Books, 1991.

Capra, Fritjof. *The Tao of Physics: An Exploration of the Parallels Between*

Modern Physics and Eastern Mysticism. Shambhala, 1975.

Carroll, Peter J. *Liber Null & Psychonaut: An Introduction to Chaos Magic.* Red Wheel/Weiser, 1987.

Case, Paul Foster. *The Tarot: A Key to the Wisdom of the Ages.* Weiser Books, 2006.

Chagme, Karma. *A Spacious Path to Freedom: Practical Instructions on the Union of Mahamudra and Atiyoga.* Snow Lion Publications, 1998.

Chia, Mantak, and Michael Winn. *Taoist Secrets of Love: Cultivating Male Sexual Energy.* Aurora Press, 1984.

Chödrön, Pema. *When Things Fall Apart: Heart Advice for Difficult Times.* Shambhala, 2000.

Cicero, Chic, and Sandra Tabatha Cicero. *Creating Magical Tools: The Magician's Craft.* Llewellyn Publications, 1999.

Coué, Émile. *Self Mastery Through Conscious Autosuggestion.* American Library Service, 1922.

Crowley, Aleister, and S. L. MacGregor Mathers, eds. *The Goetia: The Lesser Key of Solomon the King.* Samuel Weiser, 1995.

——, eds. *The Goetia: The Lesser Key of Solomon the King.* Samuel Weiser, 1995.

Crowley, Aleister. *Magick in Theory and Practice.* Dover Publications, 1976.

——. *The Book of the Law.* Dover Publications, 1976.

——. *The Book of Thoth: A Short Essay on the Tarot of the Egyptians.* Samuel Weiser, 1974.

——. *Liber 777.* Samuel Weiser, 1977.

——. *Liber II: The Message of the Master Therion.* Ordo Templi Orientis, 1913.

——. *Liber LXV: Liber Cordis Cincti Serpente.* Ordo Templi Orientis, 1907.

——. *Magick in Theory and Practice.* Samuel Weiser, 1997.

Cunningham, Scott. *Wicca: A Guide for the Solitary Practitioner.* Llewellyn Publications, 1988.

Dalai Lama XIV and Howard C. Cutler. *The Art of Happiness: A Handbook for Living.* Riverhead Books, 1998.

Dalai Lama XIV. *Ethics for the New Millennium.* Riverhead Books, 1999.

DuQuette, Lon Milo. *Enochian Vision Magick: An Introduction and Practical Guide to the Magick of Dr. John Dee and Edward Kelley.* Weiser Books, 2008.

——. *The Magick of Aleister Crowley: A Handbook of the Rituals of Thelema.* Weiser Books, 2003.

——. *Understanding Aleister Crowley's Thoth Tarot.* Weiser Books, 2003.

Echols, Damien. *Angels and Archangels: A Magician's Guide.* Sounds True, 2020.

——. *High Magick: A Guide to the Spiritual Practices That Saved My Life on Death Row.* Sounds True, 2018.

Eliade, Mircea. *Shamanism: Archaic Techniques of Ecstasy.* Princeton University Press, 2004.

Farber, Philip H. *Meta-Magick: The Book of Atem: Achieving New States of Consciousness Through NLP, Neuroscience, and Ritual.* Weiser Books, 2008.

Fortune, Dion. *Psychic Self-Defense.* Weiser Books, 2001.

——. *The Mystical Qabalah.* Ernest Benn Limited, 1935.

——. *The Sea Priestess.* Samuel Weiser, 2003.

Frankl, Viktor. *Man's Search for Meaning.* Beacon Press, 1959.

Gawain, Shakti. *Creative Visualization.* New World Library, 2002.

Goddard, Neville. "A Lesson in Scripture." October 23, 1967.

——. *Feeling is the Secret.* DeVorss & Company, 1944.

——. *The Power of Awareness.* DeVorss & Company, 1952.

Goldstein, Joseph. *The Experience of Insight: A Simple and Direct Guide to Buddhist Meditation.* Shambhala, 1993.

Greer, John Michael. *The New Encyclopedia of the Occult.* Llewellyn Publications, 2003.

——. *The Druid Magic Handbook: Ritual Magic Rooted in the Living Earth.* Weiser Books, 2008.

Gunaratana, Henepola. *Mindfulness in Plain English.* Wisdom Publications, 2002.

Hammer, Olav. *Claiming Knowledge: Strategies of Epistemology from Theosophy to the New Age.* Brill, 2003.

Hand, Robert. *Planets in Transit: Life Cycles for Living.* Schiffer Publishing Ltd, 2001.

Hanegraaff, Wouter J. *Esotericism and the Academy: Rejected Knowledge in Western Culture.* Cambridge University Press, 2012.

——. *Western Esotericism: A Guide for the Perplexed.* Bloomsbury Academic, 2013.

Jake Kobrin

Hanh, Thich Nhất. *The Miracle of Mindfulness: An Introduction to the Practice of Meditation.* Beacon Press, 1975.

——. *The Art of Happiness.* Riverhead Books, 1998.

Harner, Michael. *The Way of the Shaman.* HarperOne, 1990.

Harris, Sam. *Making Sense: Conversations on Consciousness, Morality, and the Future of Humanity.* Ecco, 2020.

——. *The Moral Landscape: How Science Can Determine Human Values.* Free Press, 2010.

——. *Waking Up: A Guide to Spirituality Without Religion.* Simon & Schuster, 2014.

Harvey, Peter. *An Introduction to Buddhist Ethics.* Cambridge University Press, 2000.

Hawkins, David R. *Power vs Force: The Hidden Determinants of Human Behavior.* Hay House, 2012.

Helmstetter, Shad. *What to Say When You Talk to Yourself.* Pocket Books, 1990.

Hine, Phil. *Condensed Chaos: An Introduction to Chaos Magic.* New Falcon Publications, 1995.

Holiday, Ryan. *The Obstacle Is the Way: The Timeless Art of Turning Trials into Triumph.* Portfolio/Penguin, 2014.

Horowitz, Mitch. *Occult America: The Secret History of How Mysticism Shaped Our Nation.* Bantam Books, 2009.

Houlding, Deborah. *The Houses: Temples of the Sky.* The Wessex Astrologer Ltd, 2006.

Huang, Kerson, and Rosemary Huang. *I Ching.* Workman Publishing, 1987.

Irvine, William B. *A Guide to the Good Life: The Ancient Art of Stoic Joy.* Oxford University Press, 2008.

Jodorowsky, Alejandro, and Marianne Costa. *The Way of Tarot: The Spiritual Teacher in the Cards.* Destiny Books, 2009.

Johnson, Robert A. *Inner Work: Using Dreams and Active Imagination for Personal Growth.* HarperOne, 2009.

Jung, Carl. "Aion: Researches into the Phenomenology of the Self," *Collected Works of C. G. Jung, Vol. 9, Part 2.* Princeton University Press, 1959.

Kabat-Zinn, Jon. *Wherever You Go, There You Are: Mindfulness Meditation in Everyday Life.* Hyperion, 1994.

King, Francis. *Magic: The Western Tradition*. Thames & Hudson, 1975.

——. *Techniques of High Magic: A Guide to Self-Empowerment*. Destiny Books, 1976.

Kornfield, Jack. *A Path with Heart: A Guide Through the Perils and Promises of Spiritual Life*. Bantam, 1993.

Kraig, Donald Michael. *Modern Magick: Twelve Lessons in the High Magickal Arts*. Llewellyn Publications, 2010.

LaBerge, Stephen and Howard Rheingold. *Exploring the World of Lucid Dreaming*. Ballantine Books, 1991.

Lachman, Gary. *Dreaming Ahead of Time: Experiences with Precognitive Dreams, Synchronicity and Coincidence*. Floris Books, 2020.

Maltz, Maxwell. *Psycho-Cybernetics*. Prentice-Hall, 1960.

Moore, Alan. Interview by Rowan Hooper. "Haunted Resonance: An Interview With Alan Moore," *The Quietus*, December 5, 2018.

Morrison, Grant. *Pop Magic!*. Disinformation Books, 2003.

Murphy, Joseph. *The Power of Your Subconscious Mind*. Wilder Publications, 2008.

P-Orridge, Genesis, ed. *Thee Psychick Bible: Thee Apocryphal Scriptures ov Genesis Breyer P-Orridge and Thee Third Mind ov Thee Temple ov Psychick Youth. Updated and Expanded Edition*. Feral House, 2010.

Pollack, Rachel. *Seventy-Eight Degrees of Wisdom: A Book of Tarot*. Weiser Books, 2007.

Pollan, Michael. *How to Change Your Mind: What the New Science of Psychedelics Teaches Us About Consciousness, Dying, Addiction, Depression, and Transcendence*. Penguin Press, 2018.

Radin, Dean. *Real Magic: Ancient Wisdom, Modern Science, and a Guide to the Secret Power of the Universe*. Harmony Books, 2018.

Rahula, Walpola. *What the Buddha Taught*. Grove Press, 1974.

Regardie, Israel. *The Golden Dawn: The Original Account of the Teachings, Rites, and Ceremonies of the Hermetic Order*. Llewellyn Publications, 2002.

——. *The Middle Pillar: The Balance Between Mind and Magic*. Llewellyn Publications, 2002.

Rinpoche, Sogyal. *The Tibetan Book of Living and Dying*. HarperOne, 1992.

Robbins, Tony. *Awaken the Giant Within: How to Take Immediate Control of*

Jake Kobrin

Your Mental, Emotional, Physical and Financial Destiny! Free Press, 1991.

Salzberg, Sharon. *Lovingkindness: The Revolutionary Art of Happiness.* Shambhala, 1995.

Seneca. *On the Happy Life.* c. 58. Translated version referenced.

Sherwin, Ray. *The Book of Results.* Revelations 23 Press, 1978.

Shoemaker, David. *Living Thelema: A Practical Guide to Attainment in Aleister Crowley's System of Magick.* Anima Solis Books, 2013.

Singer, Peter. *Practical Ethics.* Cambridge University Press, 2011.

Skinner, Stephen. *Techniques of Graeco-Egyptian Magic.* Golden Hoard Press, 2014.

——. *The Complete Magician's Tables.* Llewellyn Publications, 2006.

Spare, Austin Osman. *The Book of Pleasure (Self-Love): The Psychology of Ecstasy.* I-H-O Books, 2001.

Stavish, Mark. *Between the Gates: Lucid Dreaming, Astral Projection, and the Body of Light in Western Esotericism.* Weiser Books, 2008.

Thanissaro, Bhikkhu, trans. *Dhammapada.* Dhamma Dana Publications, 1998.

Three Initiates. *The Kybalion.* The Yogi Publication Society, 1908.

Tolle, Eckhart. *A New Earth: Awakening to Your Life's Purpose.* Penguin, 2005.

——. *The Power of Now: A Guide to Spiritual Enlightenment.* New World Library, 1999.

Trungpa, Chögyam. *Cutting Through Spiritual Materialism.* Shambhala, 2002.

Turner, Robert. *Enochian Magic for Beginners: The Original System of Angel Magic.* Llewellyn Publications, 2002.

Urban, Hugh B. *Magia Sexualis: Sex, Magic, and Liberation in Modern Western Esotericism.* University of California Press, 2006.

Wang, Robert. *The Qabalistic Tarot: A Textbook of Mystical Philosophy.* Weiser Books, 1983.

Wilhelm, Richard, and Cary F. Baynes, translators. *The I Ching or Book of Changes.* Princeton University Press, 1967.

Zalewski, Pat. *Golden Dawn Rituals and Commentaries.* Rosicrucian Order of the Golden Dawn, 2010.